RAFFAELE MATTIOLI LECTURES

In honour of the memory of Raffaele Mattioli, who was for many years its manager and chairman, Banca Commerciale Italiana has established the Mattioli Fund as a testimony to the continuing survival and influence of his deep interest in economics, the humanities and sciences.

As its first enterprise the Fund has established a series of annual lectures on the history of economic thought, to be called the Raffaele Mattioli Lectures.

In view of the long association between the Università Commerciale Luigi Bocconi and Raffaele Mattioli, who was an active scholar, adviser and member of the governing body of the University, it was decided that the lectures in honour of his memory should be delivered at the University, which together with Banca Commerciale Italiana, has undertaken the task of organising them.

Distinguished academics of all nationalities, researchers and others concerned with economic problems will be invited to take part in this enterprise, in the hope of linking pure historical research with a debate on economic theory and practical policy.

In creating a memorial to the cultural legacy left by Raffaele Mattioli, it is hoped above all that these lectures and the debates to which they give rise will prove a fruitful inspiration and starting point for the development of a tradition of research and academic studies like that already long established in other countries, and that this tradition will flourish thanks to the lasting partnership between the Università Commerciale Luigi Bocconi and Banca Commerciale Italiana.

D1388502

CAUSES OF GROWTH AND STAGNATION
IN THE WORLD ECONOMY

RAFFAELE MATTIOLI FOUNDATION

Nicholas Kaldor

CAUSES OF GROWTH AND STAGNATION IN THE WORLD ECONOMY

CAMBRIDGE
UNIVERSITY PRESS

CAMBRIDGE UNIVERSITY PRESS
Cambridge, New York, Melbourne, Madrid, Cape Town, Singapore, São Paulo

Cambridge University Press
The Edinburgh Building, Cambridge CB2 8RU, UK

Published in the United States of America by Cambridge University Press, New York

www.cambridge.org
Information on this title: www.cambridge.org/9780521561600

Edited by Carlo Filippini, Ferdinando Targetti, A. P. Thirlwall

© The Estate of Nicholas Kaldor, 1996,
Exclusive licensee 1996-1999
Banca Commerciale Italiana, Milano, Italy

First published 1996
This digitally printed version 2007

A catalogue record for this publication is available from the British Library

Library of Congress Cataloguing in Publication data
Main entry under title:
Kaldor Nicholas
Causes of growth and stagnation in the world economy / Nicholas Kaldor
(Raffaele Mattioli Lectures)
Includes bibliographical references and index.
ISBN 0-521-56160-4 (hc)

1. Economic development.   2. Equilibrium (Economics).
3. Stagnation (Economics).   4. Competition, International.
I. Title.   II. Series.
HD75.K338   1996   338.9--dc20
95-46603 CIP

ISBN 978-0-521-56160-0 hardback
ISBN 978-0-521-03985-7 paperback

CONTENTS

Preface   XI

Acknowledgements   XII

FIRST LECTURE

Equilibrium Theory and Growth Theory   3

SECOND LECTURE

Alternative Approaches to Growth Theory   21

THIRD LECTURE

The Problem of Intersectoral Balance   39

FOURTH LECTURE

The Effects of Interregional and International
Competition   55

FIFTH LECTURE

Policy Implications of the Current World Situation   71

DISCUSSION   93

Amedeo Amato, p. 95; Giacomo Becattini, p. 97;
Luigi Pasinetti, p. 101; Paolo Sylos Labini, p. 109;
Siro Lombardini, p. 112; Salvatore Biasco, p. 120;
Terenzio Cozzi, p. 123; Mario Monti, p. 127;
Giovanni Bellone, p. 129; Fabrizio Onida, p. 130;
Carlo Angelo Cardani, p. 132; Carlo Filippini, 134;
Guido Tabellini, p. 136; Ferdinando Targetti, p. 138.

NICHOLAS KALDOR, A BIOGRAPHY,
by A. P. Thirlwall   143

1. Introduction, p. 145.   2. Early Life, 1908-1939, p. 150.
3. The War and Immediate Post-war Years, p. 163.
4. Tax Matters, p. 168.   5. Growth and Development, p. 172.
6. Adviser to Labour Governments 1964-1970 and 1974-1976,
p. 179.   7. Monetarism, p. 182.   8. The Challenge to
Equilibrium Theory, p. 186.   9. Conclusion, p. 189.

CONTENTS

BIBLIOGRAPHY OF THE WORKS OF NICHOLAS KALDOR,
compiled by Ferdinando Targetti   191

BIBLIOGRAPHY OF WORKS CITED   217

LIST OF ABBREVIATIONS   221

INDEX   223

PREFACE

Professor Nicholas Kaldor delivered the Mattioli Lectures on 'Causes of Growth and Stagnation in the World Economy' in May 1984. The participants were numerous and listened to the lectures with attention and – one dares to say – passion. Many looked forward to reading the written version because the Author both expanded and detailed the dualistic growth model based on the interaction between two sectors – agriculture vs industry or developing countries vs developed ones – and offered many insights – sometimes quite provocative – on fundamental problems.

As usual one Italian scholar acted as liaison between the Author and the Scientific Commitee – Professor Carlo Filippini. The preparation of the volume was suspended because of Professor Kaldor's death in 1986. As time was rapidly passing and many works were being published either on Kaldor's ideas and theories or as collected papers, a few problems arose on how to edit the material – a provisional written text and the recorded one delivered at Bocconi University.

Many urged the print of the book because of the relevance of the topics dealt with in the 1984 Mattioli Lectures and of the contributions they offered. In the end, Professor Antony P. Thirlwall was asked to edit the Lectures avoiding major alterations to the text while providing if and when deemed necessary additional notes, references and tables. Professor Thirlwall accepted and provided the final text with Professor Ferdinando Targetti as coeditor. The volume now published has been long awaited: the joint efforts of many people and institutions – namely Banca Commerciale Italiana and Bocconi University – have resulted in further evidence of the depth and originality of Professor Kaldor's thought.

ACNOWLEDGEMENTS

For permission to reproduce and insert in this volume a large biographical essay and a bibliography we wish to express our gratitude to:

Professor A.P. Thirlwall, *Nicholas Kaldor 1908-1986*, © The British Academy, 1988, Proceedings of The British Academy, 1988, Proceedings of The British Academy, vol. LXXIII (1987), Lectures and Memoirs;

Professor Ferdinando Targetti, *Bibliography of the Works of Nicholas Kaldor*, from *Nicholas Kaldor. Teoria e politica economica di un capitalismo in mutamento*, © Società Editrice Il Mulino S.p.A., Bologna, 1988.

NICHOLAS KALDOR

CAUSES OF GROWTH
AND STAGNATION IN THE
WORLD ECONOMY

The *Raffaele Mattioli Lectures* were delivered by
Nicholas Kaldor at the Università Commerciale Luigi Bocconi,
in Milano, from 21st to 25th May 1984.

FIRST LECTURE
Equilibrium Theory and Growth Theory*

Since the very beginning, the study of economics has served two purposes, though economists are not always conscious of this duality. One concerned the problem of how in a de-centralised, "undirected" market economy, scarce resources are allocated among different uses in the *right* proportions – in the proportions in which they give the highest satisfaction to consumers as a body – in a specific Pareto sense that no one could be better off with any alternative allocation, without making someone else worse off.

The second object has been to explore the determinants of economic progress – what are the critical factors which make for continued growth, be it through the growth of productive resources or the improvement of knowledge or technology; and how far the results or the characteristic features of "equilibrium economics" (which is the subject matter of the first inquiry) have their counterpart in the second.

The first aspect involves the detailed analysis of the charac-

---

* Lord Kaldor introduced his lectures with the following remarks:

It is a great honour for me to be invited to give the Raffaele Mattioli Lectures. Although we lived in different countries, I met Raffaele Mattioli frequently, both in Milan and in Rome, during many trips that I made to Italy after the World War II. We had a common friend in Piero Sraffa, and it was Sraffa who first introduced me to him in Geneva in the summer of 1947 when I had just arrived to be the Research Director of the newly created Economic Commission for Europe (ECE). I and my wife stayed with him in his 'fattoria' in Tuscany and we once had a holiday together on Lake Garda, visiting various towns in Northern Italy. He was a very clever man, of great personal charm, and a great collector of books with a special interest in economics books. In the late 1940s, here in Milan, Mattioli collected around him an extremely able group of young men, some of whom, like La Malfa, made important public careers.

Raffaele Mattioli and I also had a common bond between us in that we were both extremely fond of Piero Sraffa, a man of quite remarkable gifts and brilliance and a fascinating person to know. One summer, I was on holiday with Piero Sraffa in Norway, when he was involved in a mountain accident and had to be taken to hospital in Oslo. I telephoned Mattioli who said he would come at once. He did so the next day. For a President of the Banca Commerciali to leave everything to fly to Oslo at a moment's notice was quite impressive. Mattioli talked to Sraffa in Italian until he became conscious again, so aiding his recovery. I wanted to make these personal reminiscences before I started my lecture.

3

teristics of the states of general economic equilibrium, considered as the ultimate outcome of an impersonal and, one might say, unconscious process of coordination of the decisions and actions of innumerable individuals, while the second aims to isolate the underlying forces which cause continued change and development.

It would be mistaken to suggest that this dichotomy is generally accepted among economists – some would regard the two as merely different aspects of answering the same question, and that a comprehensive and fully successful treatment of the first should automatically provide the answer to the second. Others would be conscious that economic laws, unless they are pure tautologies, are not eternal but are conditioned by history – they are relative to a particular stage of human evolution. Adam Smith, whose main purpose was to show the politics of prosperity, was clearly aware that the economic institutions of society are not static but are in a constant state of evolution and the policies and institutions appropriate in certain stages of development may become inappropriate in another. He divided history into four or five separate stages, distinguished by the prevailing modes of production – in much the same way as Karl Marx did in the Communist Manifesto seventy-two years later (though, to my knowledge, Marx never accorded Smith a proper acknowledgement). On the other hand, Ricardo wrote as if he was almost oblivious of history, and he regarded the social divisions, the property laws and the market institutions of early 19th-century England, as if they formed the natural way for organising society. His main concern related to matters that were within, and fully consistent with, that framework, such as his opposition to the Corn Laws which, in his view, benefited a small group in society at the expense of all others.

More recent writers tended to divide the subject between "statics" and "dynamics" where the first part related to almost everything taught in classes and described in text-books, while the second mainly consisted of future work still to be developed. As it happened, the increasingly precise elaboration of the first aspect proved more of a stumbling block than a necessary introduction to the second. I shall employ the term "equilibrium

4

theory" for theories dealing with the first aspect, and "growth theory" (for want of a better name) for the second.

Looking at post-war literature – the outpouring of books and articles in periodicals – the so-called "neo-classical" economics continues to occupy the centre of the stage, and most of this work is based on the principles of Walras' original model of general equilibrium, published over 100 years ago, and its application in special contexts, such as the theory of international trade. In this respect, the post-World War II period meant a retrogression in comparison with the great innovative period of the 1930s when, following Keynes, it looked as if interest in the new "macro-economics" – which in contrast to equilibrium theory operated with empirically derived and empirically refutable hypotheses – might replace the traditional concern with the theory of value. But in fact there was a tremendous growth in mathematical economics which, in the nature of the case, concentrated on exploring the implications of *a priori* assumptions and their logical consistency with no regard as to how this work can be applied to empirically observed phenomena and how it can be made to serve the understanding of observed economic changes. As a recent survey article in the *Journal of Economic Literature* put it, "the equilibrium story is one in which empirical work, ideas of facts and falsifications played no role at all".[1]

The main purpose of the theory, from Walras down to the most recent crop of Nobel prize-winners, is to specify the necessary axioms (or basic assumptions – they are basic in the sense that they cannot be derived from some other assumptions or from observation) under which an economy will possess a unique set of equilibrium prices, which if established will possess a certain stability in that stochastic disturbances will not cause more than temporary deviations from them. One of these axioms is that prices constitute the sole source of information on which decisions (of purchases or sales) are based, so that the allocation of resources between different uses is solely determined by prices. The core of the theory consists of the demonstration that, given certain properties concerning preferences and the linearity of all

---

1. Roy Weintraub, "On the Existence of a Competitive Equilibrium, 1930-1957", *Journal of Economic Literature*, March 1983, p. 37.

processes of production, a set of prices will exist which "clears" all markets; that is to say, it achieves full coordination between the economic activities of different units (these are normally called "economic agents", presumably to cover cases in which the unit of decision-making is a family, or an individual enterprise with several owners or controllers and not just a single person) and such a state of affairs is "Pareto-optimal" with each unit's want satisfaction maximised subject to the level of satisfaction of all other units being given. Also, each "productive resource", be it labour, capital (whatever that may be taken to mean) or a natural resource (such as a plot of land, or a waterfall, or minerals under the soil), will earn at least as much in their existing use as in any alternative use – hence no one could change their dispositions as a buyer or seller without making someone else worse off in the process.

This result is subject, however, to a large number of restrictive "axioms" which rob it (in my opinion) of any interpretative value. Of a long list, made considerably longer, and more restrictive by a number of mathematical economists,[1] than Walras originally thought them to be, are the following:

1. All resources, whether human or material resources, are taken as given; so are the preference schedules (or preference maps) of their owners.

2. All technical processes of production (capable of transforming the crude products of nature into finished goods) are given; all these processes are linear and homogeneous (i.e. the general rule of constant returns to scale applies).

3. Prices are given parametrically to all agents, i.e. there is perfect competition in all markets, on both the seller's side and the buyer's side.

4. There is no time dimension. The decision to produce (and actual production), and the decision to consume (and actual consumption) are simultaneous and take no time at all. Hence no commodities are carried over from the past or carried forward into the future. Indeed, strictly speaking, past and future are extraneous to the model.

1. Chiefly Abraham Wald, Kenneth Arrow, Gerald Debreu and Ian McKenzie.

5. All transactions take place at the equilibrium system of prices which is established *before* any transactions are made. This is in fact an unrealisable condition, for reasons set out below.

Though the mathematical theory of general equilibrium attained its final form thirty years ago, and nothing has been added to it since, attempts have been made to make the model more life-like by introducing time (divided into periods of unit length, such as a day or a year), so that all quantities are "dated" and there are markets for each commodity for all future dates as well as for the current dates: if there are n separate commodities for m periods, there are $n(m)$ markets, the prices of which are all interdependent. This means that nothing can happen in the future which is not perfectly foreseen in period 1, and economic transactions in all $n(m)$ markets are a once-and-for-all affair. (From period 2 on, life must become very boring!)

It was not possible, however, to relax the model in other vital respects – such as changes in technical knowledge occurring in the future (except those perfectly foreseen), or to allow for economies of scale (increasing returns), or for the presence of imperfect competition where markets do not "clear" since sellers sell less than the maximum amount they are prepared to sell at the ruling price. None of these features of the real world is compatible with Walrasian general equilibrium.

In fact, the extension of Walrasian general economic equilibrium to cover the case of intertemporal equilibria makes the whole theory more absurd than it was in its original timeless state. For it assumes the constancy over time of the two factors which are known to be constantly changing – human tastes and the technical knowledge available for satisfying them. It is one thing to postulate that in some basic, not precisely definable, sense there are basic human wants which by their very nature are permanent – such as the want for food, for protection against the elements through clothing and shelter, etc. But it is quite another thing to express these wants in terms of precisely specified "commodities" which are (in greater or lesser degrees) substitutes for one another. Food is a primary want and the consumption of bread is one of numerous ways of satisfying it; but one could hardly speak of a demand for bread before the milling of the wheatgerm into flour was invented, and the method of making bread out of it. Or, to take a more fashionable example, can one include computers as a variable of the preference map of "economic agents" for periods *before* computers were invented? In the sense required by the set-up of a general equilibrium model there must be a *finite* number of precisely defined commodities, which cannot be allowed to change as between one period or another. This means that as yet uninvented commodities must also be included (with an infinite price, for periods before their invention) which pre-supposes, of course, that all future inventions are perfectly foreseen. And the same goes for all other factors which enter into decision making. The question which the theory of equilibrium is designed to answer – how it is that all the different goods and services are produced and made available in the markets in the proportions which best correspond to the preferences of consumers – is posed in a manner which treats factors as exogenous and stable in time which are in fact continually evolving as a result of the operation of economic forces.

The Walrasian model, with all its absurd axioms, was intended to be no more than a starting point. It was intended, as with any theory, to develop a model of the second, third, etc. approximations, in the course of which the "scaffolding" (which served to erect the building) was gradually removed. In fact it proved impossible to relax the initial assumptions – on the contrary, the development of the theory meant the addition of more restrictive assumptions than were originally thought to be necessary. As a result, economic theory based on the theory of general equilibrium has led to a *cul-de-sac*, which, far from assisting the absorption of accumulating knowledge and experience, has inhibited progress and has created a brake on the development of an integrated system of knowledge.

One reason why Walras' model failed to provide a reasonable starting point was its exclusive concentration on the role of prices as the sole means of communication between "agents" and hence the sole instrument in the allocation of resources among industries or commodities. Granted the premise that the main problem with which economics is concerned is to explain how an undirected, decentralised system functions, it was wrong to sup-

8

pose that this function is fully performed by the price-system, and that markets can function without either reserves or intermediaries, neither of which features in Walras' model. The model assumes only two classes of "economic agents" – producers and consumers; and it is designed to prove that if all transactions take place at equilibrium prices, all markets will "clear"; the activities and decisions of myriad individuals will be consistent with one another, and everyone will be as well off as possible, in the Pareto sense.

But how is this price-system established, and what happens if it is not established? Various authors, Walras and Edgeworth included, tried to solve this problem by introducing the notion of provisional or hypothetical bids which become binding in stated circumstances – circumstances which bear some family resemblance, but no more than a family resemblance, to sales by auction where, after numerous conditional bids, the actual sale goes to the highest bidder. In the real world the auction method is confined to transactions with special characteristics – to the sale of rare books, rare pictures and coins, and occasionally, to the sale of real property, land or houses. It is inconceivable as a method in a situation in which both sellers and buyers operate in all the markets simultaneously and in which both bid prices and offer prices depend on the prices in many or all other markets, where the same process takes place simultaneously, and where a bid does not refer to a fixed quantity (like a Rembrandt self-portrait) but to a variable amount, depending on the price offered or demanded.

Yet if these conditions are not satisfied, the market will not be in equilibrium but in a state of disequilibrium; and economic theory is silent on the subject of disequilibrium. The technique of "comparative statics" which is employed on all possible occasions is a method of analysing the effect of extraneous changes of all kinds, in terms of the difference it makes to the state of general equilibrium. In other words, it predicts the effect of changes in exogenous variables by comparing two equilibrium states, without saying anything on *how* the system moves from one state of equilibrium to the other.

Until comparatively recently, nobody has pointed out that the

Walrasian model leaves out the existence of a third class of economic agent essential to the functioning of markets – professional intermediaries who are both buyers and sellers simultaneously without whom markets as an institution could hardly function. It is the professional dealers or merchants who make a "market" by being always ready to do business – by providing the facilitiy which enables producers to sell and consumers to buy without appearing simultaneously in all markets; and who are enabled to do this by carrying at all times stocks of the commodities in which they deal in large enough amounts to tide over any short-period discrepancies between "outside" buyers and "outside" sellers. In practice, they fulfil the role assigned to the "heavenly auctioneer" of Walras who conducts the preliminary "tatonnement" necessary for establishing the set of equilibrium prices *before* any transactions are made. Professional merchants or dealers are always "open" to do business during business hours – i.e. they quote prices at which they are ready to buy or to sell (up to certain quantities). They necessarily always quote a pair of prices, one for the buying and one for the selling.

They are not required under the actual rules to buy or sell only at equilibrium prices (still less, in unlimited quantities), but it is their behaviour in the face of an excess demand or excess supply by "outsiders" which brings about the tendency for prices to settle around the level at which the outsiders' demand and supply tend to become equal to each other. The important point is that it is the regular dealers in the market (they were called "jobbers" in the phraseology of the old London Stock Exchange)[1] who initiate the price changes necessary to align outside supply and demand (or production and consumption) to one another. They make their living on the difference between their buying price and their selling price (the so-called "dealers' turn"). The more highly organised a market is, and the greater the competition between dealers, the smaller the "turn" is likely to be, as a proportion of the price – though it must always be large enough to cover the carrying cost of stocks (including interest and all storage charges), as well as their profit, which is the compensa-

1. *Editors' Note*: After the financial reforms of 1987, the nature of the old London Stock Exchange changed.

tion for the risks inevitably entailed in carrying stocks. Any discrepancy between outsiders' demand and supply over a given time interval must simultaneously be reflected in a corresponding change in the volume of stocks carried by the "market" (meaning by the dealers collectively). Experience has taught them how large their "normal" stocks need to be in relation to their turnover in order to ensure continuity of dealing because a dealer's reputation (or "goodwill") depends on his ability to satisfy his customers. Refusal or inability to deal is likely to divert customers to others. To avoid this, dealers must protect their stock by varying their bid and offer prices – raising them when stocks are falling and lowering them when they are rising.

The size of the price variation induced by a change in the volume of stocks held by the market depends on the dealer's expectations of how long it will take before prices return to "normal" and how firmly such expectations are held. The stronger the belief in a "normal" price, based on "normal" costs of production, the smaller is the *temporary* price-variation which occurs during the period of adjustment to disequilibrium, and this in turn is influenced by the traders' experience of how far production is likely to be stimulated, or consumption restricted, in response to a price-rise in an "excess-demand" situation, and how far the opposite happens in an excess-supply situation. Since neither outside demand (or "flow demand") nor outside supply (or "flow supply") can adjust instantaneously to discrepancies created by unexpected changes (such as a bad harvest, for example), it is evident that the commodity reserves carried by the market provide a vital element in the functioning of markets – they provide a "breathing space" for the necessary equilibrating adjustments to take place. They provide an addition to supply out of stocks in an excess-demand situation, and an addition to demand in an excess-supply situation. In both cases, however, the inducement for providing the facility (in the truly competitive market where neither the individual producer nor the individual consumer can influence the market price by his *own* actions) depends on the dealers' belief that the current price is too high (or else too low) in relation to prices in the future, so that by reducing their stocks below normal (or in the opposite case, by absorbing stocks above their normal amount), they *reduce* the risks which they inevitably carry in their business as traders.[1] It also follows, however, that whilst the activities of intermediaries make the adjustment of supply to changes in demand (or *vice versa*) a smoother process than it would be otherwise, the very mechanism of adjustment of quantities (bought or sold) through price-changes entails that any needed adjustment calls forth *temporary* price-variations that are larger, and may be much larger, than those which are ultimately necessary for the re-establishment of equilibrium. This is the reason why, in the absence of deliberate intervention by the government or other public agencies for stabilising prices, commodity markets regularly display large short-term variations in prices which are reversed, in most cases, within a year of their occurrence. Thus, Keynes calculated, in an article published in 1938,[2] that in the case of four commodities (rubber, cotton, wheat and lead), the *average* difference between the highest and the lowest price within a single year, amounted, for the *average* of ten years, to 67 per cent. The calculations of St Clair Grondona[3] showed that the scale of short-term fluctuations in the post-World War II period was even larger.

If our analysis is correct, it is inevitable that any difference between accruals (from producers) and absorptions (by consumers) should call forth *immediate* price changes that are larger than those which are ultimately found necessary: indeed, without such an excess, the mechanism of short-term adjustment through the reduction or enlargement of traders' stocks could not be brought into operation.[4]

1. In this respect they must be sharply distinguished from "speculators" who deliberately *assume* risks by their activities for the sake of expected gain – risks which they would not incur if they "stayed out" of the market, but whose activities provide facilities to traders as well as manufacturers who carry stocks to insure against such risks by "hedging" operations.

2. JOHN MAYNARD KEYNES, "The Policy of Government Storage of Foodstuffs and Raw Materials", *Economic Journal*, September 1938, pp. 440-460 (reprinted in *Collected Writings*, Vol. XXI).

3. ST L. CLAIR GRONDONA, *Economic Stability is Attainable*, London: Hutchison Benham, 1975.

4. It is possible that the price movements in highly organised markets are exaggerated by the activities of non-professional speculators. The activities of professional speculators (who act on "rational" expectations) should in principle moderate price fluctuations, and thus reinforce the activities of the regular dealers.

Yet while the variations of traders' reserves, occurring in response to price changes, enable the market to function in a state of disequilibrium and to bring into train the set of adjustments necessary to establish equilibrium, they reveal the competitive market as a pretty crude and inefficient instrument of adjustment – something which certainly does not emerge from Walras' model of general equilibrium, or indeed from any modern treatise on the theory of value. This is because, as was mentioned already, value theory (or general equilibrium theory) restricts itself to a statement of the properties of equilibrium, and it analyses the effects of changes by the method of comparing the new equilibrium (resulting from a particular change in the "data") with the previous one, with little systematic analysis of how the markets behave under conditions of disequilibrium. Yet it is evident that on any rigorous meaning of the term, economies – the world economy, or any national or regional economy – are always in a state of disequilibrium, since the underlying conditions change too rapidly to permit full adaptation to any particular constellation of the "data" (i.e. to changes in exogenous variables).[1]

Moreover, the assumption that supply and demand are brought into equality through the movement of prices in a competitive market is only true of a particular sector of the economy, relating to basic foodstuffs (such as wheat) or industrial materials produced by agriculture or mining (such as cotton or copper), and in some ways these are the sectors with the least satisfactory features of capitalist market economies. They exhibit the largest instabilities, with prices going regularly up and down like a yo-yo, even when the differences between the rates of production and consumption are relatively small. Moreover, as Professor Sylos-Labini has shown recently, the fluctuations in commodity prices associated with changes in world industrial production

1. ALFRED MARSHALL is one of the few economists who attempted to deal with this problem by making a sharp distinction between relatively quick and relatively slow adaptations; and he established the method of dealing with the behaviour of the economy in terms of analysing "short period" equilibria which assumes durable equipment of all kinds, and hence the short-term productive capacity of all industries to be given as a heritage of the past. This device proved very fruitful in the hands of Marshall's Cambridge successors, including Keynes.

have been three times as great in the most recent decade as previously.[1]

However, in much the greater part of economic activities (at least in developed economies), prices play a subsidiary role in the continuing adjustment of production to changes in demand. These proceed directly as a result of quantity signals rather than price-signals. At any one time, prices are quoted by sellers. Buyers, directly or through the intermediary of merchants, give orders to buy at those prices, and changes in the rate of orders are immediately reflected in changes in the amount of stocks carried by manufacturers or traders (or, where goods are made individually on the buyer's specification, in the change of the producers' order book). There is thus a channel of rapid communication in the system which is not dependent on price changes for its operations. Price changes may accompany the process, but if so, they are incidental to the process of adjustment which is not dependent on it.

This implies, however, that over much the greater part of the field, the assumptions of equilibrium theory are inapplicable. The sellers of goods (whether merchants or manufacturers) are normally in an excess-supply situation (that is to say, they sell *less* than they would be prepared to sell at the prices quoted by them) which is incompatible with the basic assumption of pure competition, and though any particular seller may be influenced in his price quotations by his competitors, it is far from clear *how* prices are determined in oligopolistic markets. In some industries there is evidence of "price-leadership", under which some firm, or a particular group of firms, set prices which other firms are compelled to follow. In other industries prices are restrained by the threat of potential competition – the fear that newcomers will invade the market if the profits earned are above normal levels. But on all this – how competition operates, and how prices are ar-

1. On the Instability of Commodity Prices and the Problem of Gold, in A. QUADRIO-CURZIO (ed.), *The Gold Problem: Economic Perspectives,* Oxford: Oxford University Press, 1982. *Editors' Note:* KALDOR addressed the question of asset market stability in his classic paper 'Speculation and Economic Stability', *Review of Economic Studies,* October 1939. This is the paper about which Hicks wrote to Kaldor 'I think that your paper was the culmination of the Keynesian revolution in *theory.* You ought to have had more honour for it.'

rived at, in quasi-monopolistic markets – our present knowledge is hazy and uncertain; and future progress is more likely to emerge from patient empirical research than from the formulation of new theoretical hypotheses of a wide-ranging character.

However, one thing seems certain: the most potent factor of competition (and one that provides the best justification for a decentralised, private-enterprise economy) is continuous technological change. At the same time this provides the single, basic factor for continual economic growth. The factors usually cited as the determinants of growth – capital accumulation, the growth of the labour force, and a given rate of growth of "knowledge" – are more properly considered as the consequences or manifestations of the changes brought about by the infusion of new technology than its exogenous determinants.

Human progress, from the earliest known history, could be described in terms of the effect of the spread of technological change, which in some historical periods proceeds relatively slowly, while in others it proceeds very rapidly.

It is for this reason that economic growth and competition are intimately linked to one another. In a competitive environment the incentives to "invade" a market, or to gain market shares, by the introduction of new products which are superior to existing products because they satisfy some particular need more cheaply or more effectively, are very powerful – since they provide the quickest way, if not the only way, of acquiring personal fortunes. At the same time, large and well-established enterprises competing with one another (intranationally or internationally) depend on the continued introduction and marketing of "new" products – or improved versions of products in order to maintain their market shares; and owing to the importance of increasing returns (economies of scale) a firm's competitive position greatly depends on its maintaining, and if possible improving, its share of the market. The motor car industry provides a very good example of how, from the very beginning, the firms engaged in it were under strong compulsion to improve the performance and quality of their products, and while some of these improvements can be quantitatively assessed – as for example, engine performance – others, such as comfort, ease of handling, etc., are qualitative and for the most part remain entirely unrecorded in the measurement of the change in real output.

Let me make some remarks on the measurement of real output which have a great significance, even if their importance has been underestimated in the applied economics of growth. The problem of the measurement of the change in *real* output (or real output per worker) over a period of time, or the comparison of differences in real output per head as between different countries (as distinct from the changes in the value of production measured in money) raises some insoluble problems which are hardly mentioned either in official documents or in public discussion. They are arrived at by applying a coefficient (or "deflator") to the estimates of the value of output (free of duplication) in money terms; the construction of the "deflator" raises all the problems of an index number in an acute form, since it needs to cope not only with the change in relative prices (which itself yields different answers according to the system of weighting adopted), but also with the change in the exact specification of the goods produced and the *range* of products offered.

Both of these raise insoluble problems. The ultimate test of a unit of "real income" is whatever gives the same psychological satisfaction to the "representative consumer". There is no way of measuring the additional satisfaction derived from the improvements of, say, a motor car of the most recent vintage, as against an earlier vintage, nor of the addition to well-being derived from the introduction of a new product which provides a hitherto unknown way of satisfying some basic want – as, for example, the invention of the cinema or television (not to speak of improvements such as colour television as against black-and-white television). In the face of such changes, the measurement of real product through the application of a "GDP deflator" is the result of a set of arbitrary conventions, not themselves derivable from an underlying principle, the sole value of which resides in the consistent application of the same set of rules. In general, no allowance is made for the improvement in well-being due to the development of new products or new industries as such (such as electric lighting or heating or televisions); their contribution to real income is measured by the value of production, which means that no allowance is made for the enlargement of choice as such, i.e. the addition of electric power valued at £x million a year has the same weight as an increase in the output of some existing product, say coal, of the same value.

Since (in the last two centuries at any rate) the invention of such new products must have formed much the most important aspect of progress, the statistical measures of increases in "real income" contain a serious downward bias, though there is no possible way in which its magnitude could be quantified. On the other hand, competition encourages all kinds of expenditure (of which display advertising is but one example) devoted to persuading consumers to *change* their preferences between different products – which tends to introduce a bias in the figures in the opposite direction. Hence, while the numerical value of calculations of changes in real income, as between different periods or places, is pretty meaningless, this does not mean that *differences* in the magnitude of changes (or in their direction) are equally arbitrary, provided the set of conventions applied in calculating the "deflator" remains identical. There is no particular value attaching to the numerical estimate of the rise in real income between two periods, say, 1983 and 1984 being 1.9 per cent rather than some other figure (say, 3.4 per cent) which would have been the result of estimating the change by a different set of arbitrary conventions. But to say that the change was only one-half as large as between, say, 1980 and 1981 than between 1979 and 1980, is a more significant piece of information, since the proportionate difference between the figures for the years could be much the same under differing sets of rules provided that they are consistently applied. Equally, it is not meaningless to say that the rate of growth of output in country X was, over a given period, say, 1.3 times as high as in country Y, provided that the precise methods of calculation are the same in the two countries. Since, however, there is no international authority to lay down such detailed rules of calculation, this can by no means be taken for granted. (In the U.S., for example, the output of the automobile industry is measured, inter alia, by the *number* of passenger cars produced, ignoring any improvement in design or in performance as between cars produced in different years. However, those *major* changes in performance – such as those due to the introduction of automatic gear-changing – are explicitly allowed for on the basis of the additional cost of the improvement.)

Let us come back to our main point, that is the relation between competition and technical change. There can be little doubt that the tremendous acceleration of technological change, and in the rate of growth of both population and production, which followed the changes in the legal system initiated by the "glorious revolution" in England of 1688 – laws concerning the freedom of commercial enterprise, of limited liability, and the law relating to bills of exchange – gave an enormous fillip to competition and must be largely responsible for the fact that the industrial revolution took place in England rather than in countries such as France, which were at least as well advanced (if not more advanced) in technological knowledge or know-how. The economic and social aspects of feudalism – entailing restrictions or protective privileges of all kinds, such as those of the medieval guild system, or the stratification of society into classes determined by birth which greatly limited social mobility – imposed severe handicaps to competition which greatly slowed down technological change, though without ever eliminating it entirely. The invention of the harness (unknown to the Romans), which made it possible to replace human muscle-power by horse-power, originates from the 12th century, though it took several hundred years before its use became general throughout Europe.

Most technological changes from the beginning of human history emerged in the course of pursuing activities of various kinds, most of which involved the invention of some durable instrument – a fishing rod or a fishing net, or some kind of a spade, to take primitive examples – which increased the efficiency of work and gave rise to the existence of capital as a "factor of production", and the production of instruments or "machines" of an ever more numerous kind taking up a rising fraction of economic activities. As Allyn Young emphasised,[1] the increase in the value of instruments employed per unit of labour emerges as a result of the subdivision of production into a larger number of

---

1. "Increasing Returns and Economic Progress", *Economic Journal*, December 1928.

separate processes which gives greater opportunities for the use of specialised machinery, but which only becomes profitable as the scale of production exceeds certain levels. Hence the existence of increasing returns to scale and the occurrence of labour-saving technical progress are different aspects of an endogenous process of growth – which requires for its continued operation that the growth of productivity engendered by the growth of output be matched by the growth of market demand.

In the process of 19th-century industrialisation, competition took the form of the emergence of numerous small, specialised firms which provided improved opportunities of cost-reducing changes of technology to other firms. At the same time, the progress of scientific knowledge pursued through laboratories and research institutions, provided the basis of new products and new industries, and of the new uses for known natural resources. As Young said, "the causal connection between the growth of industry and the progress of science runs in both directions, but on which side the preponderant influence lies, no one can say".[1] In the last fifty years, however, alongside the growing concentration of enterprises in the modern science-based industries, technological progress of both labour-saving and the land-saving (or natural resource-saving) kind (a distinction which I shall discuss more fully in the next lecture) have become increasingly a full-time professional activity pursued by highly trained scientists and research workers in laboratories maintained by the enterprises themselves for the purpose of enabling them to produce and market a steady stream of new products. Here, again, it is the competition between these large, frequently transnational or multinational enterprises which generates the rapid technological change in an environment of expanding total demand, which is both the cause and the reflection of the growth in markets.

1. *Ibid.*

SECOND LECTURE
Alternative Approaches to Growth Theory

One of the ideas I wished to convey in my first lecture was that the type of economic theory which is the core of the subject as taught in western universities – and that covers North America, Western Europe, Australia, and so on – is pretty useless and indeed harmful for developing an understanding of the laws of motion of capitalist market economies. It is expressed with a phoney kind of precision or "scientism" of a most pretentious kind, using highly sophisticated, mathematical techniques for proving propositions which have no interpretative value of real-world phenomena, for the simple reason that they are based on *a priori* axioms which have no relation to the conditions which can be empirically observed. All this is aggravated, not helped, by the use of mathematics. Alfred Marshall, who was himself a first-rate mathematician (he was second Senior Wrangler in Cambridge in the year in which Lord Rayleigh, one of the leading English mathematicians of his age, was the first Wrangler), wrote towards the end of his life that he found that "a good mathematical theorem dealing with economic hypotheses was very unlikely to be good economics" because "every economic fact, whether or not it is of such a nature that it can be expressed in numbers, stands in relation as cause and effect to many other facts; and since it *never* happens that all of them can be expressed in numbers, the application of exact mathematical methods to those that can is nearly always a waste of time, while in the large majority of cases it is particularly misleading, and the world would have been further on its way forward if the work had never been done at all."[1]

Walras, along with Karl Menger in Austria and Stanley Jevons in England, elevated the scarcity of resources capable of satisfying wants, and their capability, within limits, of being substituted for other scarce resources, as the central operating principle of economics. And the allocation of resources through the instrument of the price-system was the key to an understanding of the

1. Letter to A. L. Bowley, 1901, quoted by A. C. Pigou (ed.), *Memorials of Alfred Marshall*, London: Macmillan, 1925, p. 774.

21

working of Smith's "invisible hand" in a competitive market economy. With this approach of "scarcity economics", the mode of operation of the economy was worked out by reference to "equilibrium" stated under "static" assumptions, which implied that the kinds and amounts of resources available, the utility maps of consumers and the production or transformation functions were taken as exogenously given. This "static" economics occupied most of the space in textbooks and in lecture courses. Problems of growth and development (attributed to an increase in the supply of resources over time and their efficiency due to technological improvements etc.) were relegated to the as yet undeveloped branch of economics which came to be called "dynamics". (Apart from some isolated attempts, such as Schumpeter's early book on *The Theory of Economic Development*, which remained without great influence, there was very little written on the subject until the post-war "growth models" of the 1950s.)

The whole school which dominated economics ever since the early 1870s came to be called "neo-classical", in contrast to the "classical school", originally developed from the French Physiocrats by Adam Smith and his successors – Malthus and Ricardo, John Stuart Mill and also by Karl Marx. The classical economists *started* with "dynamics". Except for Ricardo's concern with problems of exchange value and distribution, their main concern was to discover the causes of the "wealth of nations"; what are the causes of comparative prosperity and poverty, and how – by what policies of the State – can prosperity and growth be best promoted? In contrast to the neo-classical economists who believed that economics should be pursued on "scientific" lines, making use of the same kind of tools as mechanics, the English classical economists saw human societies as being in a continuous process of evolution, and the generalisations that can be made about the nature of this process have more in common with the laws of biology (including the basic unpredictability of the lines of development) than with the methods of the sciences concerned with inanimate matter, such as physics.[1]

1. This was the view of Alfred Marshall who could not be said to "belong" to either category, as his sympathies lay with the classics, but his value theory was subjective and in sympathy with the marginal utility school.

Indeed, perhaps the single most important scientific hypothesis which originated from economics, but could just as well be classed as part of biology, was Malthus' law of population which was put forward as a basic generalisation relating to all living matter and which the great biological discoveries of the mid-19th century served to confirm. Its essence lay in the proposition that all species of the "vegetable and animal kingdom" have the innate property that their powers of reproduction are greatly in excess of the needs of mere replacement, and these excess powers provide the mechanism which secures survival and recuperation in the face of large erratic shocks due to natural calamities (floods or drought), contagious diseases (such as the Black Death in the Middle Ages) or now, the danger of an all-out atomic war, which, according to the latest pronouncements of experts, might make a large part of the planet uninhabitable for decades or even centuries. Even the latter may not mean the end of humanity, and if it does not, it will be due to Malthus' population law. The small percentage of mankind who survived would, in these circumstances, multiply progressively as gradually more of the earth's surface became fit again for human habitation.

Malthus was denounced by Marx, among others, as an out-and-out reactionary since the proposition that only misery and starvation can impose a limit to the density of population carried the message that anything done to alleviate or improve the lot of the poor, or to increase the fertility of the soil, would cause extra population growth until, on a per capita basis, things became as bad as they were before.

This may have been the message of the first edition of *An Essay on the Principle of Population* (1798). But in the second edition (published in 1803)[1] he introduced the distinction between "preventive" and "positive" checks. The former serve to modify the operation of the law (by reducing the amount of excess fertility) so as to make it possible to stabilise population levels at higher levels of real income per head, or even put the mechanism out of operation altogether if fertility is sufficiently reduced.

All social institutions or customs which serve to reduce excess

1. THOMAS ROBERT MALTHUS, *An Essay on the Principle of Population*, 2nd edition, London: J. Johnson, 1803.

fertility make for higher standards of living by reducing the density of population corresponding to any particular level of real income per head. Such institutions and customs have taken many forms in the course of history, from primitive customs such as the exposure of first-born babies (as was said to be the case with the Trobriand Islanders), to monogamy and lateness of marriage, down to the latest forms of birth control through the pill, which might put the Malthusian survival mechanism out of action altogether. Anyhow, Ricardo's doctrine of a "natural" price of labour at which alone the population can be stationary, was clearly intended to take account of preventive as well as positive checks, so that it was compatible with relatively high or relatively low wages, and in this respect differs from Marx's "cost of reproduction" concept. In a dynamic context, where production and population are continually growing, the Malthusian principle may serve to determine not the level of the real wage, but the maximum growth of the labour force; this will be consistent with steadily rising wages if the rate of growth of output is higher than that of population.

It is one of the best-known facts of history that the density of population over any given area has increased with the evolution of society and the introduction of superior technologies due to land-saving technical progress (Ricardo's "improvements in the art of cultivation"), though by and large the population response was not as great as to prevent some gradual improvement in living standards. Nevertheless, none of the classical economists believed (with the possible exception of Marx) that such land-saving improvements can put off the operation of the Law of Diminishing Returns more than temporarily; and the operation of this Law must bring all economic growth through capital accumulation and increasing population sooner or later to an end. Hence the doctrine of the stationary state as the *final outcome* of economic development – an idea which figures prominently already in Adam Smith (when describing ancient civilisations like China, which in his view had already exhausted, possibly some centuries before, its growth potential). Land-saving technological progress – such as occurred with the domestication of animals, the invention of crop-raising by the cultivation of the soil

– must, in their view, have some limit. Later economists introduced the idea of changing modes of production due to the change of technical or scientific knowledge as something which is largely exogenous to the economic system – it may go on at a certain rate in time but its occurrence is independent of economic pressures.

Yet the one thing that seems clear to us now is that technological progress, whether it is of the land- or the labour-saving kind, is no more exogenous than population growth itself. If the growth of population presses against the means of subsistence owing to increasing scarcity of land (or more generally, of natural resources), voyages of discovery will be stimulated and a lot of new land discovered, as happened in the 15th and 16th centuries. Necessity is the mother of invention – as the proverb goes. Many of the momentous technological changes occurred in response to need created by scarcities. The greatly increased scarcity of wood in 18th-century Europe due to rapid deforestation, partly caused by the growth of ship-building, led to the invention of producing coke out of coal, thereby making iron-making independent of the growing scarcity of charcoal. This was one of the most important inventions of the industrial revolution.

Such examples could be multiplied almost ad infinitum. Anyhow, Ricardo and his followers firmly believed that as the population grows, a steadily rising share of labour and capital will be required for food production, leaving less available for satisfying other needs through manufacturing activities and the provision of services.

There are not many predictions that have been so completely falsified by subsequent history. Instead of more and more of the community's resources being pre-empted by the "primary sector" for producing food and raw materials, the very opposite occurred – the proportion of population occupied in agriculture and mining has fallen since Ricardo's day in the most dramatic fashion, from over 50 per cent in early-19th-century Britain to less than 3 per cent in present-day Britain. The same kind of process has occurred in most industrialised countries, and on a more moderate scale in the developing countries. In terms of *total* agricultural production, or in output per hectare, the rate of growth has been less spectacular than in terms of output per head, but these differences are deceptive since there is always "disguised unemployment", or surplus population on the land, so that the reduction in *numbers* occupied in agriculture tends to be larger than the reduction in the volume of man-hours of work. As Italy's own experience has shown most conclusively, the transference of labour from rural to urban employment, or from agriculture to industry and services, had no adverse effects on agricultural output. To a lesser degree this is also true of transference of labour within the industrial or service sectors in which, on account of the prevalence of imperfect competition, there may be "work-sharing" by enterprises and not only by workers, so that an expansion of the demand for labour in a fast-growing sector may cause a transference of labour from other sectors without adverse effects on the amount produced in those latter sectors, other than a concentration of output among a smaller number of firms. This has therefore the same kind of effect as that associated with the absorption of "open" or "disguised" unemployment.

It is difficult to visualise, therefore, that the labour supply should be the effective constraint on production in any particular "economy", except for short periods which do not leave time for the consequential movement in the flow of labour as between geographical locations or as between industries or sectors.

The meaning of the term "economy" is capable of numerous interpretations. It may refer to an area united by a single political sovereignty; and no doubt this is the meaning which writers most frequently have in mind. But it may also refer to a region within a country (such as Scotland) or a group of countries with common institutions (such as the European Community) or to the world as a whole. The geographical mobility of labour will, of course, be different according to the definition adopted, but it can be assumed that, allowing time for adjustment, it is always taking place, as the post-war experience of Europe has so eloquently shown. It is difficult, therefore, to envisage that the "productive potential" of an economy is determined by the "full employment" of its labour force. The latter assumes that the labour force in a particular economic sector or area cannot be augmented by a re-allocation of labour between sectors or enterprises. Neither of these statements is true.

Malthus' prediction that an increase in the "means of subsistence", or, as we would say, in the production of "wage goods", will lead to a growth of population, or in more extreme cases, will be attended by a population explosion, has frequently been confirmed by historical experience. The rate of growth of populations of different countries appears to be fairly closely geared to the rate of economic growth. This was true of European countries in the 18th and 19th centuries when the industrial revolution led to an explosive increase in numbers, in one country after another. It is true of India and China in the present century. Thus, India's food production doubled in the last twenty-five years – from 70 to 140 million tons of food grains – but over the same period, population also increased by 75 per cent, from 400 to 700 million, leaving room only for a very small improvement – of the order of 0.6 per cent a year – in food supplied per head. China's population over the same period has increased by nearly as much – by two-thirds, from 600 million to 1,000 million. Hence, it is true to say in both cases, that much the greater part of the increase in production has been pre-empted by the requirements of population growth, and only the smaller part – one-quarter or one-third – went to increase consumption per head. However, both countries are now taking far-reaching steps to reduce their birth rates through the spread of methods of birth control.

Despite the fact that in low-income countries, like India and China, increased density of population is a response to enlarged food supplies, the proportion of population in the primary (agricultural) sector is falling, and that in the secondary and tertiary sectors is growing – which is only possible if land-saving innovations, or the land-saving aspect of technological changes, are at least as important, or more important, than the labour-saving technical progress in the secondary and tertiary sectors. For if technical progress were mainly labour-saving, the scope for employment in the secondary sector (which is the sector that requires primary products as its direct or indirect inputs and transforms them into finished products, whether consumption goods or capital goods) and the tertiary sector (including distribution and all other services) would be reduced relative to that in the primary sector.

Assuming that food consumption per head is much the same in all three sectors of a self-sufficient economy, the proportion of the population outside agriculture is really determined by the excess of food production in agriculture over the self-consumption of agricultural labour. As Adam Smith emphasised, the scope for industrial and service employment depends on the size of this "agricultural surplus".

Most new techniques, whether they are land- or labour-saving or both, need to be "embodied" in new commodities or new instruments of some kind; hence they create the need for new investments for their realisation. Indeed, the assumption that the capital accumulated by society in relation to labour (the capital/labour ratio) is the main factor responsible for the level of productivity (or real income per head) being high or low, implies the assumption that there is at any time a stock of known but as yet unadopted superior technologies (resulting from *past* inventions) the adoption of which has been delayed, or set aside for the time being, because they require capital accumulation – that is to say, additions to saved-up income – which can only be realised gradually, over a period. Capital accumulation, in the classical view, was governed by the savings propensities out of currently accruing income. The social (or legal) institution of property rights, whether in real property or in man-made instruments of production, can be looked upon as institutional devices evolved by society for pre-empting a proportion of current production for saving and accumulation, so that the amount available for increased consumption (and the resulting population increase) is reduced.

This way of looking at the problem rationalises the classical approach which regarded the growth of capital as the main factor for determining both the rate of growth of the demand for labour and the rate of growth of output. Labour and capital were regarded as complementary factors, in contrast to the neo-classical view which regards them as substitutes. However (failing the continued invention of new technologies, which was never seriously entertained), as the stock of known but as yet unadopted

28

superior technologies is gradually depleted, the rate of profit on new investments will fall. Accumulation will cease altogether when profits, in the words of Ricardo, "are so low as not to afford [the manufacturers and traders] an adequate compensation for their trouble, and the risk which they must necessarily encounter in employing their capital productively".[1]

However, if we allow for a flow of new technologies resulting from new discoveries, or new ideas or advances in scientific knowledge, there is no need for the rate of capital accumulation, or for the rate of profit, to fall – it will remain the same when as much is added to the stock of yet unexploited technologies at one end as is withdrawn from the stock at the other end, for example. Then accumulation can go on indefinitely as it just keeps pace with the rate of technical progress. The trouble with this view is that it takes the accrual of new technologies as something exogenously given, and the (long run) rate of capital accumulation to be governed by it, whereas in fact it is a case of mutual interaction. The feedback resulting from the change of techniques, occurring in consequence of a certain rate of capital accumulation, may influence the accrual of new technologies, as much as the other way round.

The dominant view of the classical economists was that the rate of capital accumulation was the most important determining factor in economic growth. This in turn depended on the size of the "surplus" of production over *necessary* consumption. In Marx's case, "necessary consumption" was defined as "the cost of reproduction of labour"; in Ricardo's, the surplus depended on the share of income accruing to manufacturers and traders who were the class that most clearly stood to benefit from the increase in production resulting from capital accumulation. Hence the importance of profits as a share of income resided in the fact

1. The rate of profit was thought by Ricardo to be determined, as Piero Sraffa has shown, at the margin of cultivation of "corn", where both output and input consisted of the *same* commodity, by the net excess of corn output over corn input – whether the latter was 'laid out' in the form of advances paid to labour (as wages) or re-invested in the form of seed. It is here that the rate of profit is necessarily the same in corn-terms as in money-terms, and hence it sets the standard for the rate of profit in all such employments where input and output are heterogeneous commodities, so that the rate of profit can only be evaluated in money terms.

that it determined the share of savings in income. As Ricardo explained in his famous essay on the *Influence of the Price of Corn on the Profits of Stock* (which contained the core of the theory developed in the *Principles*), the importance of the free importation of corn was that, by keeping corn prices low, it kept wages low as a share of *industrial* output (since wages were assumed to be fixed in terms of corn), and thereby increased the share of profits of the manufacturer's output. Profits in industry were thus regarded as the residual part of income which is left after deducting first the rent to be paid to the landlord (on the marginal principle), and then the amount paid in wages.

In growth theories based on Keynesian economics, the chain of causation is reversed: the investment decisions of entrepreneurs, which serve to create capital goods (or "non-available output"), represent the prior claim on output, since entrepreneurial outlays are backed up by purchasing power which is very much greater, in relation to their expenditure over a given period, than that which finances the wage-earners' consumption. Investment expenditure determines, in turn, the share of profits because profits must always be sufficient to provide the residual amount of saving required to finance investment.[1] Hence the famous statement attributed to Kalecki that the wage earners spend what they earn, and capitalists earn what they spend!

On this theory, so far from profits being determined by the excess of output over necessary consumption (the Ricardo-Marx view), it is the share of wages in income which will be residual, depending on the share of output which is not taken up by entrepreneurial claims (as well as the landowners' claims) and hence available for the wage-earners' consumption. The Ricardo-Marx view on wages is more plausible in circumstances in which wages are constant in real terms, even when output per worker is rising; the alternative view is more plausible in situations in which output per worker is rising, but the share of investment in output remains constant, so that wages rise at the same rate as output per worker.

1. The savings of wage-earners (which the classical economists ignored as something negligible) reduces the amount which is left to be financed out of profits, and hence it has the effect of reducing profits by an equivalent amount.

The view that entrepreneurial expenditure, whether on investment or on consumption, represents a prior claim on output is making the same assertion as is involved in saying that it represents an exogenous component of demand, which is not dependent on, or financed by, the profits accruing out of current production. This is the basic assertion underlying Keynes' principle of effective demand, and it constitutes the essential difference between the Keynesian view, according to which production is governed by demand, and the classical view of Ricardo, Say, and John Stuart Mill (as well as the neo-classicals) according to which demand has no independent role to play in the determination of either the total volume of production or its distribution. To understand the meaning of the Keynesian revolution, as well as the post-Keynesian theories of growth and distribution, it is worth setting out the opposing view, and the hypotheses on which they are built, in some detail.

The classical economists (with the sole exception of Malthus, whose under-consumptionist views were difficult to reconcile with the subsistence theory of wages based on his population theory), maintained that production is determined by capital, which, at any one time, is the cumulative result of saved-up income. Capital determines production partly because (as the modern view would emphasise) it determines physical production capacity, but partly also (as Ricardo and Mill would have emphasised) because wages are paid-out capital, since they are paid in advance of the accrual of the product of labour. The demand for commodities, on the other hand, is nothing else but the production (or supply) of commodities looked at in a different way; demand therefore is limited by production, which excludes the opposite assertion that it is production which is limited by demand.

In a barter economy, where goods and services are directly exchanged with one another, this point is obvious. In a money economy, landowners, capitalists and workers receive money incomes, the total of which is necessarily the same as the value of output created; their money income in turn is expended on the goods and services produced. Hence the famous "law of markets" of J.B. Say which proclaims (in the words paraphrased by John Stuart Mill) that "supply creates its own demand"; if output were doubled overnight, so would the purchasing power to buy that output.

The fallacy in this argument is that whereas in a barter economy savings inevitably set up a demand for goods – whether for purposes of accumulating a reserve of goods for future use, or for acquiring some instrument of production – this is not the case in a money economy, where the natural or automatic form of saving is to refrain from spending within the "day" all the money acquired during "day" from selling goods, so that the value of the goods *bought* by an individual during the day need not equal the value of the goods *sold*. The difference is unspent money which can be carried over to the next "day" or further for the purpose of future spending. The importance of "money" is thus that it provides a link between the present and the future which does not exist in a barter economy, and thereby it makes it possible to save in the form of general purchasing power, and not only through the purchase of durable goods of particular kinds. More generally, a money economy makes it possible to accumulate financial assets (money is but one form of such assets) which cannot exist in a barter economy.

Hence Keynes' principle of "effective demand" is best described as a refinement or a development of Say's Law rather than a simple rejection of it. Keynes did not deny that incomes are derived from productive activities, so that "incomes" are merely a different aspect of costs incurred, so that they provide both a measure of the value of the goods produced and a source of demand for goods. What he denied was that there is a necessary equivalence between the costs incurred in production and the demand generated by the costs incurred. The novelty in Keynes' approach was to make production the resultant of expenditure decisions which must be on a sufficient scale to make it possible for the producers not only to recover their costs but to leave a surplus over these costs for profit.

A private enterprise economy requires such an excess: the receipts obtained from the sale of output must *exceed* the entrepreneurs' outlays on production. If we supposed, for the sake of simplicity, that entrepreneurial outlays consisted entirely of outlays for hiring labour, then the total outlays of entrepreneurs as a group will be equal to the total income of wage earners. Even if we abstract from compulsory levies on income imposed by the government etc., and if we supposed that wage earners spend the *whole* of their wage income on purchasing goods in the same period, without saving anything for a rainy day or for retirement, their total outlay on goods *cannot* be greater than the total costs of these goods incurred by the entrepreneurs, leaving nothing over for profit, the expectation of which was the entrepreneurs' sole motive in producing goods for sale. To make it possible for entrepreneurs as a class to realise a profit over and above the costs incurred, there must be an additional source of demand which is autonomous (or exogenous) in character which does not flow directly from income receipts generated by current production, and thus will determine at what level of output total demand and supply will match one another. Keynes' *principle of effective demand* asserts that this point will be given by the particular level of output at which the sum of endogenous demand (derived from incomes generated in production, in the manner described above) and exogenous demand (which are the expenditures of the entrepreneurs themselves on new investment and on their own consumption) exceeds the total outlays of entrepreneurs by no more (or no less) than the profit, the expectation of which induces them to incur outlays on production on that particular scale.[1] If receipts prove to be greater than expected, entrepreneurs will be tempted to expand their scale of operations; in the opposite case they will contract it, but given the size of the exogenous component of demand (which is assumed to be invariant to output) realised receipts will rise less than expected receipts with any rise in output, and fall less with any contraction of output.

Hence, ultimately, it is the exogenous component of demand which will determine what the level of output in the aggregate will be, subject to the proviso that effective demand thus determined is less than the maximum output at full employment. In Keynes' original model in the *General Theory* (published in 1936) he assumed a "closed economy" with no foreign trade and an ex-

1. JOHN MAYNARD KEYNES, *General Theory*, p. 24, assumes that entrepreneurs require a certain "expected profit" for any particular scale of operation, and one which is positively related to the scale of total outlays.

ogenously given labour force, as well as a given productive capacity, as in the Marshallian short period. His own analysis did not extend beyond the short period, as he did not consider the effects of investment on productive capacity and its repercussions on future investment.

However, Keynes' new way of posing the problem by asking the question how output as a whole is determined (in the circumstances of the Great Depression of the early 1930s it was difficult to uphold the view that production is constrained by the scarcity of resources); his assertion that expenditure decisions which govern aggregate demand, provide the primary determinant, and the level of output is derived from it, instead of, as in all traditional theory, the other way round, and the importance accorded to business profits which was implicit in the model (since profits *ex post* will always be sufficient, and no more than sufficient, to provide the residual savings that makes *ex-post* savings equal *ex post* investment), ensured that from then onwards economics took a different turn. It did not take long before the Keynesian model was extended to deal with problems of growth and fluctuations, with the relationship of growth and distribution, and finally, with the role of international (or interregional) trade and the mechanisms which make the growth of primary production keep in line with the growing requirements of secondary and tertiary production.

The first important step came with Harrod's *Essay in Dynamic Theory* published in 1939, which posed the question of the conditions required for a steady rate of economic growth to be sustainable. In Keynes' short-period model, physical output capacity was considered as given, as a heritage of the past, and as we have mentioned, Keynes did not consider the effect of investment on the change in output capacity (or the capital stock) over a period of time, nor the effect of changes in output on the decision to invest. He regarded investment decisions in any given period to be determined by the prevailing state of expectations, which, owing to the uncertainty of the future, are liable to sudden changes in sentiment which are not related to the facts of experience in any stable or rational manner.

This applies if any particular time or "short period" is taken in isolation. Over a period of time, however, investment decisions must themselves be governed by changes in the level of production (as determined by demand); so if production is rising, productive capacity in any particular industry, or in industry as a whole, must grow at the same rate, or roughly the same rate, as production. If it grows less, the growth of output will be constrained, sooner or later, by a shortage of capacity; if it grows by more, there will be an increasing amount of surplus capacity which must progressively reduce the attraction of further increasing capacity through new investment. Now the resource cost of a net addition to capacity depends on a technological relationship which Harrod (and some years after him, the American economist, Domar, who independently reached the same result) took as given; the amount of capital required for providing a unit-flow of output is known as the "capital/output ratio".[1] Now, if the proportion of investment in total output is assumed to be determined by an exogenously given savings coefficient (s), there is a unique rate of growth of output and capital which can be sustained, which is given by the savings ratio (s) *divided* by the capital/output ratio (v) which Harrod called the "warranted" rate of growth, $G_w = s/v$.

The growth of production requires that capacity should be capable of being activated by the use of labour. It is necessary, therefore, that the growth of the productive potential looked at from the labour side (which is the sum of two elements, the growth in the available labour force, and the growth in the productivity of labour, resulting from technical progress), which Harrod called the "natural" rate of growth $G_n = (l + t)$,[2] should be in line with the growth of the productive potential on the capital side, G_w. Hence there are four determinants of growth which, on this view, are four exogenously given constants. Hence, on these assumptions, steady and self-sustaining growth could only come about by a fortunate accident. Moreover, differences be-

1. Domar took the reciprocal of this expression, the so-called capital coefficient (or the productivity of investment), which shows the additional output capacity resulting from investment as a fraction of the value of investment. Since $v = 1/\sigma$, the two come to the same thing.

2. Where l is the symbol of the percentage rate of growth of the labour force and t is the symbol of the percentage rate of growth of productivity per man.

tween the warranted and natural growth rates are bound to set up increasing divergences in either direction. If the warranted rate exceeds the natural rate, physical output capacity would tend to grow at a faster rate than actual output, owing to the fact that production will be increasingly hampered by labour shortages. This means that a state of full employment will be unstable since it involves a faster rate of growth of capacity than the rate of growth of production (which is limited by the "natural" rate of growth) which causes planned saving to exceed planned investment which leads the actual growth rate to fall below potential. In the opposite case, when savings at full employment are insufficient to secure the growth of output capacity that is capable of increasing the volume of employment in line with the growth of the *effective* labour force (after allowing for labour-saving technical progress), there will be a tendency for effective demand to be excessive, resulting in inflationary pressures and over-full employment.

The basic shortcomings of this approach (which also are true to a certain extent of the *General Theory*) are that it takes all the critical elements in the situation as exogenously determined, irrespective of the actual performance of the economy – whereas, in fact, most of these "independent variables" cannot be taken as independent since they respond to needs revealed by the development of the economy. We have already discussed in the previous lecture how the frequency and duration of technological change responds to incentives created by needs. If labour threatens to become scarce, this will stimulate the invention and introduction of labour-saving devices of all kinds; it will also stimulate labour mobility both inter-regionally and inter-industrially. There is therefore no such thing as a "natural" rate of growth which is determined by exogenous factors independently of the demand for labour.

An even more important shortcoming, which characterises both Harrod and subsequent growth models constructed on traditional lines, is the assumption of an exogenously given *savings* ratio. This is due to the failure to recognise the special role and characteristics of profits in a capitalist economy.[1] Profits are a

1. In this respect Keynes' position in the *Treatise on Money* was much in advance of his treatment of the subject in the *General Theory*.

species of income *sui generis*; they represent the reward of enterprise, the amount of which can only be ascertained *ex post* over the whole life of an enterprise, though there is a conventional accounting measure of the profit attributable to a given period, such as a year.[1] It is a fallacy to regard profit as the payment made for the use of "capital" on a par with wages as the payment for hiring labour, or rent as the payment for the use of land. Profit is the reward for running an enterprise, the expectation of which alone induces entrepreneurs to incur the risk and trouble of organising and running a business; it is best regarded as the excess of sales proceeds over costs, and it can be negative as well as positive.[2] It is a universal feature of capitalist enterprise that profits are the prime source of the accumulation of business capital. Hence, in a growing economy, a large proportion of profits are "retained" or "ploughed back" into the business, because without such internal savings, a growing enterprise will find itself in an increasingly perilous financial position, since the more it is dependent on capital obtained from external sources (whether in the form of loans or ordinary shares sold for cash), the greater the danger that a firm may be forced into liquidation as a result of losses. Hence, contrary to the conventional view of economists (though significantly, *not* that of businessmen), internal and external sources of finance are *complementary* to each other, and not substitutes; to be in a "safe" position, the entrepreneurs' own capital and reserves must grow at the same rate as the scale of operation of the business.

The classical economists assumed that profits are the source of *all* savings, and were inclined to assume also (for simplicity) that *all* profits are saved. The landowner who derives his income "from a safe and permanent source" (and one that tends to grow

1. The calculation of the latter necessarily involves an arbitrary element due to the particular accounting conventions adopted for valuing stock at the end of the period, as well as the valuation of stock inherited from the past at the commencement of the period.

2. In neo-classical economics it is assumed to be the same as the rate of interest which is strictly speaking the payment made for loans that are necessary to bridge the period between the payments made for labour, materials, etc. and the sale of the resulting output. Interest is more properly regarded as the payment made for the use of working capital, and as such they are part of the costs incurred which the entrepreneur recoups from the subsequent sales proceeds.

automatically in time without any savings on his part) has no incentive to save, whereas the wage earner who is barely able to satisfy the urgent needs of himself and his family, lacks the ability to do so. Since Ricardo's time, real wages in industrial countries have risen well above the subsistence level, and a large part of the working population now makes regular contributions to pension schemes or life assurance policies, so that these "outside" savings can no longer be considered as negligible – though, of course, as a proportion of incomes, they are only about one-tenth as large as savings out of profits.[1]

Hence, so long as investment expenditure is larger than savings out of non-business incomes (as they must be – for otherwise the sales-proceeds of entrepreneurs as a class would fall short of their outlays and the capitalist system couldn't function), the *share of profits* in output will always tend to be such as to provide the residual savings required to finance the investment expenditure (and also the personal consumption expenditure) of entrepreneurs as a class. In order for the capitalist system to function, the share of investment out of income must therefore be smaller than the share of savings out of profits, and larger than the share of savings out of wages. It could not function if this condition is not satisfied and this condition has come to be known, in the literature, as the Pasinetti-Kaldor inequality. The assumption of a fixed savings coefficient, which underlies the Harrod-Domar type of growth model, lacks any empirical or theoretical justification.

The problems of a steadily growing economy do not arise in the field of savings or investment at all. As I shall attempt to demonstrate in the next lecture, they arise out of the difficulty of keeping the growth of the availability of primary commodities in line with the growth of the absorptive capacity of the industrial sectors of the world.

1. Even so, they threaten to undermine the profit system, since the net savings out of wages, etc., diminish the sales proceeds of entrepreneurs *relatively* to the costs incurred, and if they go far enough, they threaten to undermine the foundations of the capitalist system. Hence, to counteract it, capitalist economies develop all kinds of devices for keeping up the propensity to consume of the working classes: modern large-scale advertising, the invention of hire purchase of durable consumer goods, and the provision of mortgage finance for the purchase of houses, are obvious examples.

THIRD LECTURE
The Problem of Intersectoral Balance

In our last lecture we considered how Keynes' short period equilibrium model gave rise to models of a *steadily growing economy* where the steady growth of the physical capacity to produce output (resulting from past investment) went hand-in-hand with the growth of the *demand* for consumable output, which in turn was "fed" by the growth in the volume of investment which generated an increase in the demand for consumer goods; and the latter, in turn, justified new investment decisions on an increasing scale. It was the discovery of Harrod and Domar which showed that with a given capital coefficient there is only one particular rate of growth which will generate a growth of demand that corresponds to the growth of productive capacity, and for that reason it could maintain itself indefinitely.

I do not wish to repeat the objections to this kind of model which takes too many factors as exogenously given and which takes no account of the structural problems of economic growth. This treatment of the problem is no different from assuming that production consists of a single homogeneous commodity which is either consumed or accumulated. Hence these models have come to be called "single sector" models, to distinguish them from "multi-sector" models which take into account the mutual interdependence (or complementarity) of different sectors, the development of each of which is closely dependent on, and also stimulated by, the development of the others.

The *traditional distinction* between economic sectors is that between primary, secondary and tertiary activities. The first refers to primary products, agriculture and mining, which are "land-based" activities – they are products derived from nature, either through the cultivation of the soil, or the production of animals fed from the products of the soil, or of things extracted from materials found below the earth's surface, such as coal and oil and metal-containing ores. The secondary sector transforms raw products into finished goods, sometimes through a long chain of processes which are called "manufacturing activities". The third sector relates partly to the transport and distribution of the product of the first two sectors, as well as all such activities as medical and legal services, education, entertainment, and so on – the output of which consists of services rendered by persons and not (or not mainly) through the agency of material products.

It is usually said that the relative importance of these three sectors in the economy (as measured by the manpower engaged in each) is a measure of the degree of development or underdevelopment of an economy. Primitive communities are entirely taken up with the provision of food; a secondary sector emerges when the food producers are capable of producing more food than is required for their own consumption, and exchange their "agricultural surplus" (the term is Adam Smith's) for goods satisfying other and less primary needs, such as clothing and shelter, which require processing and adaptation of materials found in nature. In the course of development, this secondary sector grows enormously in relative importance, and there are strong reasons for believing that the manufacturing sector provides the true dynamic element – the fundamental "engine of growth" of an economy. It is the sector in which the major advances in human knowledge are reflected in the development of wholly new products and wholly new industries, the possible existence of which is quite unforeseen until new scientific discoveries create an opportunity for the satisfaction of new wants and thereby transform and enlarge the whole structure of human preferences.

Manufacturing is also the sector in which productivity increases more or less automatically with an increase in the size of the market. With an expansion of total production, new subsidiary industries appear using specially constructed instruments, the use of which becomes profitable only when the aggregate size of production is large enough to make their use economical. In the words of Adam Smith, productivity depends on the 'division of labour' and the latter depends on the size of the market, which in turn depends on the division of labour – which means that the process of expansion is self-generating. In this case, the changes which occur in response to rising demand become difficult to disentangle from changes in technology which induce increasing demand by making things relatively cheaper.

Finally, there are services which take up a rising proportion of total resources with economic progress, but where the recorded increase in productivity is relatively low – partly because of difficulties in measuring "productivity" (in measuring the output of administration, for example, a unit of output is measured by input), but partly also because it is the sector where imperfect competition is most likely to induce an excessive number of enterprises, involving higher costs, due to subnormal utilisation of capacity.

With the exception of agriculture, imperfect or monopolistic competition is universal, which has far-reaching consequences on the mode of operation of markets. Prices are determined, in most cases, not by the market, acting through independent middlemen, but by the sellers (or producers) with the result that prices are far more stable than those of primary commodities, and they are based on costs to a greater or lesser degree, whilst changes in demand appear to have no direct influence.

In manufacturing, owing to the importance of economies of scale, competition is likely to be concentrated among few producers. In the tertiary sector, on the other hand, the strength of demand in the economy in general is likely to influence the number of enterprises by raising (or lowering) the minimum turnover (or "break-even point") on which an enterprise can subsist.

In the following sections I shall concentrate on the mode of operation of a single two-sector model, agriculture and industry, which I believe is capable of bringing to light aspects of the economic problems that tend to be neglected both in micro- and in macro-economics. It is assumed that each sector is dependent on the other in a *dual* capacity: as a market for its products and as the supplier of the means necessary for its own production.

The industrial sector depends on the primary sector for its essential inputs (e.g. agricultural raw materials like cotton and wool; minerals – ores and the ferrous and non-ferrous metals derived from them; and finally, all forms of energy, whether timber, coal, oil, water power or nuclear power), and also for the supply of food, indispensable for industrial employment.

The primary sector depends on the industrial sector for its requirements for capital goods of all kinds. It is assumed that agricultural production, at any given technology, requires both labour and instruments of various kinds. Since land is scarce, increases in production, using the same technology, are subject to diminishing returns to capital and labour, but with the passing of time, agricultural output per acre rises as a result of land-saving changes in technology (which does not exclude that many of the inventions or innovations are labour-saving as well as land-saving) and their adoption requires capital investment for their exploitation (a tractor, or a combine harvester, or even a new type of seed which promises higher yields but is more costly than previous types). Hence we shall not attempt to isolate the effects of capital accumulation and that of land-saving technical progress. In other words, we shall assume that there is a certain rate of land-saving inventions that represent an accrual of new technology, the adoption of which requires additional investment for their realisation.

We shall assume that agriculture produces "corn" (a generic term denoting agricultural products of all kinds), whereas industry produces "steel" (another generic term denoting capital goods of all kinds). In order to highlight the essential inter-relationships and the problems to which they give rise, we shall ignore numerous features, such as that the industrial sector produces consumption goods, as well as capital goods, and the agricultural sector's investment may consist partly of its own products (as, for example, increasing the size of animal herds), and of activities which are *internal* to the sector (such as ditching, irrigation work, terracing the surface of land, etc.) as well as the acquisition of the products of the industrial sector. We shall assume that industrial production serves investment purposes only, whilst agriculture alone produces consumption goods, even though the proportion of consumption expenditure spent on food is only one-quarter or one-fifth of total consumption in developed industrial countries; the rest represents either manufactured consumption goods or the output of services which are ignored here altogether. Moreover, we shall assume that the proportion of consumption spent in the two sectors remains the same.

We shall also assume a community with surplus labour, most

of whom are formally attached to agriculture (if only because of the prevailing system of land tenure by families; the family represents a kind of social security system where each member is expected to participate in the work, and to share in the goods available for consumption). Industry, on the other hand, hires workers for wages and is faced with an unlimited supply of labour, provided that the wage offered (in terms of "corn") is sufficiently above real earnings in agriculture to induce whatever migration is necessary for providing the increase in industrial employment.

Each sector accumulates capital by saving part of its current income (or output), but there is an important difference in the nature of the accumulation process in the two cases. In the case of agriculture, an act of saving involves a decision to refrain from consuming a part of current output,[1] which is sold in the market in exchange for the capital goods which the introduction of new technology requires. The rate of accumulation, and hence the rate of introduction of land-saving innovations, depends, therefore, partly on the proportion of output saved, and partly on the terms on which "corn" is exchanged against "steel". In the case of the corn producers, therefore, it is correct to suppose that savings is the primary decision which determines, together with the terms of trade, the rate of capital accumulation. In the case of the steel producers, on the other hand, it is the other way round. Investment is primary, and saving secondary; it is the decision to invest which *causes* corresponding profits, and hence savings, to accrue. For the steel producers accumulate capital by retaining a proportion of current output for purposes of expanding the steel capacity, and selling the remainder in the market. Assuming that their cost *consists* of the payment of wages, and wages are fixed in terms of corn, the total amount of corn sold by the agriculturalists determines the total amount of employment; and if the steel output per worker, at the given technology, is taken as a constant,

---

1. This may be done voluntarily by each family of owner-cultivators; it may be done under a system of ownership vested in non-cultivators who extract part of the produce as payment for the use of land, which they do not require for their own consumption but sell in the market, the proceeds of which are lent to the cultivators in the form of loans which finance the investment.

the total output of steel is determined, irrespective of the price of steel. The minimum price of steel will equal the cost per unit (wl), where w is the wage (fixed in terms of corn) per unit of labour, and l is the amount of labour required per unit of steel – the reciprocal of labour productivity. Below this minimum price, steel will not be produced, because it would be unprofitable to do so. Above this minimum, there will be a relationship between the degree to which price exceeds costs, and the proportion of steel output reinvested, and the resulting profit over costs will be exactly sufficient to provide the savings for the finance of investment which is undertaken.

We are now in a position to exhibit the nature of interdependence of the two sectors, and their responsiveness to demand and prices by way of a simple diagram, where the price of steel in terms of corn (p) – or the industrial terms of trade – is measured on the vertical axis, and the growth rate of each sector is measured on the horizontal axis (Figure 3.1).[1] The agricultural growth curve is labelled g_A and the industrial growth curve is labelled g_I.

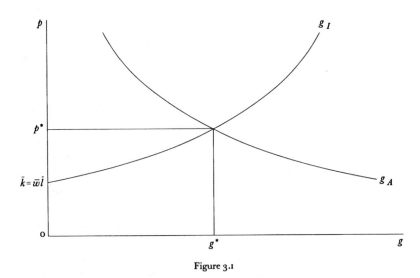

Figure 3.1

1. This section of the lecture has been rewritten by the editors in order to clarify the model presented.

There is an inverse, non-linear relation between the industrial terms of trade and the growth of the agricultural sector because the cheaper agriculture can obtain inputs from the industrial sector, the faster it can grow for any given savings ratio. Because of diminishing returns, however, more and more investment in agriculture will reduce the productivity of investment in agriculture and shift the g_A curve inwards, unless it is offset by land-saving innovations in agriculture which will shift the g_A curve outwards.

There is a positive, non-linear relation between the industrial terms of trade and industrial growth because the cheaper is "corn" (or food), the more of its own output the steel sector can invest, and hence the faster its growth. In the limit, if food were "free" (i.e. if p were infinitely high), growth would equal the productivity of capital in industry with all steel output reinvested. At the other extreme, there is a limit (k) below which there will be no growth because price just equals wage costs and no reinvestment is possible. All steel output goes to the agricultural sector to pay for food. Given the pricing equation $p = wl\,(1+\pi)$, where π is the percentage markup on unit labour costs, the g_I curve will shift with changes in the real wage (w) and changes in labour productivity ($1/l$). An increase in labour productivity will shift the g_I curve outwards, but an increase in real wages to match the productivity increase will shift the g_I curve inwards by an equal amount. Where the two curves cross gives the equilibrium terms of trade (p^*) and the equilibrium growth rate (g^*) for the system as a whole at which the supply and demand for agricultural and industrial goods are in balance.[1] At a terms of trade above p^*, steel capacity will grow faster than steel sales, which will cause steel producers to reduce the scale of investment, hence lowering the steel price and the terms of trade towards p^*. At a terms of trade below p^*, it will be the other way round. Hence, as far as the steel industry is concerned, steel investment will vary in an equilibrating direction whenever the price is above or below the equilibrium level.

---

1. The growth rates of the two sectors are equal to each other. In practice, the growth of industry is likely to be greater than the growth of agriculture because the income elasticity of demand for manufactured goods is higher than the income elasticity of demand for agricultural goods. The model may be modified to take account of this.

In the agricultural sector, assuming the corn producers are passive as far as the steel price is concerned, and will sell the amount of corn available for sale, their demand for steel will exceed the supply at any price lower than p^* (since the increase in their purchases indicated by g_A will exceed the increase in steel supplies, indicated by g_I), and this will drive the price up. Above p^* the discrepancy will be the other way round, and this will drive the price down. The difference between the two sectors is only that whereas the steel producers act so as to bring the growth of capacity in line with the growth of sales, the competition between agricultural buyers will act so as to bring price – the terms of trade – to a point where the growth rates of the two sectors are equal.

Of course, the situation depicted here, and its underlying assumptions, are simple in the extreme, and are based on several simplifying hypotheses. It should also be mentioned that, in practice, the growth rates of industry and agriculture are by no means equal; industrial and service output grows annually at two to three times the rate of agricultural production, because of the

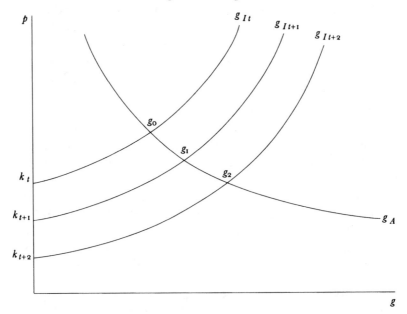

Figure 3.2

46

higher income elasticity of demand for industrial and service output. All these complications could be introduced into a more complex model without destroying its important characteristics – though it might weaken some of them.

As far as the present model is concerned, the important feature which emerges from it is that the critical factor in continued economic growth is the persistence or continuance of *land-saving innovations* – man's ability to extract more things, and a greater variety of things, from nature. Thus, in the simple model just presented, land-saving technical progress in agriculture is the only kind of technological change assumed, and this is sufficient to keep the system growing at a constant growth rate, at least as long as growth is not hampered by the scarcity of labour – so long as labour exists in super-abundance. Taking an all-inclusive view, this has hitherto always been the case. There may be places and periods (generally in special situations, such as during war time) when unemployment, open or disguised, virtually disappears in *certain parts of the world*. Taking into account the fact that obstacles to immigration, imposed by sovereign states or even by subordinate authorities, such as cities or cantons, are the consequence of an insufficient demand for labour, they tend to disappear in the face of excess demand. Taking an all-embracing view, we are nowhere near the point where world production is likely to be constrained by a labour shortage. Although the decennial growth rates of world population seem to have passed their peak, the proportion of world population effectively employed, according to the estimates of the World Bank, has been diminishing, and unemployment has been a growing problem on a world scale, even before the setback to world prosperity caused by the oil shocks of the 1970s.

The above model, as indicated, assumes technological change only in one sector, agriculture. If we introduce exogenous labour-saving technological progress in industry, then assuming constant wages in terms of corn, the g_I curve will shift outwards throughout its length, shifting the whole curve to the right. In this case, the combination of land-saving technical progress in agriculture and labour-saving technical progress in industry will lead to higher growth rates from g_0 to g_1 to g_2 in Figure 3.2.

The above assumes a constant rate of decrease in labour input per unit of output. Verdoorn's Law, however, suggests that the decrease of labour input per unit of output is greater the faster the growth of industrial output. One explanation would be greater economies of scale resulting from new techniques of large-scale production. If this is so, the g_I curve will shift outwards in the manner depicted in Figure 3.3.[1]

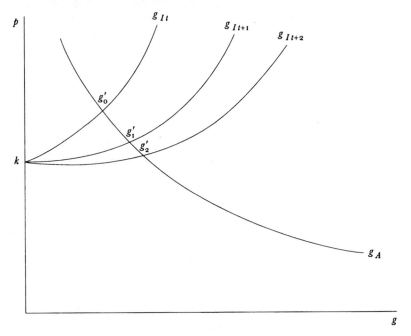

Figure 3.3

In this case, the combination of land-saving technical progress in agriculture and increasing returns in industry will lead to a steadily accelerating growth rate from g'_0 to g'_1 to g'_2 in Figure 3.3.

1. *Editors' Note*: Kaldor did not realise that Figure 3.3 cannot depict a situation of dynamic increasing returns to scale as he wished, because every g_I curve shows the rate of growth of industrial output in relation to the terms of trade *given* l, the labour input coefficient. But increasing returns to scale implies that for every different g_I curve there will be a different l. The only solution is to introduce a further equation in the system and instead of having curves in two dimensions, to depict the solution of the system by means of three dimensions.

However, both the cases mentioned above assume that while labour productivity is rising, wages per unit of labour remain constant in terms of corn. A rise in the corn-wage per unit of labour will, by contrast, shift the g_I curve in the opposite direction. If the rise in the wage just cancels the rise in productivity, the position of the g_I curve remains unchanged. If the rise in wages exceeds the growth in productivity, then, provided agricultural prices remain the same during the interval needed to establish a new equilibrium, the latter will lead to a new and lower growth rate, with less favourable terms of trade to agriculture.

But changes need not always work out as neatly as that. In our analysis so far we have assumed a stable curve of growth rates as a function of the terms of trade, p. In reality, the curves are far from stable. In agriculture the vagaries of the weather can cause the curve to shift around, and because major technological ideas do not occur at an even rate in time, the curves will shift outwards at different rates. Suppose the g_A curve shifts to the right by a relatively large amount from g_{A_1} to g_{A_2} in Figure 3.4, owing to a technological revolution, or an exceptional harvest, or the introduction of a new super-crop, or a combination of these events.

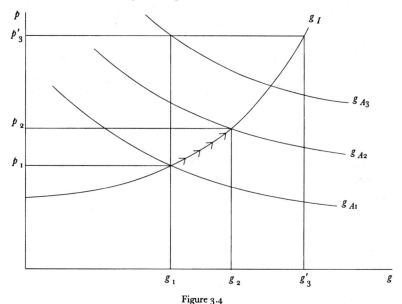

Figure 3.4

49

As a result, the quantity of "corn" offered in the market becomes excessive in relation to the current demand by a considerable margin. The resulting price fall may be gradual, however (following the arrows), if merchants and middlemen regard the supply situation as a temporary one and if they have the financial resources for increasing their commitments in the market. In that case, the total receipts of the producers and their purchasing power to procure steel will increase. The steel producers will sell more and more steel at a higher and higher relative price (from p_1 to p_2) – at any rate in the longer run, through enlargement of their capacity which is a movement along the g_I curve. The process can be presumed to continue, prompted by the (potential) excess demand for steel, until a new equilibrium is reached at a higher steel price in terms of corn, but also at a higher growth rate of both steel and corn at g_2 where again, $g_A = g_I$ (Figure 3.4).

However, we must bear in mind the difference in the nature of competition in the two markets, and in order to understand this it is best to introduce a third commodity, money, so that corn is initially sold for money, and the proceeds are then used to buy steel with money. As far as the terms of trade are concerned (the price of steel measured in terms of corn), the introduction of money as an intermediary makes no difference; however, from the point of view of a study of disequilibrium, due to an inequality between the demand and supply of steel,[1] it does make a difference whether the prices quoted by the steel producers are in corn or in money.

Supposing that the increase in the supply of corn due to the shift of the g_A curve causes a *big* fall in prices, because merchants, having expected this to happen, are unwilling to increase their commitments until the price has fallen to abnormally low levels.[2]

---

1. There is no such inequality in terms of corn, because we assume for purposes of this model, that corn has no reservation price; whatever the amount of corn supplied to the market on any particular day, it is sold for the best price it will fetch.

2. As was shown in Lecture 1, the mechanism of operation of a competitive market tends to generate fluctuations in prices that are excessive in relation to the requirements of equilibrium.

In that case, the steel price *in terms of corn* might rise to, say, p'_3. The steel producers will find that their sales are restricted by "effective demand" because the rate of growth of demand is g_1 though at that price they would be willing to increase their capacity and sales to g'_3. They will be faced with growing surplus capacity, which will reduce their investment in new capacity quite drastically, which would be shown by a leftward shift in the g_1 curve until the excess supply is eliminated. Also, this process, by curtailing the purchases of corn (with the fall in industrial output), would cause a further fall in corn price in a cumulative deflationary process.

In the above example, though, the terms of trade become exceptionally favourable as a result of the fall in corn prices, the rate of growth of industrial output is very greatly reduced owing to lack of demand; and the growth of agricultural output is also reduced, despite the outward shift in the g_A curve, owing to the unfavourable change in the terms of trade.

I have dwelt on this situation at some length in order to show that a favourable change in circumstances – the greater productivity, and the higher rate of growth of output of agriculture – may yet lead to a slump and over-capacity in manufacturing industry, with the rate of growth of agricultural production also being lower, not higher, than before, owing to the excessive fall in corn prices.

The basic reason for such irrational results is fundamentally, I think, the difference in the marketing organisation in agriculture and industry, respectively. In the field of primary production the market price is given to the individual producer or buyer, and prices move in direct response to market pressures in the classical manner. In industry, on the other hand, prices are "administered", i.e. they are fixed by the producers themselves on the basis of direct costs of production (both labour and material costs) to which a percentage addition is made, first for overhead costs (including overhead labour costs), and then for profit; the percentage added for profit reflects the entrepreneurs' judgement as to the financial requirements of their business for investment in the future. The finance for additions to capacity must invariably come in large part (normally a predominant part) from *internal* resources (i.e. from ploughed-back profits) and not from external borrowing. In these circumstances, a fall in the demand (or in the *trend* of demand) for the commodity will result in excess capacity (or, rather, in *more* excess capacity – for under monopolisitic competition producers normally maintain a larger capacity than they actually use so as to be able to exploit new opportunities for expanding their businesses) leading to a downward revision of investment plans and a further fall in the *net* demand for steel. (The history of the last few years has given an eloquent example of this.) If both the steel industry and the corn industry had been under the *same* regime for marketing, such absurd results could not have occurred because the price of the one commodity could not have fallen so as to reduce the producers' purchasing power of the other commodity.

The remedy to be sought is not in making the manufacturing industry go back to the 19th century and have market-determined prices (that didn't save them from periodic price fluctuations, and in any case was only possible when manufacturing meant the production of simple commodities, like woollen textiles and cotton shirts, and where those wholesalers who dominated the market gave specific orders to manufacturers, and then sold their products under their own brand name, competitively), but to eliminate the large fluctuations in the markets of primary commodities – a proposal I have already mentioned in a previous lecture – by means of publicly owned and operated buffer stocks, preferably by an international public authority, rather than a national authority, who would do no more than fulfil the function that the private merchant is supposed, but is unable, to fulfil. He is not wealthy enough, determined enough, or altruistic enough to prevent excessive price fluctuations. But, basically, a successfully operated buffer stock would fulfil the same functions which the merchants are supposed to fulfil in making the market work – to ensure, in the face of disequilibrium due to temporary conditions or permanent underlying changes (in our example, the rise in the g_A curve), that the ensuing excess supplies or excess demands do not give rise to such violent fluctuations as to generate even larger disturbances.

The great slump of 1929-32 had many of the features that fit our example. For example, in the latter part of the 1920s, the production of grains and other primary commodities rose faster than consumption – in the period 1925-29, end-year stocks rose by a third with only a moderate fall in prices – because traders held favourable expectations concerning the future growth of demand and were willing to hold larger stocks, in response to only a moderate fall in prices. But when the Wall Street boom broke in October 1929, expectations changed and the prices of primary commodities fell catastrophically, and this, so far from stimulating the expansion of industrial activity, had the very opposite effect. The fall in demand for industrial goods coming from the agricultural sector, and the fall in investment by the industrial countries in the expansion of the primary sector – in opening up new areas, etc. – as well as the fall in investment in the industrial sector itself, caused a big fall in industrial activity. Thus the excessive supplies of primary products, instead of giving rise to accelerated industrialisation, ushered in the greatest economic depression in industry. Keynes alluded to these tendencies in his 1942 Commod Control scheme for the stabilisation of primary commodity prices. Keynes remarked "at present, a falling off in effective demand in the industrial consuming countries causes a price collapse which means a corresponding break in the level of incomes and of effective demand in the raw material producing centres, with a further adverse reaction, by repercussion, on effective demand in the industrial centres; and so, in the familiar way, the slump proceeds from bad to worse. And when the recovery comes, the rebound to excessive demands through the stimulus of inflated price promotes, in the same evil manner, the excesses of the boom".[1]

None of this would have happened if international buffer stock schemes had been in existence which held up the price of commodities in the face of rising supplies and increased the purchasing power of agriculture in line with the rise in output. Since this would have meant that the primary producers' receipts rose relatively to the consumers' outlay, there would have been an ex-

1. D. Moggridge (ed.), *The Collected Writings of J.M. Keynes*, Vol. xxvii, *Activities 1940-1946 Shaping the Post-War World: Employment and Commodities*, London: Macmillan, 1980.

pansion in demand for industrial products which in turn would have stimulated the consumption of primary products until the excess supply was eliminated. So the buffer stocks would not have meant the indefinite accumulation of stocks. By accumulating stocks it would have started a cumulative process that could have ended in bringing consumption up to the new level of production. In a well-functioning world economy it is the availabilities of primary products which should set the limit to industrialisation – the expansion possibilities of which are limitless, or rather are only limited by demand – and not the other way round. Excess supplies of primary products, leading to sharp falls in commodity prices, are one important cause of market failures. As we shall see, however, they are by no means the only cause; the recession in the 1970s, for example, had quite different origins.

FOURTH LECTURE
The Effects of Interregional and International Competition

We have so far not considered the economic problem in its *spatial aspect* – except indirectly, in dealing with the trade between primary products and industrial goods, which may be supposed to involve the exchange of goods produced in different areas. Since primary products are "land-based industries", they are geographically spread. Industrial activities, on the other hand, for reasons we have not yet considered, tend to be concentrated in urban areas. The exchange between agricultural products and manufactured goods can also be looked upon as an exchange of the products of town and country.

There is a certain difference between the two kinds of activities in that, while both benefit from specialisation and exchange, the individual producer devotes only a part of his product (if any) to his own consumption (and that of his family) and obtains the greater part by way of exchange; the agricultural producer could, in theory, produce *only* for his own consumption. The industrial producer, on the other hand, can only operate in a social setting: his activities are dependent on the *demand* for his services, or on the products of his labour, by others. The industrial producer, whether he is an artisan producing on a small scale mainly by his own labour, or a manufacturer with many employees, is engaged in producing for the *market*, and his success or failure depends on the strength of the market demand for his products.

The world is divided into sovereign political entities (some 150 of them or more), but more important, it is divided into relatively rich and relatively poor areas, with very large differences between the two groups in terms of both material welfare and cultural status – as measured by literacy, the proportion of the population possessing specialised skills and training, and so on. The question is, how have these differences arisen, and what is their basic cause? As various investigations have shown, these tremendous differences between rich and poor nations are comparatively recent in origin – they are the cumulative result of per-

55

sistent differences in annual growth rates that occurred during recent periods of history of not more than a few centuries at most. Two or three hundred years ago, the differences in living standards, or in the "stage" of both economic and cultural development *between* countries, were much smaller than they are today.

The standard explanation for these differences in economic theory is in terms of "resource endowment" – rich areas are those which are rich in resources and in their ability to support life due to differences in climate and geology. But since human beings are mobile and are endowed with excess powers of reproduction, one would expect that differences in the fertility of different areas would tend to be offset by differences in the density of population, leaving living standards pretty nearly the same. In a very *broad* sense this is correct. There are fewer people per square kilometre in Greenland than in India. The fact that these two countries are both "poor" countries suggests rather that *natural* resource endowment cannot explain the large differences in living standards, and at best it can only explain a small proportion of them. Neo-classical economists would proceed to say that the rich and developed countries are those which are *well endowed* with capital, whilst the poor countries are *poorly endowed* with capital. This is true in a sense, but it leaves the problem of how these differences in capital endowment have arisen entirely in the air. Since capital is the result of savings, the immediate answer that comes to mind is that the rich countries are rich because they lived frugally and saved a lot, whereas the poor countries were spendthrifts who spent most of their income and saved only a little.

This explanation, however, in terms of differences in psychological proclivities or preferences – whether it is wholly false or not – is beside the point. Because, as we have discussed in the previous lecture, the savings which financed the accumulation of the prosperous countries came from the reinvested earnings of successful businesses – 90 per cent of the business capital of the industrialised countries was built up out of reinvested profits; and the reinvestment of profits in a business is not a matter of psychological choice but of competitive necessity. It would be more true to say that *all* the prosperous countries are industrialised, in the sense that without exception they possess a technically highly developed modern industry – this is true also of those rich countries whose exports are largely agricultural, as has been the case with New Zealand or Denmark until fairly recently. It is industrialisation and all that goes with it – the "fall out" in terms of social, political and educational institutions, and so on – which is mainly responsible for countries having a high income per head.

And industrial activities, unlike agricultural activities, are not "self-sustaining" – they are dependent on the demand for their goods coming from *outside* the industrial sector. This does not imply, however, that such "outside demand" accounts for the whole or even the major part of industrial activities. It implies only that the element of "outside demand" is the ultimate causal factor which accounts for all other activities, since it is the proportion of incomes derived from sales to outsiders which determines how much income will be generated in other industrial groups as a result of sales to insiders. Any additional sale to outsiders sets up a "multiplier" effect in terms of domestic activity which amounts to $1/(1\ p)$ times the original sale, where p is the proportion of income receipts which are spent on goods produced *within* the sector.

From a very early stage of history, a community of farmers must have practised trading of some kind, whether by direct exchanges or the intermediation of some object which served as a unit of account (a common unit in which exchange values were expressed), since it is unlikely that any individual farmer should have produced things in the same proportions in which they were needed for his own consumption – not unless he restricted his own activities below his potential.[1]

Since such exchanges are effected more advantageously when each potential trader has a facility of inspecting the goods offered by all other traders, it was in the general interest of traders to conduct such transactions at the same time and place. It was just as

1. ADAM SMITH, in describing the peculiarly human trait of the propensity to truck or barter, contrasted this with the absence of such habits among dogs who have never been seen exchanging one bone against another bone – leaving out of account that without further specification of the differences between the two bones and/or differences in tastes among the two dogs – there would be no more propensity to truck or barter one bone for another bone amongst humans than amongst dogs.

natural that goods which underwent a certain amount of processing (making wood, or other materials, into shapes in which
they are better adapted for some particular use) should be
offered, along with the others, at the same time and place.

Once the habit developed to meet at a certain time and place for
purposes of trading, a beginning was made for the development
of a market town, offering auxiliary services. It is evident that persons engaged in processing activities should cluster around the
market place since they were dependent on the primary producers, both for obtaining the raw materials and for the sale of their
products. The growth of marketing activities was therefore the
original reason both for the emergence of urban centres and for
industrial activities to be concentrated in such centres.

There was, however, an additional reason for the urban concentration of industrial activities. As manufacturing activities developed, it became evident that considerable economies could be
gained by dividing and sub-dividing the making of an article into a number of separate operations, each of which may have as-
sisted in the making of a number of separate articles at the same
time. As Allyn Young said in a famous paper[1]: in the course of industrial development, "an increasingly intricate nexus has insert-
ed itself between the producer of the raw material and the consumer of the final product". This process tends to cluster around
geographic centres for two reasons: firstly, because its success so
largely depends on the existence of highly specialised manpower
of the most variegated kind, the services of which are most likely
to be wanted when different processes making different goods are
likely to require the assistance of the same kind of specialised
skills; and secondly because the stimulus derived from continuous and easy communication between men with similar experience, as well as joint production between small specialised firms,
involves frequent transfer of an unfinished product between numerous firms with differing specialisations.[2] These kinds of "dynamic" economies of the geographical concentration of manu-

1. "Increasing Returns and Economic Progress", *Economic Journal*, December 1928,
pp. 527-42.
2. cf. the example of gun-making in G.C. Allen, *The Industrial Development of Birmingham 1816-1927*, p. 57.

facturing activities are not peculiar to manufacturing industry (it is also true of certain specialised services, such as banking), but it is inherent in the nature of industrial activities as such. Hence the fact that in all known cases the development of manufacturing activities was closely associated with urbanisation must have deep-seated causes which are not dependent on particular technologies or on particular sources of power.

The above is one aspect of a most important phenomenon, which was largely ignored in traditional economic literature (at least in the sense that its consequences have not been explored), and that is the existence of increasing returns, or the economies of *large-scale* production, in addition to which there are the economies of *large* production (as measured by the output of the aggregate of all industries) as Allyn Young put it. These economies are only partly due to the fact that, with the methods of mass production made familiar by American techniques such as the belt-line assembly or the single-purpose machine tool, the optimum size of plant for making chemicals or motor cars and numerous other things may be very large in comparison to the size of the market as a whole.[1] An even more important aspect, emphasised by Young, relates not to the *size* of the individual plant as such, but to the fact that the larger the market for a commodity, the greater will the number of specialised processes tend to be (i.e. the greater the sub-division of a production process into a larger number of stages) which makes it possible to introduce automation (i.e. to use specially constructed equipment made for a particular task) and thereby greatly enhance the productivity of labour. It is therefore more the growth of the number of different *kinds* of specialised undertakings, rather than just the use of large-scale plant, which is responsible for the phenomenon of increasing returns. It is also responsible for con-

---

1. Fundamentally, scale economies are the simple consequence of the three-dimensional nature of space, which makes the costs of any enclosed space (whether a pipeline, the size of an engine, or the floor space of a factory) more or less proportionate to the area of the enclosure, whilst capacity increases with the volume of the area enclosed. This holds equally in a wide variety of things, like electric generating stations, the size of oil tankers, etc., where the cost per unit of the service provided is all the lower the large the unit which supplies it – *provided only* that the construction problems involved in making larger units are solved.

tinual improvements of technology which is, indeed, but one aspect of it.

The existence of increasing returns makes a very large difference to the way markets develop and competition operates; the remarkable thing is only why its consequences have up to now been so largely ignored, even if the facts were broadly familiar to everybody.

I am thinking here first of all of the classical theory of international trade which was invented by Ricardo, and elaborated by a succession of famous economists: John Stuart Mill; the Swedish economists Ely Heckscher and Bertil Ohlin, and finally, Paul Samuelson, all of whom concluded that free trade necessarily improved the real income of all participants. The basis of the doctrine is the theory of comparative costs, according to which, under conditions of free trade, each area, region, or country exports those goods in which its *comparative advantage* is greatest, and imports those in which it is smallest. It is, therefore, not absolute productivity which matters, but only comparative advantage; a poor under-developed country may derive just as important an advantage in trading with a rich country as the latter does with the former.

Ricardo proceeded to demonstrate his law in terms of an example of trade between England and Portugal, where Portugal is assumed to be the rich country, with a high productivity per head, whose comparative advantage in making wine is greater than in making cloth. In that case, Portugal would be better off by concentrating on wine production and importing cloth from England, giving wine in exchange.

This proposition is valid under two suppositions, neither of which is explicitly stated. The first is that the total volume of employment in both trading countries is no smaller after the opening of trade than it was before. The second is that there are *constant costs of production* to transferable factors in both industries – which means that the productivity of labour and capital in either industry is the same after the opening of trade than it was before. Under these two assumptions, it is easy to demonstrate that both countries stand to gain from free trade. Portugal will be richer, having more cloth at its disposal than before, with the same amount (or possibly more) of wine; while England will have more of both commodities, or in an extreme case, more of one without having less of the other.

However, in the absence of the assumption of constant costs, either on account of diminishing returns to transferable factors, or increasing returns due to economies of scale, the proposition ceases to be true, and it is an extraordinary fact that this has never, to my knowledge, been properly acknowledged in the literature of international trade theory.

Take first the case of *diminishing returns*. Suppose the amount of wine produced in Portugal is limited by the amount of land suitable for viniculture (while only a limited amount of labour can be used with advantage on any one hectare of land). Production could then be limited by a *land constraint*, not a *labour constraint*. If the maximum number of people who can be usefully employed on the land is smaller than the total number available to work, the remainder can only be employed in industry or services. In the absence of international trade, the people who are not wanted on the land will be engaged in making "cloth", in the ratio, say of 1 yard of cloth = 10 litres of wine. In England, on the other hand, 10 litres of wine cost the same as 10 yards of cloth. The opening of trade will mean that the price of *cloth* will fall so much, both in terms of money and in terms of wine, that it will no longer be profitable to produce cloth in Portugal – the Portuguese textile trade will be ruined. (This is not just an imaginary example: according to Friedrich List this is what *actually* happened as a result of the Methuen Treaty with Portugal of 1704). Now, if all the workers freed from cloth-making could be employed in increasing the production of wine, in proportion to the increase in labour, all would be well: the real income of Portugal would be greater than before. Portugal would have *more* cloth and *more* wine to consume than in the absence of trade. However, if land is limited, this is not possible. Nor will it be possible to save the cloth-trade by reducing wages. For there is a minimum wage (in terms of wine) below which the cloth workers could not subsist. Hence, the result might be that while Portugal will export more wine to England, the national real income of Portugal would shrink, since the addition to its wine output may not compensate

61

for the loss of output of the cloth trade. Portugal could well end up by being a much poorer country than before – there would be less employment and less output.[1]

The whole classical and neo-classical conception that the opportunity to trade with abroad will necessarily benefit a country by re-allocating resources in such a way that each unit of labour will directly or indirectly make a greater contribution to the national output than it did before, is a false one. Or rather, it will only be true under highly restrictive and unrealistic assumptions.

The most important assumption on which both classical and modern international trade theory is based is that of constant returns to scale – the existence of homogeneous and linear production functions for each particular commodity which are the *same* in different countries – i.e. that technology and the efficiency of its exploitation are the same everywhere. Under these assumptions, as Heckscher and Ohlin have shown, differences in the relative prices of commodities in different countries can only arise owing to differences in relative factor prices which must in turn be due to differences in relative factor endowments. Suppose there are two "agricultural" countries in one of which the land/labour ratio is more favourable than in the other. In the first country, rents will be low relative to wages, in comparison to the second country. Hence products requiring relatively more labour (like potato-growing as against grains) will be dearer in the country with relatively more land, and so on. With free trade, each country will export those goods which contain more of the factors with which it is relatively well endowed; hence trade will reduce the differences in factor price ratios, and in favourable circumstances will eliminate them altogether. Hence it brings about the same tendency to equalisation of factor prices (mainly wages

1. The example involves England being able to manufacture cloth much more cheaply in terms of wine than Portugal, and not solely on account of the unsuitability of the British climate for wine production. The example also supposes that England uses a technology in cloth production, involving a smaller outlay of labour per unit of output, otherwise it could not sell cloth at a price which is below the *minimum* cost at which it can be produced in Portugal, even when wages are at the minimum quantity of wine on which workers can subsist (unless English workers can subsist on so much less wine than Portuguese workers, which is unlikely!).

and interest rates) as the free mobility of factors would cause (abstracting from the cost of movement in each case).

From this it follows, in turn, that trade must necessarily *reduce* the differences in real income per head between different areas, and in favourable circumstances eliminate them altogether.

It has already been shown that under the assumption of constant returns to scale and perfect competition, a country cannot be made poorer, only richer, by the opening of trade. Also, countries will end up (under Paul Samuelson's "factor price equalisation theorem") with the *same* real income per head as would happen under completely free mobility of factors. It therefore follows that while everybody gains, the poorer countries will gain most, and the richer countries will gain least. When factor prices are equalised, real income per head will be the same in all countries (assuming, of course, that all countries have the same factors – only the proportions differ).

The observed trends in income per head for the past 200 years, during which international trade has increased very substantially in relation to total world income, have been the very opposite. Differences between wealthy countries and poor countries have grown enormously – the very opposite of what the theory predicts.

The reason for this is that, apart from the existence of diminishing returns in agriculture, there are increasing returns in industry, so that the countries which were ahead in industrialisation will gain an increasing lead with every enlargement of the market for their products.

But the absurdity of the assumptions of neo-classical theory lies not only in the exclusion of increasing returns, but in the very idea that each commodity has a clearly defined "production function", which is equally applicable to the enterprises of each of the trading countries.

Backward countries are less efficient in production, which means that they require greater inputs per unit of output, not just in terms of one particular factor, but of all factors.[1]

---

1. Of course, they could be expressed by saying that the less-efficient country possesses 'lower quality' factors; in which case the proposition becomes tautological.

63

The case of increasing returns has never been properly explored in economic theory – beyond the famous statement of Alfred Marshall (and of Cournot and Walras before him) that increasing returns lead to monopoly because some producers get ahead of their rivals and gain a cumulative advantage over the others whom they will drive out of business – hence increasing returns (or falling marginal costs) could not exist under conditions which prevail in a *competitive market*. When, in the 1930s, the new theories concerning the imperfection of markets suggested that this need not be – falling costs and competition can co-exist – economists, in general, shied away from exploring the consequences.

However, businessmen could never ignore the existence of diminishing costs. It is on account of the economies of large-scale production that a rising market share means success and a falling market share spells trouble. And it is on that account that in a growing market a business *cannot* stand still: it must grow if it wishes to survive.[1]

Owing to increasing returns in manufacturing, success breeds further success, and failure begets more failure. Another Swedish economist, Gunnar Myrdal, called this "the principle of circular and cumulative causation".

It is as a result of this that free trade in the field of manufactured goods leads to the concentration of manufacturing production in certain areas – to a "*polarisation process*" which inhibits the growth of such activities in some areas and concentrates them in others.

This is just what has happened as a result of the industrial revolution and the transport revolution of the 19th century. Areas which were wholly isolated previously became drawn into the world economy. But one cannot say that the enlargement of markets brought about by these technological revolutions benefited *all* participating areas in the same way. The manufacturing industry of Britain (at first chiefly the cotton industry, later iron and steel and machinery) received an enormous stimulus

---

1. The only economist of the 19th century who fully recognised this was Karl Marx. In neo-classical theory, each firm has an optimum size; when the output of an industry grows, it is the *number* of firms, not the size of the existing firms, which increases.

through the opening of markets in Europe, in North and South America, and then in India and China. But, at the same time, the arrival of cheap factory-made goods eliminated local producers (of hand-woven textiles and so on) who became uncompetitive as a consequence, and it made these countries "specialise" in the production of raw materials and minerals which, however, could only offer employment to a limited number of workers. As a result of this, the countries dependent on the exports of primary products remained comparatively poor – the poverty was a consequence, not of low productivity of labour in their export sectors, but of the limited employment capacity of their "profitable" industries.

On the other hand, the "polarisation process" was counteracted by the successful *spread* of industrialisation to other countries. Ever since Britain started the industrial revolution in the closing decades of the 18th century, there was the prospect that her new techniques based on the factory system, of the use of new types of machinery and of new sources of energy, would sooner or later be emulated by other countries. And so they were. In the second half of the 19th century, France, Germany, Italy and many of the smaller countries of Western Europe began to industrialise behind the protection of newly erected tariff walls, and this happened also outside Europe, in the United States, and still later in countries like Japan, India, the countries of Oceania, and many others. All this time the spread of industrialisation over wider and wider regions was counteracted by the "polarisation" effect which is nothing else than the inhibiting effect of superior competitive power of the industrially more efficient and more developed countries, as compared to the others. The economic unification of Italy probably provides the best-known example of the polarisation effect. Since the unification occurred at a time when the industries of the North of Italy were rather more developed than those of the South (though the difference was not very large; industrial productivity was supposed to have been some 20 per cent higher in the North than in the South), it was quite sufficient for free and guaranteed access of the Northern industries to the Southern markets to inhibit the development of the latter at the same time as it accelerated the industrial development of the North. The interaction between these forces – i.e. that of polarisation which leads to concentration of development in successful areas, and of imitation or emulation which leads to the *spread* of industriali-sation into a wider range of areas – has never, to my knowledge, been properly explored.

The fact remains that all the countries which became industri-alised (other than Britain which started off the process) did so with the aid of protective tariffs which were high enough to in-duce a substitution of home-produced goods for imports. This was true of Germany (particularly after Bismarck's famous tariff of 1879), of France (which abandoned the earlier free trade pol-icy of the 1860s), of Italy, and most of the smaller European countries, with the possible exception of Sweden. It was also true of the United States which became increasingly protectionist at the end of the 19th century, culminating in the McKinley tariff of 1900. In some cases (of which Japan is the most important ex-ample), the form of protection relied more on state subsidies, financed out of a tax on agriculture, than on import duties. But without some such instrument, industrialisation could never have started. However, what distinguishes the successful industrialis-ers from the others was the use of relatively moderate tariffs – no greater than was necessary to make domestic industries prof-itable – and a protective tariff that was carefully designed in favour of those industries that had the capability of developing an export potential, and not just a substitute for imports. As against that, the less successful industrialisers were those who used a high degree of protection rather indiscriminately and who developed industries whose costs in terms of primary products were much too high to enable them to break into the world mar-kets. (In many of these countries, e.g. the countries of Latin America, the emergence of many highly inefficient industries was not the result of a policy of protection introduced as a matter of choice, but more in the nature of a largely unforeseen by-product of widespread import prohibitions, which were introduced by sheer necessity to conserve foreign exchange at a time when earn-ings from their traditional exports collapsed during the Great Depression of the 1930s.)

International statistical comparisons have firmly established that differences of growth rates of GDP are mainly explicable in terms of differences in the growth rates of the manufacturing sector; countries with high rates of GDP growth have invariably been those whose manufacturing industry has grown at an even faster rate and whose exports of manufactures have grown at a still faster rate. Harrod[1] has shown (three years before the publication of Keynes' *General Theory*), in his theory of the "foreign trade multiplier", that changes in export demand have multiplier and accelerator effects which operate so as to adjust, via changes in the general level of output, the level of imports to that of exports. On this theory, the foreign trade of countries which are mainly exporters of manufactures is brought into balance through changes in the level of output and employment, and not through changes in relative export and import prices. Recent statistical research has shown that the prices of manufactured goods are based on costs and on customary markups for profit and are quite insensitive to changes in demand. Under these circumstances, it is variations in real incomes, not of relative prices or changes in exchange rates, which provide the major force tending to keep imports and exports in balance. It follows, moreover, that the growth rate of exports, together with the *income* elasticity of imports, govern the growth rate of the economy. Thirlwall has shown[2] that a simple formula based on these two factors explains much the greater part of the differences in recorded growth rates of the industrialised countries. Table 4.1 shows the actual growth experience of various countries over the two time

1. R. Harrod, *International Economics*, London: Macmillan, 1933.

2. 'The Balance of Payments Constraint as an Explanation of International Growth Rate Differences', *Banca Nazionale del Lavoro Quarterly Review*, March 1979.

Harrod's original formula was that assuming exports (E) of a particular country are given exogenously, and imports are a simple linear function of income ($M = mY$, with $0 < m < 1$), and there are no other 'leakages' from income (Y), so that

$$Y = \frac{1}{1-k}E, \text{ (the general 'multiplier' formula)}$$

where $1 - k = m$, so that $E = mY$, or $E = M$.

The 'dynamised version' of this formula, given by Thirlwall, is $\dot{y} = \frac{\dot{e}}{\pi}$

where $\dot{y}$ and $\dot{e}$ are the logarithmic *growth rates* of income and exports respectively, and π represents the *income* elasticity of demand for imports.

periods 1951-73 and 1953-76, and then shows the predicted growth rate from the dynamic Harrod trade multiplier formula obtained by dividing the rate of growth of exports by the income elasticity of demand for imports. The correspondence between the actual and predicted growth rates is very close. The economic interpretation of these findings is that the balance of payments is the effective constraint on growth and it permits any particular country's growth rate to be all the higher the greater is the income elasticity of demand for its products by its trading partners and the lower is the country's own income elasticity for foreign products.[1]

Table 4.1
A comparison of the actual growth rate with that predicted
from the dynamic Harrod trade multiplier

Country	Growth of Real GNP (y)		Growth in Export Volume (x)		Income Elasticity of Demand for Imports (π)	Predicted Growt Rate from the Harrod Trade Multiplier (%)	
	1951 to 1973	1953 to 1976	1951 to 1973	1953 to 1976		1951 to 1973	1953 to 1976
USA	3.7	3.23	5.1	5.88	1.51	3.38	3.89
Canada	4.6	4.81	6.9	6.02	1.20	4.84	5.02
W. Germany	5.7	4.96	10.8	9.99	1.89	5.71	5.29
Netherlands	5.0	4.99	10.1	9.38	1.82	5.55	5.15
Sweden	–	3.67	–	7.16	1.76	–	4.07
France	5.0	4.95	8.1	8.78	1.62	5.00	5.42
Denmark	4.2	3.58	6.1	6.77	1.31	4.65	3.17
Australia	–	4.95	–	6.98	0.90	–	7.76
Italy	5.1	4.96	11.7	12.09	2.25	5.20	5.37
Switzerland	-	3.56	-	7.20	1.90	-	3.79
Norway	4.2	4.18	7.2	7.70	1.40	5.14	5.50
Belgium	4.4	4.07	9.4	9.24	1.94	4.84	4.76
Japan	9.5	8.55	15.4	16.18	1.23	12.52	13.15
UK	2.7	2.71	4.1	4.46	1.51	2.71	2.95
S. Africa	–	4.97	–	6.57	0.85	–	7.73

Source: Thirlwall, *Ibid.*

1. For a full discussion of this model and other empirical evidence, see J.S.L. Mc-Combie and A.P. Thirlwall, *Economic Growth and the Balance of Payments Constraint*, London: Macmillan 1994.

The growth of a country's exports thus appears to be the most important factor in determining its rate of progress, and this depends on the outcome of the efforts of its producers to seek out potential markets and to adapt their product structure accordingly. The income elasticity of foreign countries for a particular country's products is mainly determined by the innovative ability and the adaptive capacity of its manufacturers. In the industrially developed countries, high income elasticities for exports and low income elasticities for imports frequently go together, and they both reflect successful leadership in *product development*.[1] Technical progress is a continuous process and it largely takes the form of the development and marketing of new products which provide a new and preferable way of satisfying some existing want. Such new products, if successful, gradually replace previously existing products which serve the same needs, and in the course of this process of replacement, the demand for the new product increases out of all proportion to the general increase in demand resulting from economic growth itself. Hence the most successful exporters are able to achieve increasing penetration, both in foreign markets and in home markets, because their products go to replace existing products.

All this, of course, is a simplified picture. Price elasticities also matter for that part of trade which is in "traditional goods" like textiles, shoes, etc., where product innovation and technical change is far less important. It is in these sectors that newly industrialised countries have traditionally achieved important and rapid gains in world trade. They did so because they were able to copy the technologies of the more advanced countries, and had the advantage of much lower wages. As Hufbauer has pointed out[2], the proper division of international trade in manufactures is not so much the traditional division between "capital intensive" and "labour intensive" trade, but between "low wage" trade and "technological lead" trade. The developed industri-

1. Italy's example is rather exceptional in that she was particularly successful in achieving a high rate of growth of exports, but at the same time she also had a high income elasticity for imports with the result that her post-war growth record was not much better than average.

2. G.C. HUFBAUER, *Synthetic Materials and the Theory of International Trade*, London, Duckworth, 1966.

alised countries with high wages must be able to export goods in which they have a technological lead over others, either on account of the design and marketing of new products (such as computers, silicon chips, etc.), or because of advanced manufacturing processes which yield comparatively high productivity. (On account of the importance of static and dynamic economies of scale, a country which has a large *home* market may thereby acquire an automatic advantage also in exports. A good example is synthetic rubber production, in which U.S. costs have traditionally been much lower than those of other countries, mainly because of the size of the U.S. home market.)

A new feature of the world economic development of the last ten years is that the newly industrialised countries became important exporters, not only in the so-called traditional products, but in technologically advanced products, particularly when these happened to be highly labour intensive (as in all the electronic products based on the transistor or the silicon chip). At an earlier stage, Japan achieved important advances as against all other countries in a number of fields, such as optics. Thus, a number of semi-industrialised, low-wage countries of South-East Asia, such as Hong Kong, Taiwan, South Korea and Singapore, acquired significant shares in the world market in the products of the latest electronic technology, but in general they did so as a result of access to U.S., German or Japanese technology, whose leading firms have increasingly tended to develop subsidiaries in these countries in order to take advantage of low wages.

FIFTH LECTURE
Policy Implications of the Current World Economic Situation

This is our last lecture, and its purpose is to bring together the various threads and to apply the theoretical considerations advanced in earlier lectures to an interpretation of the current world economic situation, and the implications of this analysis for the policies required in order to restore fast growth and high employment levels to the world economy.

The post-World War II period – or more precisely, the twenty-five years elapsing between 1948 and 1973 – witnessed the most rapid, the most widespread and the most even rate of economic growth recorded in all modern history. There was no equivalent to this, either in the 19th century or in the first half of the present century. And it was no less remarkable for being so unexpected – because it was in sharp contrast to the aftermath of World War I, which witnessed a severe post-war slump, then a weak recovery, and then the greatest economic depression in history which lasted ten years. After the Second War, on the contrary, high growth rates of productivity and of real income came to be taken for granted, and when a sharp break occurred at the end of 1973, this was just as unexpected, and it took some time before the true magnitude of the change began to be grasped.

But during the twenty-five "good years", the rate of progress was much faster than any one could have foreseen. Professor Arthur Lewis, writing in 1952[1] predicted, on the basis of an extensive study of world production and trade in the previous ninety years, that if economic recessions were successfully avoided, world food production in the decade 1950-60 might rise at the rate of 1.3 to 2 per cent a year, though, owing to various adverse factors, he held the lower figure as more likely. He put the possible growth of world manufacturing production at 3.9 to 5 per cent, depending on the availability of raw materials and the success of economic and financial management in avoiding slumps.

---

1. W.A. LEWIS, 'World Production, Prices and Trade, 1870-1960', *Manchester School*, May 1952.

As it turned out, world manufacturing production, according to U.N. estimates, increased by 6.7 per cent a year, both in the decade 1950-60 and also 1960-70, while world food production increased by no less than 2.7 per cent in both decades.

The fall in growth rates after 1973 was also remarkably uniform among the *developed* countries. In the United States, taking the period 1960 to 1973, real national income grew by 4.5 per cent a year. In the period 1974-81 this rate fell by more than one half to 2.1 per cent a year. In the countries of the European Community the contrast was even larger: whereas in the period 1960-73, real GNP increased by 4.5 per cent annually, in the period 1974-81 the growth rate was only 1.7 per cent, and in the final two years it was even less. Similarly, in Japan there was a considerable fall in growth rates, but from very much higher levels – an average of 9.5 per cent a year in 1951-73. In relation to that, the growth rate of Japan since 1973 (at 3.7 per cent a year) represented much the same proportionate fall as in the EEC, though it continued to be very much higher than either that of Western Europe or the United States.

The large fall in the growth of output was paralleled by a large fall in productivity growth. In the countries of the EEC, the fall in output per head was nearly as large as the fall in total output: 2.6 per cent a year as against 2.9 per cent. In the United States the fall in productivity growth was even greater – in important sectors of the economy it actually turned negative. In the 1973-80 period, annual productivity growth for the economy as a whole declined by 0.3 per cent; in industry it rose at only 0.5 per cent. No one had a satisfactory or universal explanation for the fall in productivity growth coming at a time when, according to all accounts, technological progress has accelerated.[1] In my view, the best explanation lies in the fall in output itself since output growth and productivity growth are known to be highly correlated. In the circumstances, the fall in productivity growth was

1. Studies of productivity slowdown include: E. DENISON, *Accounting for Slower Growth*, (Washington DC: Brookings Institution, 1979); R.C.O. MATTHEWS (ed.), *Slower Growth in the Western World*, London: Heinemann, 1982); Symposium in the *Economic Journal*, March 1983; and J.W. KENDRICK (ed.), *International Comparisons of Productivity and Causes of the Slowdown*, Cambridge, Mass.: Ballingers, 1986.

in some ways a blessing in disguise, since, without it, the increase in unemployment would have been very much greater. In America unemployment increased from 4.9 per cent in the 1960-73 period to 6.9 per cent in the 1974-81 period (reaching over 9 per cent in 1981). If the productivity trends of the pre-1973 period had remained, unemployment would have been 20 per cent or more. Similarly, it has been estimated that unemployment in Western Europe could possibly have been nearly three times as high (30 million instead of 13 million) if the fall in the rate of growth of production had not been accompanied by an almost equivalent fall in the growth of productivity.

The first question to ask is why the post-war boom (if one can call it such) lasted so long. The trade cycles of the 19th century clearly had a great deal to do with the fact that the growth of primary products either ran ahead of, or lagged behind, requirements, resulting in either unduly low or unduly high commodity prices, and both could have been the cause of the periodic economic crises which led to a slow-down or stagnation of industrial output before a new cycle started with a fresh recovery. As we have argued earlier, continued economic growth is only possible if the increase in the availability of primary products is in line with the increase in requirements resulting from the rise in industrial production. This does not mean, however, that these two sectors must grow *at the same rate* for the growth of production to continue without encountering structural obstacles.

The rate of growth of primary production – with one or two conspicuous exceptions – like oil – was consistently lower than that of secondary or tertiary production. The main reason for this was that the *value added* by fabrication, transport and distribution took up a steadily rising proportion of the final price of the average commodity. Even in the case of foodstuffs which are sold to the final buyer without any transformation by processing – other than packaging or breaking bulk – like vegetables and fruit, for example, the proportion of the final price received by the producer or grower tended to diminish relative to the prices paid by the consumer. In this case, clearly the difference in the nature of competition – the perfect competition situation confronting farmers, for whom the price is given and which they cannot influence by withholding supplies, and the imperfect or monopolistic competition which is prevalent along the whole chain of processors and distributors whose mark-up on the buying price tended to rise (though actual statistical evidence for this is rather scanty) – meant that the percentage of the final price going to the original producer tended to diminish. In the case of manufactured goods, moreover, it is possible to argue that the transformation of basic materials through processing became more complex and required more labour on average than before. One only needs to compare a modern motor car with the horse-drawn vehicle of the pre-motor age to become convinced that the cost of fabrication, in terms of labour and capital, despite all the labour-saving progress of technology, increased relatively to the labour and capital engaged in producing the raw material which was transformed by manufacturing.

In addition, there is Engel's famous law, according to which the proportion of income spent on food diminishes and that spent on other things increases with any rise in real wages. There again, it is difficult to disentangle the changes which are due to technical factors, or which are the consequence of consumers' preferences, from those that came to be known as the "Prebisch Effect" – that is to say, the fact that a rise in productivity in primary production is passed on to the consumer or buyer in the form of lower prices, whilst in the case of manufacturers or distributors, the gains in productivity are, by and large, retained by the producers in the form of higher profits and wages.[1] No doubt this difference in the factors governing price formation must have been an important factor in the more rapid growth of the secondary and tertiary sectors.

In the period after World War II, a large deterioration of the terms of trade of manufacturing countries was feared, owing to raw material shortages and the rapid growth of population. Various bodies, like the F.A.O. (the Food and Agricultural Organisation of the United Nations), kept making the most gloomy predictions about a threatening famine due to insufficient world food production which in the event has never materialised.

1. See R. PREBISCH, *The Economic Development of Latin America and its Principal Problems*, New York: ECLA, U.N. Dept. of Economic Affairs, 1950.

(There was a sharp increase in the prices of raw materials and foodstuffs at the outbreak of the Korean War – owing to a widespread expectation that it would lead to a third world war – as a result of which the prices of primary products shot up by 50 per cent, purely as a result of speculative buying, but within two years this speculative boom collapsed, and prices were back again where they started.) Taking the inter-war period as a whole, the United Nations index of the export prices of commodities in dollar terms was the same in 1970 as it was in 1950 (though individual commodities fluctuated up and down). This was not true of the export prices of manufactures which rose by some 25 per cent over the period, so that on first glance the terms of trade appear to have moved fairly strongly against the primary producers. However, as I mentioned in an earlier lecture, the index of prices of manufactures contains a serious upward bias, due to making no allowance for the improvement of quality and performance of manufactured goods, nor for the introduction of new products with high initial prices which did not exist earlier.

Hence one can say that effectively the terms of trade between primary producers and manufactured goods remained pretty stable, until the first "oil shock" towards the end of 1973. This stability was not the result of growth of primary production remaining on the required path of expansion in relation to the growth of industrial production. In fact, agricultural production, as a result of the progress of land-saving technology, increased faster than consumption, leading to growing surpluses in the main grain-exporting countries. Under pre-war conditions this would have led to a collapse of agricultural prices, sooner or later. However, as a legacy of the experience of the 1930s, the United States and other large grain producers introduced agricultural price support programmes which maintained prices by accumulating publicly owned stocks (chiefly of food grains) until about the middle of the 1960s. From then on, to ease the financial burden of carrying huge stocks, the excess stocks of the United States, the largest grain exporter, were gradually dissipated by means of soft "food loans" to Third World countries offered on highly favourable terms, and reinforced by a policy by acreage restrictions. Equally, raw material and energy production kept pace, until the final years of the 1960s, with the greatly enhanced growth requirements of the industrial countries, and their prices were kept stable by policies of strategic stockpiling.

The question which we must now discuss is what could have been the motive force of the rapid and almost uninterrupted growth, both in Western Europe and in the rest of the world, in the twenty-five years ending in 1973?

The main (or the primary) engine of growth was the continued growth in demand for manufactured goods in all the main industrial countries, which had important "spill-over" effects on the growth of services in housing and construction, as well as on the demand for primary products. There is no doubt that the continued increase in *demand* was the primary factor; otherwise the vast structural changes in employment and the large-scale importation of foreign "guest workers" in the fast-growing countries cannot be explained.

How far was this the consequence of policies of demand-expansion deliberately pursued in the principal countries, and how far was it the consequence of the growth of international trade fostered by the post-war international agreements and treaties in the international trade and currency field? How far was it a consequence of the change in attitudes to the scope of governmental responsibilities which can be traced to the Keynesian revolution in economics? I do not think that these questions admit a simple answer since the dominant considerations which guided policy were not the same in different countries.

The United States, which emerged from the war with a unique commanding position, laid the greatest stress on institutional arrangements which aimed at restoring a liberal capitalist system, through the speedy liberalisation of trade, the reduction of tariff barriers, the restoration of general currency convertibility at least on current transactions, and on generous financial aid, partly given by the United States itself (through the Marshall Plan for the speedy recovery of the war-torn economies of Europe[1], and later as aid to the development of Third World coun-

---

1. Incidentally, the operation of the Marshall Plan unintentionally led to a great deal of forward investment planning, in both the public and private sectors of the industries of the recipients of Marshall Aid. I am sure that this was not the intention of the Gov-

tries), and partly through the two Bretton Woods institutions of the International Monetary Fund and the World Bank. But beyond the passing of the Employment Act, which laid the responsibility on the President of the United States to follow policies that secure maximum employment and purchasing power, and to submit an Annual Report to Congress aided by a Council of Economic Advisers, there was no attempt to use fiscal policy as an instrument for regulating demand except in the early 1960s under President Kennedy.

In Britain, on the other hand, Keynes himself introduced during the war the system under which the State Budget is placed in a national accounting framework, and Keynesian policies of demand management were consistently followed after the war, by aiming at a level of taxation and expenditure which secured the growth of demand that was in line with the assumed growth of productive potential. The difficulty was that there was very little to indicate what the growth of productive potential was. Many of us had the suspicion that those who framed policy assumed a very low rate of growth of productive potential based on past experience. If they had assumed a somewhat higher rate, something more ambitious might have happened.

In France, the same spirit of government-induced economic growth led to the formulation of a succession of five-year plans which succeeded in coordinating the expansion of capacity in the public and the private sectors and to secure an average annual growth rate of 5 per cent, which was among the highest in the industrial world, and in sharp contrast to France's pre-war performance.

In the case of West Germany and Italy, economic growth was not, as far as I know, consciously engineered by fiscal policies, but these were, next to Japan, the two countries showing the highest

ernment of the U.S.; it happened unintentionally – it happened because the State Department had to sell the Marshall Plan to Congress, to allow for what they called "detailed plans" concerning investment requirements and intentions for five years ahead, but plans which did not exist, and in order to support the application for Marshall Aid, governments called together committees of various industries and made them fix targets for the extension of capacity. In order to justify how much money they would require for investment, it was important to get growth under way, and once under way, it developed its own momentum.

growth rates of exports (an average of 11-12 per cent a year in the period 1951-73). The resulting rapid growth of manufacturing industry led, in the case of Germany, to the rapid absorption of several million Germans who were expelled from the lost German territories of East Prussia, Silesia and Bohemia, and later, when all these immigrants found jobs, to the importation of several million "guest workers" from countries of south-western and south-eastern Europe. Italy's rate of growth of manufacturing output did not lead to the same kind of labour shortage as Germany's, possibly because her income elasticity of imports was greater, but mainly because the scope for mobilizing labour reserves in agriculture for the expansion of industry was much greater.

Thus the primary impulse in the case of many countries was the growth of international demand – in exports – which was partly the cause and partly the response of the increase in investment expenditure in industry, commerce and social infrastructure. To a considerable extent, the forces making for expansion communicated themselves from one country to another – the increase in A's exports involved an increase in income and hence in demand by A, which meant in turn an increase in exports by B, and so on.

Though the question of causation is far from settled, I would attribute primary importance to the role of the United States dollar which, after the adoption of the Bretton Woods arrangement concerning currencies, became *de facto* the international reserve currency, so that America had, in fact, an unlimited borrowing power – she was able to borrow automatically by incurring deficits on "basic transactions" (on current and capital accounts taken together) and thereby provide other countries with additional reserves, thus enabling them to expand their economic activities without running into a balance of payments constraint.[1]

Moreover, the balance of payments of the United States, after the large-scale currency realignments of 1949, turned into a

---

1. This was an incidental (and unforeseen) consequence of the Bretton Woods Agreement and was due to the fact that the dollar was adopted as the universal "intervention currency" – i.e. each member country was deemed to have fulfilled its obligations under the Treaty if it kept its local currency in parity with the United States dollar in its *own* market.

deficit on "basic transactions" (i.e. on current and capital account), and remained in deficit in almost every single year until
1971. At first this was due to *net* foreign investment (public and
private) exceeding her current account surplus. Later, in the
1960s, it was supplemented by a growing deficit on current account. Deficits of *both* kinds implied an addition to the demand
for goods and services in the world outside. They implied an increase in world investment which had much the same international "multiplier" effects as if the annual production of gold
had increased by an equivalent amount. For the rest of the
world, it meant increasing reserves (in the form of ever rising
dollar balances) earned through rising exports or externally
financed domestic investment.

But with the wide passage of time, the whole financial basis of
the Bretton Woods system became increasingly precarious. At
the beginning, the world was hungry for dollars and was de-
lighted to accumulate dollar reserves, which yielded interest, in
preference to gold, which did not. But as countries had more and
more dollars, and as the U.S. official liabilities began to exceed
several times the total value of gold in their possession (at the
official price, which until March 1968 corresponded also to the
market price), the willingness to accept dollars was progressively impaired – especially when the U.S. deficit assumed larger dimensions during the Vietnam War. France demanded to be paid
in gold; Germany revalued her currency repeatedly in a vain attempt to stem the speculative flight from the dollar into the
Deutschmark, and in the end the whole Bretton Woods system
collapsed in August 1971 with America's formal abandonment of
convertibility coupled with a demand for a large-scale readjust-
ment of currency parities.

A new system of parities was laboriously erected in the so-
called Smithsonian Conference, but it did not last long. Two
years later, the new parity rates were abandoned, and since that
time, large-scale and unpredictable variations in exchange rates
– between the dollar and the EEC currencies, and for some years
also between the dollar and the yen – continued, which must have
been one of the factors preventing economic recovery, though it
is impossible to assess its precise importance.

79

However, while in terms of price instability and an accelerating trend in inflation, clouds were gathering from around 1968 onwards, in terms of productivity growth and employment growth the world boom continued for a time at an accelerated pace. With President Nixon's abandonment of a fixed gold par value for the dollar, currencies became floating in varying forms and degrees, and Governments were relieved of the necessity to put the brakes on whenever the current account deficits threatened the parity of the exchange rate. This was in contrast to the period up to 1971 when there were always some countries which had to pull in the reins for the sake of the balance of payments, whilst others went full speed ahead. But after August 1971, no one felt the necessity to put on the brakes for the sake of the exchange rate; hence world industrial production accelerated and reached an annual rate of around 10 per cent in the latter half of 1972 and in early 1973. Commodity prices started rising for a number of apparently disconnected reasons. There were two bad harvests in Russia and a bad harvest in China. Both countries made large grain purchases in the U.S., which meant that U.S. grain reserves were suddenly emptied, for the first time for forty years or more. The U.S. internal price of wheat, which up to then was considerably *above* the world price, was suddenly well below it, so the world price of wheat doubled in a remarkably short period. With the faster growth of industrial output, the absorption of a number of non-ferrous metals (e.g. copper, tin, nickel, etc.) passed beyond current accruals; hence stocks diminished and prices rose.

There is evidence also that speculative investment in commodities greatly increased on account of the inflationary expectations engendered by the suspension of the gold convertibility of the dollar. Such speculative investment extended to "soft" commodities (such as cocoa, coffee and sugar) where there was no evidence of pressure on supplies due to increased consumption, as well as to non-ferrous metals. Moreover, as Professor Sylos Labini recently demonstrated,[1] from 1971 onwards the prices of raw

1. 'On the Instability of Commodity Prices and the Problem of Gold', in A. QUADRIO-CURZIO (ed.), *The Gold Problem: Economic Perspectives*, Oxford: Oxford University Press, 1982.

materials became far more sensitive to variations in world industrial production than they were before. Whereas in the period 1950-71 the rise and fall of raw material prices coincided with corresponding changes in the growth rate of world industrial production, the percentage range of variation in prices was smaller on the whole than that of industrial production; *after* 1971, the extent of price fluctuations was nearly three times greater. This highly increased price-sensitivity can only be explained on the supposition that speculation which took the form of "movement trading" (i.e. which increased in response to a price rise and *vice versa*) became a much larger share of the total. Thus the sharp rise in prices of 1972-74 was followed by an almost equally sharp fall in 1974-75 which was again abruptly reversed when world industrial production recovered in late 1975 and in 1976; in fact, there can be little doubt that the sharp rise in raw material prices in 1976 (and again, following another sharp fall, in 1978) was the main factor which nipped world industrial recovery in the bud. These extraordinary changes reflected changing expectations concerning world inflation, far more than varying pressures of demand coming from outside the markets, and this is best seen by the close correlation between movements in the gold price and of commodity prices.

In addition to this, the rate of inflation also accelerated on account of the sharp rise in the annual increase in money wages in the industrialised countries from around 1968-69 on. It started with the *événements* in France in June 1968 when the French Government was compelled to grant a general increase in wages extending to all industries of 15 per cent as a means of ending a general strike. This seems to have acted as a signal to other countries, like Germany, Britain, Sweden, etc., who all had double-digit wage increases in place of the 5-7 per cent annual norm for wage increases in previous years. As a result, the rate of increase in the prices of manufactured goods in international trade (in terms of U.S. dollars), which had fluctuated around the rate of 1-2 per cent a year, increased to over 5 per cent a year in 1969 and subsequent years.

All this meant that the rate of inflation of consumer prices rose from a customary 1-2 per cent a year, which was the average for all OECD countries from around 1948 on, to 4.8 per cent in 1969 and 5.6 per cent in 1972. However, in the following three years it averaged just over 13 per cent a year, something for which there was no precedent, certainly not for the twenty-five "developed" countries who are members of the OECD. The major factor in this jump was the formation of the OPEC cartel and the fourfold rise in the world price of oil in the last quarter of 1973. This was the most important price increase, not only on account of its highly inflationary effects (particularly when indirect effects are taken into account, as well as the direct effects which alone added some 4 per cent to the cost of living index), but because of its far-reaching consequences on world production and employment. Up to that time, accelerating inflation went hand-in-hand with accelerating output and a boom in employment, but after 1973 inflation in *money* terms was associated with a slow-down in *real* terms: the annual percentage change in industrial production, which rose from 3.1 per cent to 8.1 per cent between 1970 and 1973, *fell* by over 2 per cent in 1974 and by nearly 5 per cent in 1975. Over those two years, average unemployment (for all OECD countries) rose from 3.4 to 5.5 per cent. Hence the new term "stagflation". The inflation was combined not with a boom, but with a stagnation, or actually a deflation and a fall in production.

In retrospect, this great increase in the oil price was inevitable sooner or later, since, without any cartel, Saudi Arabia *alone* could have raised her own price several-fold and carried the world price of oil with it. It is not perhaps generally known that for the eight years before 1973, the world became increasingly dependent on the Middle Eastern countries, not only in terms of oil, but also of total energy requirements. Middle East oil extraction increased by 166 per cent between 1965 and 1973, and provided a wholly disproportionate part of the total energy requirements of the non-Communist world, which over the same period increased by only 5 per cent. This meant that Middle East oil production provided 70 per cent of the increase in *total* energy supplies (including coal, hydro and nuclear energy and natural gas, as well as oil) of the non-Communist world in that period with an annual increase in Middle East production of 13 per cent a year, whilst total world consumption of *all* forms of energy increased by 5.5 per cent.[1] It is clear that this could not have continued for long without a premature exhaustion of the reserves of the Middle East or without any countervailing benefit to themselves.

However, as the members of OPEC were unable to increase their external spending immediately, the net effect of the huge rise in the oil price was the equivalent of imposing a huge deflation in *real* terms – it was the equivalent of a 4 per cent cut in real disposable incomes of the world's consumers without any countervailing increase in demand. It had the same effect as if all consuming countries had suddenly imposed large additional taxation without any increase in public expenditure. In balance of payments terms it meant that the OPEC countries had a cumulative current account surplus of $350 billion in the years 1974-80, reaching its peak after the second oil shock of 1979 (which more than doubled the 1974 price) of some $110 billion in 1980, after which the surplus fairly quickly disappeared on account of the very rapid increase in external expenditures of the Arab countries, becoming negative in 1983 to the tune of $35 billion. However, in the years 1974-77, and again in 1979-80, the OPEC surplus was the major factor which imposed a demand deficiency, and a balance of payments constraint on expansion, on the rest of the world.[2]

From 1980 on, however, there was a new wave of recession, which in contrast to earlier recessions was largely confined to the countries of Western Europe, and particularly to members of the European Community. For this new recession I hold Britain largely responsible on account of the unfortunate coincidence of North Sea oil and Mrs. Thatcher coming on stream more or less at the same time. On account of North Sea oil, the balance of

1. After 1973 the situation was reversed in that Middle East oil supplies *fell* by 3 per cent a year in the 1973-80 period, while total world energy consumption went on rising, though only at the modest annual rate of 1.1 per cent.

2. Through international private bank lending on a very large scale, the developed countries managed to offset the deficit by additional exports to the borrowing countries (largely concentrated on Latin America), thus concentrating the deflationary effects of OPEC on those non-oil developing countries who were not creditworthy enough to receive loans from private banks.

payments on current account had a turn-around of nearly 9 billion dollars (from minus 1.4 to plus 7.5 billion) between 1979 and 1980, rising by a further 5.5 billion to 13.2 billion in 1981. The deflationary policies of the "monetarist" government of Mrs. Thatcher caused a turn-around of total real *domestic* demand by 6 per cent of the gross domestic product (from +3 per cent in 1979 to 3 per cent in 1980) and a further fall of 2.5 per cent in 1981, causing a rise in registered unemployment of nearly two million.

At the same time, Britain's three major partners in the European Community – Germany, France and Italy – had a total deficit of 29.6 billion dollars in 1980 and 19.3 billion in 1981. The cost of oil imports was largely responsible for the deficits of the EEC countries other than Britain. Since Britain's oil exports went mainly to other countries of the EEC, clearly the pressure on continental countries would have been greatly eased, and Britain's own economic situation and prospects greatly improved, if the new source of income from oil (all of which represented a net improvement in the balance of payments, through reduced imports and increased exports of oil) had been combined with a bold policy of expansion of both public and private investment, that would have made it possible for the Continental countries to pay for oil with additional exports of investment goods. Instead, Britain's gain from oil was wholly offset by the 15 per cent fall in her manufacturing output, due to a wholly artificial exchange rate.[1] At the same time, the purpose of the government's policy, to reduce the inflation rate by monetary stringency, failed on account of the inability of the government to restrict the money supply in the face of an accelerated increase in prices – which in turn was the direct result of a large increase in the taxation of commodities.

Thus, in the years 1980-82, Britain's policies were the cause of a deepening recession in Europe, in much the same sense in which the United States was the *cause* of the world-wide recession in 1929-32, and the Arab oil producers were the *cause* of the world-wide stagflation after 1973.

1. This was allowed to rise to levels at which, on IMF calculations, British unit costs were 50-60 per cent higher in dollar terms than those of other industrialised countries.

Mrs. Thatcher, whose monetarist views showed a strong resemblance to the old and long discredited ideas of the pre-war
Austrian economists, cannot be held responsible, however, for
the triumph of monetarism in the 1970s. She was merely swim-
ming with the tide. The astonishingly rapid and widespread con-
version of politicians, bankers, journalists, and other leaders of
public opinion to the most primitive ideas on the causation of
inflation – according to which the *sole* cause of a universal rise in
prices is to be found in the excessive prior increase in the money
supply – whose advocacy was pursued for many years by Professor Milton Friedman of Chicago, but by practically no one else
(except for the Austrians, von Mises and von Hayek). Then,
within a year to two, all opinion-formers and "decision makers",
at least in the Anglo-Saxon world, but also in France, Germany,
and possibly in Italy, were converted to it – except for the great
majority of professional economists who could not bring themselves to forget Keynes in favour of the simple and crude notions
of the old quantity theory of money. But for anyone else, the
"new monetarism" answered the needs of the hour. It was simple, it offered simple remedies; and, more importantly, it offered
the prospect of reversing the growing imbalance between the
power of labour in relation to the power of capital which was the
result of the full employment situation of the previous decades.[1]

So, in the elections that took place towards the end of the
1970s, right-wing monetarist governments came into power both
in Britain and in the United States, and "monetarist" policies
were formally adopted by the leading Central Banks, most importantly in the United States under Paul Volcker. The practical
result was that in the futile effort to reduce the growth of the
money supply, interest rates, both short-term and long-term,
were driven to extraordinary heights – at one time the money
market rate rose to 20 per cent in America – whereas in all previous economic recessions, interest rates were kept low so as to encourage borrowing.

The result of all this has been a complete paralysis of policy-
making at the international level, combined with the impossibil-

1. This was a consequence of the view that *any* general rise in prices is a manifesta-
tion of excess demand; monetarism denies the existence of cost-inflation.

ity of any one country taking the initiative for improving its own economy and those of others. Countries in exceptional circumstances, like Britain had in 1980-82, *could* have done it; America *could* do it – perhaps she *is* doing it already, owing to her enormous fiscal deficit and its reflection in a large excess of imports over exports, except for the fact that the Federal Reserve tends to offset this by continuing to raise interest rates, and thereby generating huge inflows of highly mobile funds which drives the exchange rate of the dollar higher and higher. Since the prices of many important commodities, including oil, are fixed in terms of dollars, the rise in the price of the dollar in terms of other currencies adds to the balance of payments difficulties of other countries, even though it improves their industrial competitiveness.

The fact that OPEC (as a group) is now in deficit on its current balance, and that Britain's current account surpluses have virtually disappeared while the United States is in a large deficit, makes it a great deal easier for other developed countries to expand their economies than at any time since 1973. But there is still need for coordinated action, at least among the members of the European Community. As the French example has shown, an expansionary budget which is out of line with the fiscal stance of the other main countries of the group, quickly gets a country into serious payments difficulties owing to the resulting imbalance in trade.

The lack of agreement on the fundamental lines of a policy for economic recovery is acutely felt, and the need for it is shown by the increasing frequency of inter-Governmental meetings at various levels: the next world summit meeting in which the heads of the leading Western powers all participate is due to take place in London in a few weeks' time.

If, by some miracle, this summit meeting, unlike all its predecessors, resulted in a constructive programme of recovery, what should its main provisions contain? I should like to end this series of lectures by suggesting the outline of a world-wide agreement on the necessary policies for recovery.[1] The programme could be summed up under four main heads:

1. *Editors' Note*: Europe is again in slump, and many of the policies advocated here have contemporary relevance.

1. The first is coordinated fiscal action including a set of consistent balance of payments targets and "full employment" budgets.[1] If this does not prove to be politically feasible, it is inevitable that the growth of unemployment will sooner or later force governments to take measures that would make it necessary for them to expand demand without being frustrated by the inevitable balance of payments consequence of expanding their economies relative to their trading partners. This means that there needs to be some form of restriction that would limit the increase in "competitive" imports to some target ratio in relation to exports. Trade liberalisation, which played such an important part in the rapid economic progress during the years of expansion, becomes a serious obstacle to economic recovery in the case of prolonged stagnation due to the inability of countries to achieve a coordinated set of policies. But, given a proper recognition of the problem, that under conditions of unrestricted free trade the actual *volume* of production and trade may in fact be considerably less than under some system of regulated trade – a system which relates the volume of imports in manufactures from a particular group of countries, such as the members of the EEC, to some mutually agreed ratio to the exports of individual members to the rest of the group – there is no reason why full employment should not be restored through policies of expansion, preferably directed by the expansion of State investment. This coordinated action by all countries, instead of isolated actions by each country, is the first and most important requirement of recovery.

2. Secondly, it is essential that interest rates should be brought down as rapidly as possible, and by as much as possible. If the United States is not willing to participate in such a change, it would be best if European countries adopted an interest equalisation tax (as was enforced in the United States before 1971) that

---

1. At present all countries have fairly large deficits in the general government budget, but these are largely the consequence of the low level of activity. On a "full employment" basis they would show a highly restrictive picture – they would show surpluses and not deficits. Contrary to appearances, the requirement of stability is for expansionary budgets – with lower taxes and higher expenditure, and not further fiscal restriction (as is advocated, for example, by M. de Larosiere of the International Monetary Fund).

makes it unattractive for European lenders to put their money into dollar balances even when European interest rates are considerably lower than those of America.

3. Thirdly, the most important requirement is to prevent the great volatility of commodity prices. This requires the creation of international buffer stocks financed directly out of a newly created international currency that is accepted by participating governments in the same way as the present SDRs are accepted by IMF members in settlement of their claims. Instead of issuing SDRs to member countries (free of charge so to speak) in proportion to their quotas with the IMF, it would be very much better if SDRs were issued to an international commodity corporation who would use them in payment of commodity purchases, and in this way – in contrast to the Common Agricultural Policy of the EEC – make the cost of accumulating stocks required for maintaining stable prices of primary commodities not a charge on the tax payer, but the "backing" (or "cover") of an international reserve currency convertible into national currencies.

Such a system could be established gradually, through a newly formed international institution, which would establish buffer stocks for commodities such as food grains and non-ferrous metals and then expand gradually into a wider range of commodities. In order to be successful it is essential that such a scheme should be started at a time when the world economy is depressed and commodity prices are low (as at present), and when it is desired to stimulate investment and the growth of future production by the assurance of stable prices. It may be difficult to convince the United States, but it is a policy which the European countries could initiate. They already have a European currency in the form of ECUs, and ECUs could be used to finance market intervention under the Common Agricultural Policy, which could be the beginning on the accumulation of buffer stocks for commodities.

4. Fourthly, the above would still leave one important problem unresolved, and this is the problem that Keynes also left entirely unresolved the tendency to chronic inflation under full employment conditions, due to the system of settling wages by sectional (or industrial) collective bargaining. It is a universal phenome-

non under capitalism that wages on the average rise faster than productivity, so that *labour costs per unit of output* have a chronic tendency to rise, almost irrespective of the state of demand. In Britain, for example, three years of very heavy unemployment of over 3 million, or 13 per cent of the labour force, have not sufficed to bring annual wage increases down to the level of productivity increase.

Therefore it is hopeless to expect that by restricting demand by monetary and fiscal measures you can get rid of cost inflation due to excessive wage increases. Despite all the present Government's efforts to weaken labour by heavy unemployment, wage increases in private industry are still running at least twice the rate of productivity increases, and this was achieved at a tremendous cost in terms of lost output due to a low level of real demand. The system of sectionally independent collective bargaining makes rapid wage increases inevitable, even at high levels of unemployment, owing to three major objectives of trade unions which are incompatible with each other. The first is the desire to preserve the *status* of their members in relation to other groups of workers (the matter of "relativities"); the second is to secure for their members a fair share of any significant increase in the company's profits, and the third is to resist any encroachment on the *attained* standard of living owing to unfavourable developments which might be wholly external in origin – such as an unfavourable change in a country's terms of trade caused by a rise in the prices of imported inputs of industry, or of food.

Since productivity increases differ enormously between different industries, and between different firms in the same industry, the second objective, in combination with the first, is bound to produce the result that wages rise faster than productivity – even in the absence of any unfavourable factor mentioned under the third objective. For the social pressures for preserving traditional wage differentials are very strong and of very long-standing. The stability of relative wages was noted in England in the 18th century or even earlier. This phenomenon by itself, however, would not be sufficient to explain the inflationary trends in the post-war period in the absence of the change in circumstances typified by the rise of modern oligopolies. Successful oligopolistic firms are likely to experience exceptional reductions in unit costs which they are not compelled, as manufactures were in the 19th century, to pass on to their customers in lower prices. As a result, they make exceptional profits and they can thus afford to raise their wages by more than is necessary to satisfy their labour requirements; and if they pay wages which are *above* the normal market rate, they reap their reward in good labour relations, in the ability to pick the best workers, and in always having a queue of workers to fill any vacancies. They do not, therefore, oppose, or not strongly, claims for wage increases due to rises in profits – in other words, they concede by their actions that their workers get a fair share of any increase in profits. This, in turn, is bound to lead to pressures for wage increases for reasons of relativities – with the result that these consequential settlements cause wages to rise faster than the average of productivity growth in the economy as a whole.

I confess I cannot see any way of resolving this problem, short of an entirely new approach which starts with a system of continuous consultation between the social partners – workers, management and the Government – in order to arrive at a social consensus concerning the distribution of the national income that is considered fair and which is consistent with the maintenance of economic growth, reasonably full employment and monetary stability.

In all countries, except those where the trade unions were decimated by the Nazis, namely Austria and Germany, trade unions are sectional, independent, and tend to belong to a common organisation which is nationwide, like the Trades Union Congress in Britain. But the power is with the individual union, not with the centre. If you take countries like France or Italy, the system is even more divided, fragmented, because in addition you have communist unions, socialist unions, Catholic unions and all sorts of other unions. After the war, the Germans and the Austrians were lucky enough to have no unions, and could start with a "tabula rasa". As a result, a new organisation was created where the central organisation is a powerful one, and the individual industrial organisations are subordinated. And the annual wage bargaining is on an overall national level, between the three social partners – between the organisation of all employers, the Government and the unions. And they agree on an annual wage increase which they say is not inflationary, which is then shared out between the unions according to various criteria. The post-war experience of Austria and West Germany shows that, starting with a new, integrated organisation of trade unions, it is not too difficult to make substantial progress on such lines.

DISCUSSION

Professor Amedeo Amato:* I would like to thank Lord Kaldor for his fascinating lectures, and also to take this opportunity to thank him for his equally fascinating lectures that I was able to attend at the University of Cambridge many years ago.

In these Mattioli lectures Lord Kaldor has gone to the heart of many of the basic problems facing the world economy. However, I would like to put forward a question on which he only touched upon here, although he has made fundamental contributions in the past. This question also involves some important aspects of his critique of the economic policy of Mrs. Thatcher (see *The Scourge of Monetarism*). It concerns the effects of fiscal actions; that is, the impact of an increase in the budget deficit when it is financed not by increasing the money supply but by the issue of bonds.

Professor Kaldor has developed an analysis of this problem which is partly different even from the view shared by most Keynesian economists. Indeed, a bitter debate between Keynesians and monetarists – a continuation of the debate between Keynes and the Treasury – has gone on for many years on this question. This debate has found a (temporary) resolution as far as neo-Keynesians and Mark I monetarists are concerned – with the conclusion that an increase in the budget deficit financed by the issue of bonds has an expansionary real effect in the short run, but is neutral in the long run. Here the terms "short run" and "long run" are quite ambiguous since they have very different meanings for the two schools. The short run, in which there is the expansionary effect, is taken to mean two or three months for the monetarists and some years for the neo-Keynesians – although in the last resort, the question becomes an empirical one. The common analysis of the two schools relates to the consequences of bond issues through resource crowding out and financial crowding out.

In some of his most recent contributions, Professor Kaldor has raised two kinds of objections to this analysis which, as I said, is by now shared both by neo-Keynesians and by Friedman monetarists (of course, the monetarists of the rational expectations

* Università degli Studi, Genova.

school further differentiate between anticipated and unanticipated increases in the budget deficit).

The first objection of Professor Kaldor is the following. As activity increases – as a consequence of an increase in the budget deficit – the higher utilisation of capacity causes an increase in the share of profits, mainly on account of lower overheads per unit of output (whether of labour costs, rents, etc., or interest payments). Thus, savings increase more than in proportion to the increase in income. If this is analysed in the framework of a "credit money economy" – as opposed to a "commodity money economy" – with endogenous money supply, investment would then increase instead of decrease. In other words, there will be a *crowding in* and not a *crowding out* effect.

Moreover, Professor Kaldor puts forward a second, possibly more serious, objection. This starts from the proposition that the cost to the buyer of purchasing long or medium term securities is the sacrifice of foregone liquidity (and not the sacrifice of foregone consumption). It is not a question, therefore, of inducing individuals to *save* but only of inducing them to commit themselves to the purchase of a long term security which is subject to the risk of a capital loss (or gain) on account of future changes in the rate of interest. This is pretty standard Keynesian-Kaldorian theory. But Professor Kaldor goes on and draws from this premise – and possibly from the theory of the term structure of interest rates – the conclusion that an increase in the issue of public securities does not necessarily imply an increase in the relevant interest rate. This perhaps means that, for instance, the present high U.S. interest rates would not be explained by Professor Kaldor with the usual reference to the increase of bonds issued to finance the budget deficit.

This last conclusion, and the analysis underlying it, are quite new even among Keynesian economists, and for their relevance they might merit some detailed exposition in this meeting. Thus I should be grateful to Lord Kaldor if he might consider this subject in his reply.

Lord Kaldor: Professor Amato asks about the consequences of a budget deficit when it is financed not by the issue of treasury bills, but by medium or long term bonds. He asks whether it will have a crowding-in effect or a crowding-out effect, and whether there will be a sacrifice of liquidity, or whether the interest rate will remain the same. The first thing that one must ask before answering this question is what is the binding constraint on the national income and output. If the binding constraint is the balance of payments, an increase in the budget deficit cannot have a crowding-in effect; it must have a crowding-out effect because output is not limited by demand, but by the balance of payments and no further increase in output is permissible because imports exceed exports. The alternative case is when the binding constraint is effective demand, which is the case considered by Keynes. In this case, there must be crowding-in, however the deficit is financed. To say that deficits crowd out private investment and are of no use assumes that output is limited by something other than demand. This is the same argument that took place in Britain in the 1920s when the Treasury argued against the public works programmes of Lloyd George and Keynes on the grounds that if money is spent on public works, business investment will be reduced. What this ignores is that as income rises, savings will rise to finance the public works. Also profits will rise, and profits are largely saved. So I honestly don't believe that the view on which Central Banks and Governments all over the world place so much importance, i.e. whether a deficit is financed by the banks or whether it is financed by the issue of long term bonds, makes any difference whatsoever.

PROFESSOR GIACOMO BECATTINI:* I would like to begin with a challenging and sweeping assertion by Professor Kaldor in the first of his lectures. Professor Kaldor states: it is more probable that the future progress of economics will emerge from patient empirical research than from the formulation of wide-ranging theoretical hypotheses. I would say that I both agree and disagree with this statement. I agree, first of all, because I share his scepticism concerning the ability of the more general and abstract theory taught in the universities to help us understand the world. In par-

* Università degli Studi, Firenze.

ticular, as Professor Kaldor says, models based on general economic equilibrium are not only useless but positively misleading for those endeavouring to interpret what today is the most important matter: namely the laws that govern change in capitalist economies. On this I agree, and I also agree that one should seek to avoid all the pitfalls awaiting those who try to apply a theory which is fundamentally ill-suited to the study of change, capitalist or otherwise. Nevertheless, I believe that Professor Kaldor's assertion that future progress lies entirely in empirical research requires qualification. What we need is a different way of considering the evolution of social facts more consonant with their nature. What different way is this? I shall try to set out in a few words what I consider to be the nub of the problem. Simplifying, the problem of development can be conceived as the problem of the progressive specification of basic wants. In every historical era, humanity has certain essential needs which always and necessarily must be satisfied, and it has available certain means with which to satisfy them. History can be viewed as the increasing articulation of these basic wants, as the discovery or invention of new ways to satisfy them. As history advances, a new structure of wants and techniques evolves. The problem of development is the problem of this progressive articulation, and incorporation in the economic system. I believe that this extremely general and generic scheme incorporates, as a particular case, the Adam Smith-Allyn Young theory of the progressive division of labour, so dear to Professor Kaldor. By this I mean that, whereas Young examines this phenomenon from the viewpoint of the productive process, I believe that it should be seen as a cultural process, in the sense in which the term culture is used by anthropologists. Thus, for example, when Professor Kaldor states that, at bottom, technological change is the *deus agitans* of progress, I would extend the meaning of technological change to include not only productive technology, but also the technology of consumption, broadening the concept to embrace the idea of a technology of life, which is indeed nothing but culture in the sense given above. I am convinced that Professor Kaldor's concept would become more fruitful, more concrete, more personal if, together with the economic-financial obstacles to the introduction of technical progress, he also considered "cultural" obstacles in the broad sense. I suspect that many major obstacles to the diffusion of new ideas arise from the fact that ideas move extremely sluggishly through our minds. One particular point in our mental space does not immediately connect with all the others; the paths are sinuous and there are many obstacles, dependent on history and on culture, which are more difficult to overcome than the ordinary economist is willing to admit. Thus, if this process of the "specification" of basic wants is married to technological progress and accumulation, I would entirely agree that this is the paradigmatic vision most consonant with study of the laws of change of capitalism.

Within this overall vision, the search for profit becomes an *acceleration factor* driving a dynamism that has its ultimate roots in the "spirit" of men "impelled for good or evil to change and progress", as Alfred Marshall put it, but it is not the factor that generates such dynamism. I discern a certain priority given to technology in the most recent writings of Professor Kaldor which strikes me as a retreat from the ideas that he held some years ago, when he always saw technology as intimately wedded to accumulation. Indeed, I would be in favour of a three-way marriage between technology, accumulation and "culture" where, as in *Alice in Wonderland*, one cannot tell whether these are three different characters or only three incarnations of the same person. I am extremely pleased to see, although it was to be expected, that Professor Kaldor continues a line of thought which can be summed up by the names Smith, Marshall, Young and, I would add, Keynes and Kaldor. In my view this line of thought is much more fruitful in the explanation of change in a capitalist economy than others which have gained wider currency in recent years. Of course, in pursuing this line, Kaldor repeatedly encounters Alfred Marshall.

On this I would make a number of brief remarks in the hope that Professor Kaldor can help us to clear up the matter. Professor Kaldor cites Marshall on several occasions, and credits him with having identified the problems and having indicated, somewhat vaguely, their solution. Kaldor also, with a particularly telling quotation, credits Marshall with an extremely up-to-date awareness of the dangers of mathematical formalism. This quotation, taken from a letter from Marshall to Bowley, is very impressive indeed; one should add, perhaps, that in the lines following those quoted by Professor Kaldor, Marshall states that he "admits exceptions". Had he not even admitted exceptions, the "scientific" study of social facts would be impossible. Professor Kaldor draws our attention to Marshall's invitation to biological analogies, stating that this effectively is the way forward, that this is the road to follow in exploring the laws of capitalist change. Professor Kaldor also appreciated Marshall's kinship with the classicals, in the sense that he was primarily concerned, like the classicals, with the supply side. Marshall's theory, despite what one might be induced to think by the "scissors" image, is a theory essentially about supply and accumulation – about development. Professor Kaldor recognises that Marshall posed in theoretical terms the problem of increasing returns. In reality, this problem, so central to Professor Kaldor's concerns, is, I maintain, absolutely central to Marshall's thought as well. I do not believe that Marshall gave a satisfactory solution to this problem. I would argue that, from his early manuscripts (recently published by Whitaker) until his last work, the principal theoretical issue addressed by Marshall was how to incorporate increasing returns into the inner core of economic theory. Therefore, in a certain sense, Professor Kaldor with his preoccupations stands very close to Marshall. One might add that the role of dealers, the auxiliary industries, the "industrial districts", which are given particular prominence in Professor Kaldor's lectures, would make Alfred Marshall happy were he still alive today. The point that misleads many in their reading of Marshall – and which may also have somewhat misled Professor Kaldor when, in the 1930s, he took part in the debate on imperfect competition – is that in Marshallian theory the exigencies of a theory of value overlap in an unclear, indeed decidedly ambiguous, manner with those of a theory of development. Marshall is a Janus. I would say that if one extracts the part which anticipates theories of development, Marshall's thought is very up-to-date – as I believe Professor Kaldor's lectures have shown.

I take this opportunity to say that perhaps we need to return to the 1930s; years which too hastily dismissed Marshall's thought in the particularly rigid and impoverished version of it propounded by certain of his pupils.

Professor Kaldor's lectures make me feel a little less an intellectual Jacobite; I foresee, although perhaps I am mistaken, the restoration of Marshallian ideas, duly dynamised.

I close with two questions. If Engel's Law and Young's Principle constitute the central nucleus of a theory of development, it is clear that political economy must establish a systematic relationship with the social disciplines that deal with other aspects of this process, which is both socio-economic and cultural at the same time. How does Professor Kaldor think that the problem of the relationships between economics, sociology, social psychology, and so forth, should be addressed: for example, the relationship between the process of accumulation studied by economists and that of socialisation studied by sociologists?

My second question is this. If, in order to understand real developments, we require new and general insights, where are we to look for them? Professor Kaldor has said: certainly not in the general equilibrium theory. Must we then seek them in Marxism, in Keynesianism, in neo-Ricardian doctrine? If I have understood Professor Kaldor correctly, he finds none of these solutions entirely convincing. Perhaps he is thinking of a Kaldorian blend. Is there room in this blend for the characteristic features of the Cambridge tradition as it was before what we may call the murder of the father took place?

LORD KALDOR: I will be very brief. I just want to clear up some misunderstandings. When I talk about the importance of empirical research, I do not want to underestimate the value of economic theory. But what I do think very strongly is that theory must be far more closely related to the results of empirical research. Far too much economic theory is based on trivial *a priori* assumptions which cannot be proved right or wrong, yet strong theoretical conclusions are derived from the models.

PROFESSOR LUIGI PASINETTI:* I am sure Professor Kaldor and

* Università Cattolica del Sacro Cuore, Milano.

the audience will realise that I speak with some hesitation, mainly because I always find myself so much in agreement with Professor Kaldor's approach to economics that I have very little to add on matters of substance. I shall, however, offer a few comments on the lectures and, at the end, I may ask a few questions.

Professor Lord Kaldor – or simply Nicky as his friends and pupils (and there are many of them here in the room) usually call him – is clearly an economist "of many seasons".

We are all familiar with the Kaldor of the 1930s, the time of his association with the London School of Economics, and the well-known economists who were teaching there at that time, especially Allyn Young, Lionel Robbins and Friedrick Hayek. And we all appreciate his contributions of that period to economic theory, mainly in the field of micro-analysis, relating to imperfect competition and welfare economics. That was a splendid vintage of Kaldor contributions – a vintage which even now some traditional economists, like Solow for example, are insisting were Kaldor's best.

Then we have known the Kaldor of the 1950s and 1960s, the Kaldor of the post-Keynesian growth and distribution theory, meaning by that the efforts at a straight generalisation to the long run of the concepts that had emerged from Keynes' *General Theory*. In this period, Kaldor produced a famous theory, which he has always defined as the "Keynesian theory of income distribution". We call it today the "Kaldor theory of income distribution", and rightly so.

In these lectures we have heard the Kaldor of a third season: we have heard a Kaldor that is reacting to the events of the 1970s. On a strictly factual level, there have been memorable events in the 1970s – the oil crisis, the inflationary movements in all Western industrial economies, the breaking down of the Bretton Woods rules of behaviour in international relations, and, above all, the reappearance of unemployment on a mass scale. On a theoretical level, there has been an all-out attack on Keynes' theories and policies. We all agree, of course, that Keynes' theories and policies have shown deficiencies, in many respects, in the face of the new situations that have arisen on the world scene. What has been surprising, however, is the surge of ideas and theories of conservative extraction that go back to pre-Keynesian approaches to economic theory and policy, and the appearance of politicians ready to revive and embrace theories and old-fashioned *laissez-faire* policies which until a few years ago had been considered discredited and definitely surpassed.

In these lectures, we have heard the response of Kaldor to these events. He has offered us a series of tools of analysis (mainly in his third and fourth lectures) and he has drawn a series of practical implications, in terms of concrete economic policy proposals (mainly in his fifth lecture).

Now, how have I been listening to all this? These new developments in Kaldor's thinking have come at a time when my association with Cambridge has come to an end, and it has been very interesting for me just to listen to him.

From one point of view, I have found the usual Kaldor – a Kaldor with very many familiar traits. Though the subject matter has been different from the one on which I used to hear him in Cambridge, the approach he has used is the same. What has always been striking to me is Kaldor's high originality, even in the details. Consider, in these lectures, his analysis of the role of intermediaries in the market, or of the role of technical progress as the most potent factor of competition, or of Keynes' principle of effective demand considered as a development of Say's Law rather than a rejection of it. Most scholars find it natural to begin to look at things from a traditional point of view – not Kaldor. Always iconoclastic with reference to traditional economic theory, always unable to stay within the traditional bounds, Kaldor abounds in ideas and thoughts that often go beyond even the very formal model he is trying to present. One may well disagree with him; yet one cannot but find him extremely stimulating and thought-provoking.

But what are the novelties of this Kaldor of the third season? I see his interests moving away – to use Baumol's expression – from that "magnificent" classical growth theory resumed by the Harrod-Domar models of strictly macroeconomic Keynesian derivation, and towards the movements of an economy through time with changes in the *composition* of the macro-magnitudes – changes in relative sizes, in relative prices, and in the terms of trade between different sectors. In other words I see his interests shifting towards the movements through time with *structural change*.

In a sense, this is not surprising; this is the direction in which post-Keynesian economic theory has found itself going naturally, being driven more and more, from Keynes' dichotomy between consumption and investment, towards a more detailed sectoral analysis. Joan Robinson went on to develop a two-sector consumption/investment model. Kaldor himself relied on a distinction between capitalists and workers in his theory of income distribution. Sraffa has proposed an inter-industry analysis, like that of von Neumann and Leontief. It seems quite natural in a sense that one should end up with a kind of multi-sector growth analysis with structural change. I personally have found myself going in this direction.

But what has Kaldor done? Kaldor has indeed gone in this direction, but in a particularly interesting way. He does not go far in the disaggregation direction – he concentrates in fact on an analysis limited to two sectors – but he does more in another direction, because he introduces a whole series of structural characteristics and of institutionally based rules of behaviour. In other words, Kaldor is trying – in a way which has always been typical of his analysis – to *stylise* the complex facts of life by encapsulating them into a basic two-sector model in which there is primary good production on the one side and manufactured good production on the other side. In this way, he gives up the richness of a multi-sector model, but at the same time he gains all the advantages of being able to introduce specific behavioural relations. Kaldor is able, by contrasting the different behaviour of the different sectors, to bring out a whole set of relations and basic characteristics that immediately bring to mind what happens in the real world. He has decreasing returns in agriculture and increasing or constant returns in manufacturing; he has technical progress which goes on saving land in agriculture and technical progress which goes on saving labour in manufacturing. He has competitive prices in agriculture, where the producers are price-takers – they behave in a passive way; and he has oligopolistic prices, or rather administered prices, in manufacturing, where the producers are price-makers. He has savings as the primary variable in agriculture and he has investment as the primary variable in manufacturing. On one side – agriculture – the supply conditions are prevailing; on the other side – industry – demand conditions are prevailing. This puts him in the privileged position of being able to deal with disequilibrium situations, which would have been impossible to do within any other theoretical framework.

One may well find some unsatisfactory features in Kaldor's analysis. For example, I would find unsatisfactory his characterisation of the relations between agriculture and industry, which is simply done on a diagram that has a price on the vertical axis, a price which represents, in fact, the terms of trade between the two sectors; also the fact that the two rates of growth of industry and agriculture are equalised (I will say a little more on this in a few moments). But at the same time, clearly, the model does illuminate a lot of other relations; it shows quite well how an economy can get into difficulties. Most of all, the model allows Kaldor to go on to investigate a series of relations in international trade that derive from adjustments of physical quantities, quite irrespective of price variations. And, moreover, the model allows him to draw a whole series of relations that are helpful in understanding what has been happening recently on the world scene. The fruitfulness of the analysis is shown at its best when the model allows him to set out a detailed programme of what to do in order to resume economic growth with full employment and monetary stability.

I shall not go into all this. I leave it to other scholars in the audience to comment on, or respond to, Kaldor's provocative proposals and to his striking indictment of the current British Prime Minister, accused of being the main cause of the present European recession. As a contribution to the discussion I shall now put to him a few questions.

The first question is this: the title of these lectures – "Causes of growth and stagnation in the world economy" – is remarkably similar to the title of the inaugural lecture Kaldor gave at Cambridge in 1966: "Causes of the slow rate of growth of the U.K. economy". But the conclusion seems to be profoundly different.

In that inaugural lecture, Kaldor insisted on labour as being the major bottleneck to the expansion of the U.K. economy. In this lecture, at a certain point, he has even said that it is difficult, very difficult, to visualise the labour supply as an effective constraint on production in any particular economy. The question is: has there been a change of mind on this? Or has there been a refinement? To what extent are the two conclusions reconcilable?

The second question is the following: One of the striking features of economic growth in all the economies that we are observing is that the rates of growth are so different from sector to sector, from time to time. (Note that reference to actual observations is not casual. Kaldor insists that we should always look at the real world before making our own assumptions.) But in his two-sector model, the equilibrium situation is that $g_A = g_I$, i.e. at a point where the rate of growth of the agricultural sector is equal to the rate of growth of the industrial sector. The question is this: isn't proportional growth, at least in equilibrium, a little bit too reminiscent of the von Neumann type of growth model? It would seem that we are confined to use the model only in situations of disequilibrium. Would it not be a better expression of Kaldor's own ideas to think in terms of differentiated growth rates? Maybe this would be the way to proceed to models with more than two sectors.

The third question relates to the conclusion emerging from the lecture on international trade. Kaldor gives an explanation of the relative poverty of the countries whose exports consist of primary products. He says that the countries depending on exports of primary products remain comparatively poor, but their poverty is a consequence not of low productivity of labour in their export industries, but of limited employment capacity in their profitable industries. Now, there has been research and theoretical developments on this subject, which might be recalled here. Arthur Lewis, for example, has made investigations of the movements of relative prices in terms of rates of growth of productivity in the export industry sector and in the non-export industry sector. I, myself, in my book on *Structural Change*, have shown the crucial importance of comparing the rates of growth of labour productivity in the export sector with those in other sectors. Would it not be more appropriate simply to say that the relative poverty of these countries is a consequence of low *comparative rates* of growth of productivity in the other sectors of the economy compared to the export sector?

Here is my fourth and final question: One of the exciting proposals that I find in Kaldor's programme, aimed at the resumption of economic growth with full employment and monetary stability, is the proposal that the countries of the European Community, independently of the United States, could turn their much criticised Common Agricultural Policy into something really new. Kaldor seems to envisage the accumulation of commodity buffer stocks, in physical terms, which could provide a real backing or cover for an international reserve currency convertible into national currencies. Could Professor Kaldor expand on this? We know, of course, his earlier proposals for a *world* currency, backed by stocks of physical commodities. Has he worked out something similar in details in terms of a new proposal relating to a *European* international reserve currency as against a world currency? i.e. in practice with reference to Europe as against the United States?

LORD KALDOR: I do not disagree with most of what Professor Pasinetti has said. We are great friends, and he knows me very well. He knows the characteristic which I share with Keynes that I never feel bound in my thought today by what I thought yesterday. I always like to look at problems afresh. If I am alive in five years' time, you will probably find that many things that I have said today, I will not agree with. It is certainly true that when I wrote my Inaugural Lecture in Cambridge in 1966 I did believe very firmly that Britain suffered from a labour constraint in a way which was not true of other countries because in all other countries there were forms of disguised unemployment, in agriculture, while in Britain there was real full employment. In Britain, I believed there was an absence of labour reserves and this was an important factor in limiting production of manufactures and exports. But I now think this was quite wrong. I said so in print in various subsequent articles, and Professor Pasinetti is quite right that it is completely contrary to what I said in these lectures which are meant to convey the idea that there has never been such a labour constraint except from a purely short term point of view. There may be a scarcity of trained or skilled labour, and labour may be relatively immobile, but these are short-term constraints. If there is one thing which exists in superabundance, it is labour.

I agree with him also when he talks about the effect of international trade in increasing the differences between rich and poor countries, instead of diminishing them, which is the thesis of all official international trade theory from Ricardo right down to Samuelson. A country may concentrate on being a great raw material exporter, and this may be its comparative advantage, but it will not make a country rich. The reason why it will not make a country rich is because it does not give much employment. Take the case of Mexico, for example, where there are enormous oil reserves. From that point of view it is potentially a very rich country, but wages in Mexico are very low because the oil industry is one industry which gives rise to very little employment.

As far as Mrs. Thatcher and the recession is concerned, the big mistake was to deflate the economy at the same time as the discovery of North Sea oil was driving the balance of payments into surplus. This drove up the exchange rate to excessive levels, destroying British industry and reducing demand for European imports at the same time. North Sea oil was a natural opportunity to reinvigorate the whole of Europe instead of exacerbating recession.

On the question of buffer stocks, I would agree that a worldwide buffer stock scheme is the solution to the problem of the world trade cycle. It would be the best solution to get the world out of the present state of stagnation and lack of demand. But the European countries could do quite a lot to improve their own situation. I would not expect the United States to do anything. In times of unemployment, when demand is low, countries should not have to contribute so much to the expenses of the European Community. The Community should print its own money, and accumulate stocks, and this would improve the economic situation in every country of the Community. There is a case for taking the Common Agricultural Policy out of its present fiscal framework and financing it by newly printed money which is accepted by a European Central Bank as a reserve against commodities. This would be a good idea for helping Europe in the absence of something better.

PROFESSOR PAOLO SYLOS LABINI:* I made the intellectual acquaintance of Nicholas Kaldor in 1941, when I was preparing my doctoral dissertation, that was already in the field of growth economics, since it was concerned with the economic consequences of inventions on industrial organisation. At that time this was a rather unusual topic: economic theory was then predominantly static. I studied an article published by Kaldor a few years before in *Economica*: "The Equilibrium of the Firm", in which he was clearly detecting some of the difficulties arising, in the traditional theory of problems of a dynamic nature. A few years later, in 1950-51, when I was a research student in Cambridge, I followed several of the lectures given by Kaldor. At that time I had asked for, and obtained, Dennis Robertson as my supervisor because I knew his important book *A Study of Industrial Fluctuations* published in 1915. Two years before, in 1948-49, I had been at Harvard, where I had Joseph Schumpeter as my supervisor. These choices were due to my interest in growth and cycles or, rather, the cyclical growth of the economy.

After Cambridge, I had several occasions to meet Kaldor; in Geneva, when he was in the Economic Commission for Europe, and, almost every year, in Rome, in the house of Gerda Blau. I realized that often I was moving on a line of thought that was similar to his own; several ideas of mine have been influenced by him, probably more than I am aware. In particular, through a particular route that goes back to my work on oligopoly, I reached the conclusion that it is theoretically necessary to separate the economy into at least two, or better, into three sectors – raw materials, industrial products and services; a conclusion, as you all know, similar to that reached by Kaldor through a different route.

* Università degli Studi «La Sapienza», Roma.

I have three short comments to make. The first one is concerned with Adam Smith who is really the founder of modern economic theory and of growth economics. In his second lecture Lord Kaldor says: "Nevertheless none of the classical economists believed, with the possible exception of Marx, that such land-saving improvements can put off the operation of the law of diminishing returns more than temporarily." Well, I would say that this statement is undoubtedly true in the case of Ricardo. But if Marx is a possible exception, so too is Smith before him. Apart from minerals, Smith distinguishes three types of products of the earth: (1) vegetable products, except wheat, (2) wheat and (3) cattle. Only for cattle, Smith speaks of diminishing returns, particularly when, in a country, free lands are finished and cattle requires increasing labour costs. For vegetable products, Smith assumes that, as a rule, returns are increasing, though more slowly than in manufacturing. Wheat is a special case, since it is produced with the help of cattle, and, as a rule, it is produced at approximately constant returns. My comment is not intended to deny or to belittle Kaldor's contention that land-saving inventions are of fundamental importance for economic growth. I would simply say that this view can, in a sense, be found already in Smith, who on this point had a position very different from that of Ricardo. Considering the general topic of Lord Kaldor's lectures, it is probably well to point out that Smith's treatment of the behaviour of returns – whether diminishing, increasing or constant – is fully dynamic; it is growth economics in the strict sense of the world. The students who are here would do well to give a high priority to the study of Adam Smith's great work.

My second comment is concerned with a statement that I found in Kaldor's last lecture, that is: "Traditional wage differentials are very strong and of very long-standing". I think that this statement applies to a great extent – though not completely – to wages in the strict sense, but, in our time at least, it does not apply to the wage-salary differential. I refer to the traditional dichotomy between "manual" and "intellectual" labour. In fact, all the statistical data that I have seen for different industrialised countries show that the gap between average wage and average salary after World War II is rapidly falling. Such a trend is an important one not only for economic theory, but also for social and political reasons.

My third comment refers to Kaldor's world-wide programme. In my view, such a programme brings into full light the main characteristic of Lord Kaldor's work, that is, his integrated and, so to say, "anti-schizophrenic" approach to economic problems. Pure and applied theory, abstract and empirical inquiries, public and private finance, often are treated as different and separate analyses, whereas Lord Kaldor tends to unify them so that, even without realizing it, he combines even the most abstract piece of theory with the most concrete type of proposal. This is also the case with Kaldor's world-wide programme, in which we find the proposal for the creation of an international commodity corporation, that would organise buffer stocks of raw materials at the world level to stabilise their prices, as a means of stimulating investment in the production of raw materials and to put an end to the present-day world-wide monetary disorder. In fact, Lord Kaldor conceives his proposal as a special kind of international monetary reform. I could not agree more with such a proposal, but I would suggest that the probability of its success would increase considerably if it were supplemented by a proper monetary reform, with quasi-fixed exchange rates and a monetary unit in some way linked to gold. Indeed, the two proposals – the buffer stock scheme and the monetary reform – are strictly connected. This was quite clear to Keynes, too, as Kaldor recalls. Only recently Donald Moggridge has published the detailed Memoranda that Keynes prepared in 1942 for the British Government to put forward these two proposals. Keynes was conceiving the international monetary reform as the basis for introducing his buffer stock scheme, whereas Kaldor considers the opposite connection.

Personally, I would consider the two proposals as strictly interdependent. In my view, the international monetary reform should create, or strengthen, an international currency similar to Keynes' "bancor" – it could be the European ECU properly reordered. As is well known, Keynes's "bancor" was tied up to gold in a peculiar way. In the early 1930s Keynes had stated that "gold is a barbarous relic"; but in the course of time he somewhat changed his mind.

LORD KALDOR: Professor Sylos Labini is another Italian economist whose writings I have known and admired, and I find myself always in agreement with his views. I agree entirely with
what he said about Adam Smith, and the conclusion of all the
great classical economists that in the end, agriculture is subject to
diminishing returns and industry is subject to increasing returns.
The tendency to increasing returns may exist in some agricultural production also, but the fact that land is ultimately limited is
the basis of the great law of diminishing returns, which in the
view of Smith and Ricardo will be the factor that governs everything in the future. Ultimately, the growth potential of the world
must reach an end because of the law of diminishing returns.
Whether true or not, it did also presuppose what Ricardo called
improvement in the art of cultivation, which is what I call land-
saving innovations. But these are temporary. You cannot have
them for ever.

This brings me to my two-sector model, which Professor
Pasinetti also referred to. In my simple diagrammatic model, the
two sectors of agriculture and industry grow at the same rate, but
they do not have to. It is not a requirement of the theory, nor is it
realistic. What I am trying to emphasise is that the two sectors
must be in a balanced relationship with each other, otherwise
overall growth will be constrained. But I want to emphasise that
in a well-ordered world economy it is the product of nature that
sets the limit to expansion. The expansion of industry is limitless;
labour reserves are abundant, and capital accumulation can be
speeded up continuously with an expansion of industrial production and employment. But these industries use the product of
nature, and at any stage of technology, nature can yield a certain
maximum and no more. Thus, in the long run, it is the rate of
growth of land saving innovations in agriculture that sets the limit to the growth of the world economy.

PROFESSOR SIRO LOMBARDINI:* I shall restrict my intervention
to four brief comments on Professor Kaldor's lectures, with
which I find myself substantially in agreement. My encounters

* Università degli Studi, Torino.

with Kaldor date back many years: his essays on the firm and on capital exerted a notable influence on the direction of my own research. What I intend to do is to confirm certain assessments made by Kaldor of the state of the theory with a series of remarks of my own regarding the following points: (a) the inability of general equilibrium models to interpret the processes of economic development; (b) the role of prices in actual practice compared with that envisaged by equilibrium theory; (c) the role of innovation in development; and (d) the light that my observations concerning the above three points may shed on the current situation.

(a) Walras' model can be used to interpret economic growth only if this is brought about by an expansion of the population which fulfils the expectations of entrepreneurs regarding both the growth of demand and the availability of sufficient labour to operate new machinery. This is substantially the interpretation of Walras' model given by Cassel. Unfortunately, however, it is an interpretation bereft of heuristic value, and for two reasons. Firstly, population growth – as Smith warned and as concrete experience has largely borne out – is not a sufficient condition (indeed, it is not even a necessary one) for economic development. In the context of general equilibrium theory, another interpretation of the growth process is possible: von Neumann's model, which is much more elegant and yields interesting insights into the relationship between growth, income distribution and the structure of demand (which can also be developed on the basis of Sraffa's model). What I wish to emphasise here is that as regards economic development, von Neumann's model confirms my judgement of the Walras-Cassel model. Unlike the latter, the former is unable to identify any market mechanism able to ensure efficiency in the use of resources (and in the choice of techniques). Competition cannot act as such as a mechanism, for the reasons set out by James Meade, who also belongs to the marginalist tradition, in his contribution to indicative planning.

There is another reason why general equilibrium models are unable to furnish significant interpretations of the process of economic development, a reason whose importance has been stressed by Kaldor's lectures: the limited availability of certain natural resources. Thus, apart from the logical difficulties generated by the problems of the existence of equilibrium (which can only be resolved by formulating hypotheses that substantially deny the importance of technical progress), of the plurality of equilibrium situations, and of stability – one need only consider these problems to realise that the dynamics of the system (contrary to what Pareto maintained) cannot be interpreted as a series of equilibrium states – real processes cannot be explained by general equilibrium models, which can in truth only be used in normative economics.

(b) If we take the theory of rational expectations to its logical extreme, we can state that the market mechanism is able to ensure the most efficient use of resources. Yet this reminds us what our older schoolmates used to tell us when we were children: to catch the bird you only need to place a grain of salt on its tail. The formation of expectations displays certain features reminiscent of others connected with technical progress, as Knight pointed out. Some discontinuities in the process are explained by the disappearance of innovative expectations or by an abrupt change in predominant expectations. I shall leave these two complications to one side. There still remains, however, the fact that every agent formulates its expectations on the basis of an interpretative model of the economy which necessarily diverges from the models more or less consciously used by other operators, and *a fortiori* from the real model. Only the marginalist proponents of theories of rational expectations are convinced that they know the mechanisms whereby the economy operates, and are confident that their knowledge can be communicated to all agents. I have appreciated Kaldor's contribution to the explanation of the mechanisms responsible for the rapid growth of the 1950s and 1960s, and the onset, to a large extent unexpected, of the recessive trends of the 1970s. I shall propose an interpretation of these phenomena which, by seeking not to explain the historical process but to aid its understanding, does not invalidate Kaldor's arguments. Every theory emphasises certain aspects of the process. This is necessary if the theory is to be formally rigorous and sufficiently simple to provide operationally significant insights.

We may move on from the hypothesis of adaptive expectations by supposing that every agent modifies, on the basis of previous experience, not only the values of the exogenous coefficients and variables in its model, but the model itself. If we could assume that the problems for all agents arise in the same form and for a sufficiently large number of time-periods, so that through progressive adjustments all agents come to know the real model, then the theory of rational expectations would certainly be valid. We would have managed to place the grain of salt on the bird's tail, and we could go on to the second task that exercises the intellectual energies of the theorists of rational expectations: capturing the bird.

Kaldor is right to say that processes are necessarily in disequilibrium. But this is not solely because changes, stemming principally from technical progress and from changes in the availability of commodities (and also from changes in economic policy), prevent the system from converging towards equilibrium; it is also due to the expectations mechanisms of a monetary economy. There are in fact two causes of disequilibria, as Katshuito Iwai has stressed. The first consists of the factors that modify the context in which operators formulate their expectations and take their decisions. The second is the inevitable incoherence among individual expectations. Of course, the second of these causes assumes particular importance because of the operation of the first, but for the purposes of correct theoretical analysis they should be kept distinct.

Now, if we replace the fantastic interpretation of the market proposed by Walras and his theory of the auctioneer with a more realistic account which recognises the role played by individual operators in determining prices and wages, and the connections that individual decisions establish among prices and wages, then it is not difficult to show that it is precisely the flexibility of prices which prevents the market mechanism from bringing the system into equilibrium. Hence it is possible to interpret both individual cumulative processes (inflation, recession) and the coexistence of cumulative processes which at first sight appear contradictory (stagflation).

(c) I come to the central thesis of Kaldor's analysis, with which

I agree: namely that the prime factor in the development process is innovation. The process of accumulation is itself closely bound up with innovation – whether one subscribes to the Smithian view that it is accumulation which induces innovation (the greater capital available to the capitalist allows him to introduce new machinery and, above all, to step up the process of the division of labour), or whether one views the connection in Schumpeterian terms (it is only through the innovation made possible by bank credit that labour productivity can be increased and higher levels of accumulation thus achieved; the greater saving then repaying the debts incurred in the credit system).

Innovation (or technical progress) has only been given caricature treatment by the marginalist school. In fact, analysis of innovation is only possible if one abandons the marginalist context (or equilibrium theory), and for two reasons. Firstly, because innovation presupposes certain kinds of interaction between the social system and the political system – as Pareto himself pointed out when he stressed the different perspectives acquired by the development process when the *residues* of the former or the latter class predominate. Secondly, because it is impossible to examine the role of innovation if one maintains the hypothesis that consumer tastes are given. Every innovation in productive processes entails the possibility of new forms of consumption. During the first industrial revolution, process innovation (the division of labour) came about downstream of innovation in products (textiles and foodstuffs). During the second industrial revolution, the development of machinery not only allowed the replacement of labour by the machine, but also created the basis for the manufacture of the automobile, which, from a rich man's toy became, also thanks to the adjustments in income distribution that Ford introduced, a mass consumption good. Electricity not only revolutionised productive processes but led to the appearance of new consumption goods (radio, domestic appliances, television) which, together with the automobile, helped to create a new model of development. We are now entering the age of information technology in which the association between innovation in productive processes and new goods and services appears even closer.

The new forms of consumption thus made possible could not be assimilated – as equilibrium theory would have it – to the satisfaction of needs that already potentially existed (tastes, in Pareto's terminology, which are unable to exert all their influence on the system because of the obstacles represented by the insufficient availability of goods). As Schumpeter reminds us, the railways did not arise because consumers advanced effective demand for those services in preference to the stagecoach. The majority of changes in goods consumed have been imposed by producers on consumers who, more often than not, have resisted the change and have had to be educated by the elaborate psycho-techniques of advertising. This consideration suffices – although others could be cited – to show that the economic process cannot be studied according to the marginalist paradigm whereby needs are given and the economic problem is essentially the optimal distribution of resources, also given, to satisfy these needs.

(d) Kondatrief long-wave cycles can be interpreted as originating in the cumulative processes that certain technical innovations engender, in that they have not only revolutionised production techniques but patterns of consumption as well.

The causes of the crisis of 1929 were multiple, and the one cited by Kaldor certainly warrants careful examination. Nevertheless, I believe that perhaps the most important reason for the crisis was that the onset of consumerism – which consisted in the revolution in patterns of consumption ensuing from the diffusion of the automobile as a mass consumption good and the advent of new electrical consumer durables – was decelerated because the diffusion of these new goods was impeded by the distribution of income, and because in other countries the distribution of income obstructed the consumption-oriented evolution of the new economic and social system (some timid attempts had been made in Germany).

This possible explanation of the crisis can also help us to understand the reasons for the unexpected and prolonged boom of the years that followed the World War II, in contrast to the recession that followed the World War I. For a variety of reasons (in Italy, the growth of exports and of public spending during the period of reconstruction), the new pattern of consumption spread rapidly through most of the European countries. This phenomenon not only induced the growth of internal demand but boosted international trade, which also intensified as a result of changes already taking place in the international division of labour and continued to expand during the 1960s. Kaldor is right to insist on the role played by the growth of demand in the boom of the 1950s and 1960s; yet this growth of demand was the result of these changes, of these interactions among technological innovation and the development of new consumption patterns, rather than of Keynesian policies which, if anything, were induced by the changes in the social structure that these interactions brought about (the growth of the middle classes and of new political/ideological attitudes among the political parties in favour of public spending, which in certain countries like Italy became the condition for the new pattern of consumption to emerge).

The abrupt growth of consumption (and indeed the oil crisis) also finds internal explanation in the interpretation of the development process that I have briefly outlined above.

However, in order to explain the present crisis and the divergences now emerging between the prospects of growth for Europe and the United States and Japan, different considerations are in order. Unfortunately, these, too, require a radical revision of the models that we have inherited from the neo-classical school, and, indeed, of the conception of the economic system on which they are based. The advent of computer technology, changes in the international division of labour, certain changes in the structure of demand stemming from changes in the distribution of income, required, in the early 1970s, profound restructurings which in the short period appeared too costly and risky for both workers and entrepreneurs. It was this situation that engendered the collusion between a proportion of entrepreneurs and trade unions that led to welfare policies of an importance and impact – not only on public finance but also on rates of productivity growth – which we are only now beginning fully to understand. The economic system conceived by the neoclassicals as an adaptive system has become a mechanism which interacts with the socio-cultural system in order to maintain its structures.

This statement applies to Europe as a whole and to Italy in particular, and explains the differences in inflation rates and in growth rates, even medium-term ones, now apparent in the European countries compared with the United States and Japan.

If this diagnosis is correct, then the therapy suggested by Kaldor must be supplemented by structural measures designed to restore flexibility to the system. I am in broad agreement with Kaldor's verdict on the economic policies adopted in Britain; that the development policy that could have been implemented was not. I would only add that such a policy can only be successful if it is combined with a policy that alters structures which, because of higher rates of productivity increase in sectors today in stagnation, enables supply to adjust to demand.

One may indeed talk of a policy of supply, but in a sense entirely different (and in direct theoretical opposition to) the notion of a policy of supply in the ideological context of the neo-monetarists and the neo-free traders. Although it may seem paradoxical, we must recognise that it is upon the success of this policy of supply that the survival of the market will depend; a market whose function is not as we have learnt from the marginalist models, but is instead as Schumpeter suggested: it is the market, in fact, which enhances the nexus between the economic and socio-cultural systems which gives maximum development to innovation, both through the maximum enhancement of entrepreneurial skills and through the constant changes in tastes and in the structure of demand which, at certain moments, bring about changes in the pattern of development itself.

LORD KALDOR: I agree with most of what Professor Lombardini says. The main point I would want to stress is that there is no single cause of economic crises. For example, in my view the economic crisis of 1929 was a classic example of a crisis caused initially by the over-supply of grains which were accumulated for years in the hope that world demand would expand, but then merchants got rid of their excess stocks, prices collapsed, and it was the collapse of grain prices which caused the collapse of purchasing power in the agricultural sector which then reduced the demand for industrial goods, reducing investment in industry and agriculture, and so on. It was a classical under-consumption type of crisis, if you like, precipitated by changed expectations.

The recession post-1973 was entirely different caused by shortages of primary products, particularly oil, which drove up their price, and precipitated a deflation of demand in the industrial consuming countries.

Both rising and falling primary commodity prices tend to produce stagnation, but for different reasons.

PROFESSOR SALVATORE BIASCO:* I should like to ask Lord Kaldor for clarification on a few points which arise in his fifth lecture. I am in full agreement with his analysis of the international situation, especially with the shift of emphasis from supply to demand factors. We live in a world where the dominant philosophy is that each country must put its own house in order before an international order can be established. This view essentially stresses supply factors, as if the growth of each economy were limited by insufficient expansion of the productive capacity, and as if weakness in demand followed from it. This sluggishness in capacity growth is thought to be exogenous (or at least independent of demand); it is seen as the result of social conditions and of the political, institutional and financing effects of the long boom, all of which now act as obstacles to expansion. Thus the crisis is seen as having many epicentres, rather than a single epicentre which must be sought at the world level. Lord Kaldor takes a global view of the system, focussing on the international economy as a whole. His analysis centres upon the generation of (international) demand and the limits it imposes on, or derives from, national economic policies. Supply forces are viewed as being induced by demand rather than as autonomous components. As this point remains implicit in Lord Kaldor's analysis (assuming that I understand it rightly), I would urge him to formulate it explicitly.

Moving on from this point, I should like to raise a few problems with regard to the matters discussed by Lord Kaldor. The extraordinary growth in production that took place in the 1950s

* Università degli Studi «La Sapienza», Roma.

and 1960s arose from ex-ante fallacies in composition which were no less substantial than those that occurred later in the 1970s and 1980s when the growth rate of the world economy was falling. For example, export led growth processes, pursued simultaneously by several countries, were possible only in the absence of recurrent external constraints that would have brought them to a halt. These countries needed to maintain a positive balance in goods and services as a guarantee of continued expansion of demand, of productivity, and finally of exports. But clearly a positive balance could not be maintained by all countries at once. Another example is the simultaneous pursuit of policies aimed at containing internal demand in order to ensure that the economy of each single country would be governed by international demand. This too implies a fallacy in composition, in that international demand is derived from the generation and dispersion of internal demands.

My interest here is not primarily centred upon these fallacies of composition: what I want to emphasise is that to some extent they have been resolved by a sort of spontaneous coordination of the market. Today, however, the requirements of the market lead not to coordination but to anarchy. Lord Kaldor stresses the role played during the period of intense growth by the United States, which certainly acted as the nth country, the one that reconciles the objectives of the others – in other words, a residual country. Though it is only a necessary but not sufficient condition for resolving *ex-ante* contradictions, the role of the nth country in the international economy cannot but fade in a regime of fluctuating exchange rates. Indeed it can no longer exist and has in fact disappeared. With a fluctuating exchange rate a country acting as an nth country – for example the U.S. in 1977-78, Germany in 1979, or the U.S. in 1970-73 – is subject to the import of inflation, the replacement of its currency in the international market, and so on. This state of affairs leads to an explosion in raw material prices and a world-wide spread of inflation; the nth country itself is forced to backtrack in its economic policies. On the other hand, these same processes affect the competitiveness of the nth country, and thus its compensatory function with regard to the other countries is endogenously destroyed. A new flow of funds structure appears on the scene, in which the currency of the central country appreciates but this does not necessarily have a stimulating effect on the world economy – or if it does, it is conditional on a deindustrialisation of that country. This is a process that cannot continue indefinitely.

Now, I wonder whether Lord Kaldor's scheme, which involves the creation of more international currencies, and which links the reform of the international monetary system to buffer stocks in the raw materials market, may be a way of recreating the function of the residual country which has been endogenously destroyed by the market. That is to say, it might be recreated by entrusting it to a specific mechanism operated by a cooperative supra-national body with discretionary powers. Is this a correct way of understanding the implications of Lord Kaldor's proposal?

I have a third question, which I shall state very briefly: in his fifth lecture Lord Kaldor hints at the need for the most important countries to serve as a locomotive for the world economy. If they do this they must to some extent accept a deficit in their goods-and-services account. But once they accept a deficit, these countries are the ones to receive a transfer of goods and services from the rest of the world. In a situation of North-South equilibrium, however, we should have flows of production from rich to poor countries, and this means that the rich countries should have a surplus in their goods-and-services account. Yet when this actually occurs in the world, we know there is deflation. Here I would like to ask Lord Kaldor if his proposal for trade regulation could be seen as a proposal to unite the two requirements which prove to be contradictory in the anarchy of the real world. I refer, I repeat, to the need for an effective transfer of goods and services towards poor countries, which can occur only through a positive trade balance on the part of rich countries, and, at the same time, the need to sustain the growth of world demand, which now occurs when the rich countries show a negative balance.

If that is the case, when a rich country has recourse to protectionist measures, should it not be forced to make unilateral transfers (to the World Bank or other international bodies) so as to compensate the countries that suffer losses through those protectionist measures? If compensation is indirect, and the World Bank uses these receipts to make transfers to poor countries, such measures might be accepted as part of the international rules of the game, and might reconcile those otherwise contradictory requirements which I mentioned before.[1]

PROFESSOR TERENZIO COZZI :* I welcome very much the lectures offered us by Professor Kaldor. I found them very refreshing from a number of points of view, but foremost because they so admirably reflect what I think is the best virtue of Professor Kaldor. He is a first rate theoretician, but one who never loses sight of reality. He never indulges, as is so common among theoreticians these days, in theorising for the sake of theorising. In the best tradition of the political economists, from Smith to Ricardo to Keynes, he has the facts in mind and looks for a theoretical explanation of these facts. He has no interest in stating absurd assumptions, in manipulating them in the most difficult but elegant way in order to reach, after a long detour, some empty and useless conclusions.

His strong attack on general equilibrium theory is a case in point. His arguments convinced me long ago and I have no reason to object now. There is only a little difference of emphasis I should like to put to his arguments. In my view, the most important shortcoming of the general equilibrium theory is to be found in the logic of the approach that considers, as the all important fact, the scarcity of the factors of production. By so doing, it precludes any fruitful analysis of technical change and of economic growth. The second big limitation comes from the assumptions of constant returns and perfect competition, with all they imply as underlined by Professor Kaldor.

As for the third criticism, that referring to the fact that an economic system is never in equilibrium, I think it is correct to stress the necessity of considering more carefully the problem of the stability of equilibrium. And I agree that many of the so-called stability analyses are nothing more than complicated ways of

1. There was not reply to Professor Biasco.
* Università degli Studi, Torino.

showing the existence of equilibrium. This criticism applies to all models that assume the working of the auctioneer and exclude transactions at false prices. By the pre-reconciliation of the programmes of the agents, the auctioneer in fact shows that they can be mutually consistent: i.e. that the equilibrium exists. As stressed by Professor Kaldor, nothing is said about what happens in the real world where there is no auctioneer.

But if we leave the criticism at this point, it seems to me that we are not in the strongest position. We can stress that the rigidities existing in the real world can prevent the system from reaching its equilibrium for quite a long time. Markets will not be cleared for that time. But, if there are at work forces making for stability, sooner or later they will bring the system nearer and nearer to the equilibrium solution which remains the state towards which the system is tending. We may be dead in the meanwhile but, from a purely theoretical point of view, the equilibrium theorists may claim to be right after all! The assumption made by the New Classical Macroeconomics is just this one. It ignores the possibility of temporary disequilibrium, and concentrates only on final states. The assumption of rational expectations serves only to reach immediately the conclusions that, in any case, with other mechanisms of forming expectations, would have been reached in the long run. There will be only the natural rate of unemployment and no involuntary unemployment. Moreover, there will be nothing that economic policy can do to change the result.

What is wrong with this position is the assumption that there exists a *unique* equilibrium of the Walrasian type. It is an assumption, not a conclusion. There is nothing, not even in the abstract world of general equilibrium theory, to warrant such a conclusion and to exclude the existence of a *continuum* of equilibrium solutions, each one of them reachable by following a particular disequilibrium path. The point is that what happens when the system is out of equilibrium – when there are transactions at false prices – will have a powerful influence on the particular solution, be it an equilibrium or not, that in due time will be approached. We cannot, in a dynamic setting, separate the analysis of equilibrium from the analysis of the path followed to approach equilibrium. The one influences the other; the short run influences the long run.

By the way, this criticism applies also to the neo-Keynesian growth models of the 1950s and 1960s. The introduction of the Kaldorian technical progress function is a step forward, but does not suffice to overcome the problem. All these models have a unique equilibrium solution, in fact a golden age one, that is too exogenous and too mechanistic. In the age of continuous and smooth growth of the 1950s and 1960s, these models had something to tell us. But they contributed to making it possible to forget one of the lessons put forward by Harrod: that of the inherent instability of capitalism. It should be no surprise that, when the situation changed so dramatically in the 1970s, scholars started to consider the theory of growth much less interesting than it used to be.

Professor Kaldor did not make this choice of throwing away the baby with the dirty bath water. He tried to move forward by considering the functioning of a model disaggregated into primary, secondary and tertiary sectors. Two important features emerged; firstly the role of technical progress in overcoming decreasing returns in primary production and emphasising increasing returns in manufacturing, and secondly the consequences of the different market forms existing in the primary sector in contrast to the other sectors.

In his model of corn and steel, Professor Kaldor has dealt with the case of a big fall in prices of the primary products and has shown that this fact can cause a reduction in the demand for manufactured products. But what will happen in the contrary case of a big increase in primary product prices? Should we expect a boom? I do not think so, and I am sure that Professor Kaldor thinks the same. It is a case of asymmetry. But our theories are not well equipped to consider the problems of asymmetries. Here, too, we have much work to do.

Lastly, I should like to ask two more questions to Professor Kaldor. The first one refers to increasing returns to scale. In the past, as reflected in Professor Kaldor's analysis, increasing returns were mainly linked with specialisation and arose at the plant, industry and the economy level. Professor Kaldor has given much emphasis to the last aspect, and rightly so, because the recent trends in technical progress seem to allow much more flexibility to the specialised plants, and these can be technically efficient at a much smaller size than in the past. Economies of scale are more and more to be found at the industry and the economy level, and less and less at the plant level. The orientation of technical progress seems also capable of giving new prospects to enterprises of small and medium size. The fewer niches that these firms have occupied in recent times seem to have largely increased in number and enlarged in scope. I ask Professor Kaldor: is there something to be added to his analysis in this respect? Should we expect changes in the prevailing market forms? Will the dominance of the concentrated oligopoly be reduced? And, moreover, shouldn't we treat the commercial, managerial and organisational innovations with at least the same attention given so far to process and product innovations? The market for the specialised products has to be the world market, where productive efficiency is only one of the conditions of success.

This consideration leads to my last question. I have the feeling that Professor Kaldor's position on the question of protection has changed a little since some time ago. It seems to me that, while in the past he advocated protection at the national level, for the U.K. to be precise, he now seems to favour wise and moderate protection at the EEC level. I strongly welcome the change, if there is any. In that case, I should like to ask whether he now thinks that no single European country has any chance of competing with the United States or with Japan; that it is necessary to have a concerted action at the European level in order to foster growth and to reduce unemployment, and that to have growth in European trade, it is necessary to avoid national (as opposed to common) protection.

LORD KALDOR: Professor Cozzi asks me my present view on protection. It would be that international trade should be balanced between groups of countries so that balance of payments constraints on demand are eliminated. This could be achieved through a system of vouchers which limits imports to the value of exports. I prepared a detailed plan along these lines at the request of the French government in 1982, and also published a plan for India along these lines in 1984.[1]

PROFESSOR MARIO MONTI:[*] In his fifth lecture, Lord Kaldor puts forward a "constructive programme of recovery"; a comprehensive and ambitious programme, seldom proposed in current years. The plan consists of four elements: a coordinated fiscal action with consistent targets across countries so as to balance the foreign accounts and the full-employment budget; a substantial and rapid decline in interest rates; the stabilisation of prices of raw materials through a buffer stock scheme; and a centralised method of wage determination able to overcome sectoral negotiations and based upon some social consensus on income distribution. Each of the four elements could, of course, be discussed at a theoretical level, but I would rather like to make an observation and to raise a question concerning the feasibility of the programme. The observation is the following. If one had to identify which method of governing the economy underlies Lord Kaldor's programme, the answer would probably be: centralisation. A centralised method is implicitly called for internationally (the coordination of budgetary and balance-of-payments policies; the buffer-stock scheme etc.), as well as at the national level (overcoming of decentralised wage negotiations). The question derives from the preceding observation. Apart from the specific theoretical objections one might have to the individual components of Lord Kaldor's programme, how feasible is this programme which would rely heavily on the centralisation of decision making, in a historical phase which, if anything, seems characterised by an ever increasing fragmentation and decentralisation? International coordination and incomes policies, whatever their potential merits, have had rather a chequered history over the last three decades, a period which was conceivably more favourable to their implementation. At the global level of

* Università Commerciale Luigi Bocconi, Milano.

1. *Editors' Note*: The French Plan was unpublished, but for a summary, see A.P. THIRLWALL, *Nicholas Kaldor* (Brighton: Harvester Wheatsheaf Press, 1987) pp. 287-288. On the Plan for India, see 'An Exchange Rate Policy for India', *Economic and Political Weekly*, Bombay, 14 July 1984.

the western economies, there was a clearer hegemony by one leading country than is presently the case. In Europe, the decision process at the EEC level was smoother and less cumbersome. Finally, individual countries had not yet experienced to a full extent those technological developments which now seem to bring about an increasing diversification within the working class, and which may well lead to a dissolution of the concept of "class" as a meaningful category in the social and economic process. On the basis of these trends, there are some who, rightly or wrongly, anticipate the end of industry-wide labour contracts themselves. In sharp contrast, Lord Kaldor argues that a much greater centralisation is necessary. The question is then the following. Does Lord Kaldor share the view that his "constructive programme of recovery", however desirable, is likely to encounter severe feasibility problems? If he does, is he prepared to extract from his programme some second-best version, less satisfactory but more likely to be implemented? Or is the programme, consistent as it is internally, to be viewed as effective only if it comes as a whole – even if this means it may not come for a long time?

The second point raised concerns the expenditure tax. His proposal of an expenditure tax, as well as his theoretical contributions to studies on the tax system in general, are among the themes that will give Lord Kaldor a place of distinction in the history of economic thought. Indeed, if there is a proposal by Lord Kaldor which is presently being considered with keen interest by several policy-makers in different countries, it is the expenditure tax, much more so, for example, than the buffer stock proposal. This is so even in the United States, a country which presently may not be said to share Lord Kaldor's basic philosophy as far as economic policy is concerned. It may thus seem slightly curious, if not paradoxical, that in his lectures Lord Kaldor has not stressed this issue. The question to him is, therefore, how he now views a tax on expenditure from a theoretical standpoint and what role it should play in his proposed design for more rational economic policies.

LORD KALDOR: Professor Monti asks me whether I think the proposal I put forward for economic recovery is feasible. I certainly think it is feasible in the technical sense. If the Governments of the major advanced countries wanted to do something, they could do something, but it seems to be in the nature of sovereign states that they can never agree on very much. Very little action seems to come out of all international summits that are held. I don't have very great expectations that the next summit meeting in London with President Reagan and all the other Prime Ministers will be anything different. All I wish to say is that if Europe could be coordinated there is quite a lot that could be done without the positive cooperation of America. America always acts with selfish motives, but sometimes these selfish motives turn out to have unexpected beneficial consequences. For example, the enormous budget deficit in America makes the world economic situation a great deal easier than otherwise would be the case.

PROFESSOR GIOVANNI BELLONE:* I have two brief questions. In the neo-classical theory of production, the question of who accumulates capital is not crucial; the roles of workers and owners are interchangeable. Once an optimising process is identified, it does not matter who will carry it out, and bring it to fruition. By contrast, in non-neoclassical theory, from Smith to Marx to Keynes, roles are well defined and not interchangeable. My first question in relation to Professor Kaldor's first two lectures is which homogeneous group of decision makers would he identify in the process of growth today? Secondly, in relation to the third lecture, where Professor Kaldor stresses the interrelationship between the industrial and the agricultural sectors and the importance of land-saving innovations, who finances the land-saving innovations and who undertakes them?

LORD KALDOR: Professor Bellone asks me how technological change is financed. One thing I did not mention in my lectures is that one of the great inventions of modern capitalism is banking. This was never stated more clearly or better than by Adam Smith in the chapter on money in Volume 2 of the *Wealth of Na-*

---

* Università degli Studi, Padova.

tions. In that long chapter you find nothing on prices, nothing on the quantity theory of money, but a great deal on how modern banks, by their ability to extend credit, enable investment to be undertaken before the savings are available to finance the investment out of the profits earned. This, of course, was also Keynes' great idea. The elasticity of credit is very important for the growth process because it finances new ideas, new inventions, and the growth of new firms. It was a vital factor in the acceleration of growth in the 18th and 19th centuries, and remains important today.

PROFESSOR FABRIZIO ONIDA:* I have a comment related to economies of scale, the topic that Professor Kaldor discussed extensively in his fourth lecture. The interdependence between internal and external economies, which was the main focus of Young's article of 1928 in the rediscovery of Marshall, has become again a very fashionable, and at the same time puzzling, argument. Adam Smith had in mind economies of scale in specific products or components, in the famous example of the pin factory. Increasing scope for the specialised supply of components, and specialised process machinery, leads to fragmentation rather than concentration of suppliers, a sort of intra-industry vertical specialisation. Since the last century many important process innovations in basic industries (such as steel, textiles, petrochemicals, consumer durables, automobiles) have led to economies of scale of the opposite type: integrated plants and general machinery, vertical integration and intra-firm specialisation.

Now, the present wave of innovation, dominated by electronics and telecommunications, seems to have an ambivalent impact. On the one hand, this stream of innovations seems to foster an increasing concentration of firms and vertical integration for at least three reasons: (a) more efficient control of an increasingly complex organisational framework; (b) the crucial role of public procurement in large scale, high-growth markets (e.g. telecommunication networks, large urban infrastructures, long-distance transport facilities), leading to integrated national

* Università Commerciale Luigi Bocconi, Milano.

and multinational suppliers: (c) economies of scale in R&D and marketing. On the other hand, available computer-aided facilities have found increasing applications in re-organising small-scale business within integrated specialised areas – the so-called industrial districts – sometimes linked to a dominant subcontracting firm purchasing specific components (e.g. car industry), but often working as an "independent" fully integrated supplier (e.g. textile-clothing, leather and shoes, and mechanical engineering in Italy). Vertical and horizontal disintegration (specialisation) involves business services (e.g. R&D, accounting, fiscal assistance and marketing) as well as merchandise goods.

In addition, a significant impulse to vertical and horizontal "disintegration" has come from the search for "optimum scale of plants" smaller than before, due to increasing entrepreneurial fears of excess capacity and labour cost rigidity in (European) countries, where expectations of medium-term real growth of final demand have been substantially reduced since the mid-1970s.

My question is rather naive: should our students still be taught that increasing returns lead to higher concentration of industry and greater monopoly power of firms?

LORD KALDOR: Adam Smith's main point was that the division of labour depends on the extent of the market, so that the larger the total production, the greater the scope for differentiation in production – in terms of both processes and products. As stressed by Allyn Young, this is the most important aspect of economies of scale. It is certainly true that in the last few years there has been a strong merger movement leading to the growth of very large firms, but it is doubtful whether this has led to economies of scale in production (as opposed to economies of scale in advertising and marketing). At the same time, the revolution in microelectronics has enabled the growth of a number of small firms to take advantage of the new opportunities. But for every 100 new things launched, 98 go bad. I still think that individual initiative remains very important, and that small firms have an important role to play in a dynamic economy. They are frequently the carriers of unexpected ideas. Technological development always takes unexpected directions – you cannot predict it – and that is what makes the whole economic system fundamentally unpredictable. That is why neo-classical general equilibrium theory is so sterile, because it makes precise predictions from *a priori* assumptions, as if we live in a world of certainty with known technologies and known tastes, when, in reality, everything is changing with time. This is the hallmark of being pre-scientific in exactly the same sense as the physics of the Greeks was pre-scientific, based on *a priori* assumptions rather than empirical observation.

PROFESSOR ANGELO MARCELLO CARDANI:* Although the share of manufacturing output in GDP has been continuously declining in the past twenty years for all major western economies, still manufacturing industry plays a key role in fostering growth, employment and wealth. The relevance of this role goes far beyond the mere approximate 35 per cent of GDP that manufacturing accounts for, and the reasons for that can be ascribed mainly to the inducement effect that manufacturing industry has on the rest of the economy. This line of argument is well rooted in Professor Kaldor's work of the 1970s, and in the debate on "Kaldor's Laws". Several tests were carried out on the empirical specification of the relationship between productivity growth and output or employment growth. While the basic tenets of the theoretical argument were never seriously questioned, the empirical specifications were challenged, mainly on statistical grounds.

I would like to refer to a specific point in that debate, and this is the role played by technical change. To estimate a stable relationship across countries, the assumption of evenly distributed growth of technical knowledge is required. If the relationship between productivity growth and the explanatory variable shifts over time because of technical change, the shift factor must be the same in all countries to allow for cross- section estimation. If the range of countries is wide, this assumption is clearly quite strong. Further, an even distribution of growth of technical

* Università Commerciale Luigi Bocconi, Milano.

change would not be sufficient to allow for similar shift factors if the output mix of the manufacturing sector is different in different countries, as it is likely to be. The risk of a different output mix still exists if we go one step further to the disaggregated sectoral level, but this is perhaps less severe. It would seem quite reasonable to assume a closer level of both technological change and output composition in terms of products and production techniques in comparing, say, French chemicals with German chemicals than if the whole of French and German manufacturing were compared.

Some preliminary regressions seem to confirm, by and large, this hypothesis. The equation $p = c + dq$, where p and q stand for, respectively, the logarithmic rate of change of productivity and output, was estimated separately on total manufacturing data for four countries: the United Kingdom, Italy, France and Germany.

Subsequently, the same relationship was estimated pooling cross-section and time series data for the same years, 1960-1980.

The usual pooling tests having been satisfied, the coefficients of the pooled estimation turn out to be:

$$p = 0.03 + 0.54q \qquad R^2 = 0.64 \quad DW = 1.7.$$
$$(0.003) \ (0.046)$$

The numbers in parentheses are asymptotic standard errors.

The same experiment was used on data for six disaggregated sectors: Iron and Steel, Building Materials, Chemicals, Food Beverages and Tobacco, Textiles, and Paper and Printing. With some exceptions (four cases out of twenty-four) the d coefficient turns out to be higher, the adjusted R-squared higher, and there is sometimes need for first-order autocorrelation correction.

Again, having satisfied the pooling tests, a pooling estimation was carried out on the data for the separate sectors across countries, the accepted hypothesis being the common technology. The results are as follows:

	c	d	s.e.	R^2	DW
Iron and Steel	0.02	0.70	0.048	0.73	2.1
Building Materials	0.03	0.64	0.048	0.70	1.8

Chemicals	0.001	0.78	0.037	0.85	1.9
Food, Bev. & Tobacco	0.01	0.88	0.055	0.76	1.7
Textiles	0.04	0.55	0.050	0.60	2.0
Paper & Printing	0.01	0.70	0.051	0.70	1.8

The coefficient values are significantly higher than the value reported for total manufacturing. This seems to confirm the hypothesis of a strong relationship between productivity growth and output growth, but also the need for detailed, disaggregated analysis.[1]

PROFESSOR CARLO FILIPPINI:* Professor Kaldor's lectures have clarified many of the economic problems that now confront us, and they have also raised a number of questions as well as the desire to increase our knowledge even further. Among the many points that merit attention, I shall restrict myself to the following.

On superficial examination of what we have heard, it might seem that there is little room in growth processes for fluctuations or economic cycles, especially those in real variables and not just in prices.

Indeed, whereas it is possible (or even probable) that an economic system may enter a phase of depression and persist in an equilibrium state of Keynesian under-employment, there are no explicit mechanisms which generate expansions and contractions in economic activity, and which are periodic and self-sustaining.

Certain economists, Schumpeter in particular but also Marx, contend that cycle and development are closely connected; indeed (in the words of Schumpeter) the cycle is the form itself of the development of a capitalist system. Steady growth is unrealistic, and it is the concentration of innovations that accounts for the specific dynamic trend of an economy.

Another position, a more restrictive one, maintains that cycles are generated in response to exogenous shocks.

In both cases it would be interesting to know whether these fluctuations are explosive or damped; whether, that is, industri-

* Università Commerciale Luigi Bocconi, Milano.
1. There was no reply to Professor Cardani.

alised economic systems possess mechanisms able to restore them to an equilibrium state (albeit one of under-employment), or whether they are highly unstable, with ceilings (for example, the productive capacities of sectors) that prevent the process from continuing *ad infinitum*.

According to the answers given to this question, the economic policy measures proposed and their contents will differ.

In particular, I would like to know whether there are substantial differences in this *possible* tendency towards self-regulation when the system is in growth, compared to when it is in a stationary state.

In recent years there has been a revival of interest in Kondratief long cycles with a duration of 50-60 years. It is perhaps worth pointing out that studies of this phenomenon reveal a cyclical trend: in fact, they desperately resort to profound and prolonged crises as a last refuge in the absence of better arguments. There are numerous theoretical explanations for these cycles. One in particular, proposed by Rostow, is based on the trend in the terms of trade between primary products and the products of manufacturing industry.

The importance of this relative price is apparently due to the fact that it is simultaneously both the cause and the expression of changes in the distribution of income, in the direction of investment, and in the century-long trend of interest rates.

I would ask Professor Kaldor whether there is room in his growth model for these long cycles or whether, instead, he considers them to be nothing more than historical phases characterised by the successive hegemonies of particular countries (Great Britain at the beginning of the industrial revolution and the United States today); a phenomenon describable by a S-shaped or logistic curve, and not by real and proper fluctuations.

Lastly, I would ask if it is plausible that, with the passage of time, different countries rise and decline, ceding their supremacy to others, so that the present industrialised economies are now preparing to hand over to their successors. The industrialised economies leave increasingly more of industrial production to the developing countries, concentrating on only a limited number of high-technology sectors, services especially.

Professor Kaldor has rightly stressed that the greatest gains in terms of productivity are to be obtained in manufacturing industry. Services are instead generally characterised by high labour intensity and high levels of skill.

It thus appears that the industrialised countries will no longer benefit from high rates of productivity growth precisely because of the decisions regarding international specialisation that they are now taking, and that they will be overtaken by the developing countries.

Are these the prospects for the medium/long period or will other factors intervene (for example, the more rapid demand for services predictable from Engel's Law)?[1]

PROFESSOR GUIDO TABELLINI :* In his first lecture, Lord Kaldor stated that, because of transaction and storage costs, and uncertainty, large fluctuations in the prices of primary commodities around their "long-run equilibrium" level were necessary in order to induce stabilising movements in inventories.

In his second lecture, he argued that such short run price fluctuations may have serious negative externalities: not all goods have flexible prices; hence the sudden and sharp change in the price of primary commodities may induce disequilibrium relative prices between goods traded in "auction" markets and goods traded in "customer" markets. This in turn may bring about quantity adjustments and set in motion a multiplier process, which could even lead to effective demand failures.

In his last lecture, Lord Kaldor proposed a remedy for this problem: a scheme of price stabilisation by means of public holdings of buffer stocks of primary commodities.

Taking for granted the validity of the points raised in Lectures 1 and 3, I wish to question the proposal on the following two grounds:

(1) How can the authorities in charge of the scheme distinguish between temporary and permanent shocks? Obviously, we want the authorities to peg the price of the commodities around their

* Università Commerciale Luigi Bocconi, Milano.
1. There was no reply to Professor Filippini.

long-run equilibrium price, and not in response to permanent shocks to either supply or demand.

(2) Even if the long run equilibrium price is correctly guessed, can price stabilisation be effective in the face of merely temporary shocks?

The first point is the standard argument of those who object to public attempts at price stabilisation in particular markets (be it the foreign exchange market, the market for agricultural products, or for primary commodities), and I need not elaborate on it.

The second point is rather novel and, I believe, quite important. The question asked above was answered in the negative by S. Salant in a paper recently published in the *Journal of Political Economy* (January 1983). He formulated a model with the following features: (i) expectations are rational; (ii) both private individuals and the public agency can hold inventories of a storable consumption (or otherwise depletable) good; (iii) the supply of such a good is subject to independent random disturbances drawn from a stationary distribution (i.e. the shocks are all temporary); (iv) the government attempts to stabilise the commodity price at a level such that expected flow consumption equals expected flow supply.

Salant proved that: (1) Speculative attacks against the public agency occur as soon as the inventories held by the agency reach an endogenously determined threshold; (2) The attacks would be successful (i.e. the agency would have to abandon the price stabilisation scheme); (3) They occur *infinitely often, independently* of the initial size of the inventories held by the agency.

But there are other ways in which the public authorities could reduce the excessive volatility of commodity prices. The simplest and most desirable one would be to reduce the uncertainty surrounding their own future behaviour. There is no doubt that the increased volatility of interest rates since 1979 has been generated to a large extent by uncertainty about the future course of U.S. monetary policy (both in the short and in the long run). Naturally, this volatility has spilled over from financial markets into commodity markets.

In this respect, it seems to me that the scheme suggested by

Lord Kaldor could aggravate the problem, by adding further uncertainty. There are a number of questions: (a) in the eventual-
ity of a speculative attack against the public agency, will the
agency resist or give in? (b) in the face of exogenous shocks to
commodity markets, will the authorities interpret the shocks to
be of a temporary nature (and thus peg the commodity price), or
will they interpret it to be of a permanent nature (and thus let the
market price adjust to the new equilibrium level)? (c) in case the
market interpretation about the nature of the shock differs from
that of the public agency, will the agency change its plans later
on, and when?

I wonder whether the results mentioned above, together with
these questions, can explain why past attempts at price stabilisation in particular markets are generally a history of failure.[1]

PROFESSOR FERDINANDO TARGETTI:* I have five questions on:
growth and distribution; technical progress; the public sector
deficit; money; and the terms of trade.

(1) In Professor Kaldor's models of growth and distribution of
the late 1950s, the change in the level of prices was due to demand in the goods market; in particular a rise in prices was due
to an excess of aggregate demand. For this to work, full utilisation (and full employment) was pre-supposed. On the other
hand, in Kaldor's 1956 article on the theory of distribution, he
criticised Kalecki's theory of distribution based on the markup
on the grounds that it was unexplained. It seems to me that in
subsequent years Kaldor has partly changed his view on this subject. First, in the articles on inflation of the 1970s, the price increase is based on a fixed markup on rising costs. The cost increases are due either to a leap frog effect (the wage-wage spiral
mentioned in the last lecture) or to an 'exogenous' push (e.g. oil
or tax) in the industrial sector plus wage resistance. Secondly, in
several articles in the 1970s (and here in the third lecture),
Kaldor has pointed out that the long term growth of the manufacturing sector could be limited by the deflationary behaviour

* Università degli Studi, Trento.
1. There was no reply to Professor Tabellini.

of the agricultural sector, or by the deflationary behaviour of fiscal and monetary policies in surplus countries. Hence the competitive pricing system and the full employment hypothesis, which were underlying the growth and distribution models of the 1950s, are both abandoned.

I wonder, therefore, how much of Kaldor's distribution theory must be amended, and how much of Kalecki's original theory of mark up, has to be regained by today's Kaldor?

(2) My second question is about technical progress. In Kaldor's 1957 and 1958 articles on growth theory, the technical progress function determines the rate of growth (it substitutes for Harrod's exogenous natural rate of growth). Subsequently in the papers of the 1960s and 1970s Kaldor has not dealt with the *determination*, but with the *limits*, of growth – which in 1966 were the supply of labour and in 1971 the balance of payment for a single country; whereas in 1976 (and now) they were the sectoral imbalance or the slow rate of growth of land-saving technical progress for the world as a whole. Now I wonder if Kaldor still thinks that, if an economy is within the boundaries of these limits, the driving force which determines the actual rate of growth is still the shape of the technical progress function. If this is so, for the same rate of accumulation a new stream of invention would raise the rate of growth of productivity. But then what emphasis does he give to the actual long run fall in the rate of growth of productivity in the OECD countries? Is it just the result of an autonomous slow down of the rate of growth of output, i.e. a reverse action of the Kaldor-Verdoorn law, or else is it an autonomous inward shift of the technical progress function, and how can this cope with the electronic revolution?

(3) My third question is about the widespread public sector deficit. Keynesians are biased to think that the public sector deficit is a cyclical phenomenon inversely related – as a *dependent* variable – to the rate of growth of output. Monetarists, on the other hand, and many new eclectic economists, are more in favour of: (a) giving a structural explanation (i.e. that the growing deficit is due to the expansion of the welfare state); and (b) giving a reverse order of causality between the growth of Public Sector deficit and the (dependent) slow-down of output growth.

Kaldor has always been a "structuralist Keynesian", and a careful observer of old and new "stylised facts" of capitalism. Does Kaldor think that the widespread growth of Public Sector deficits is a structural phenomenon? Does he think that it has some consequence for the growth and distribution of income? Finally, does he think that the stabilization policies, having to deal with this new situation, have to undertake some major changes? (In particular, the active use of the deficit spending to rescue western countries from the actual recession).

(4) My fourth group of questions are on money. First: Kaldor has always held that we have learned from Keynes that an economy is a monetary economy where wages are settled in money and not in real terms (and, as a consequence, that money wages are a residual distributive variable). Can one then deduce that, if a widespread indexation prevails, or if the wage bargaining is frequent and a Hicksian wage-resistance behaviour prevails, we are back to a non-monetary economy? What are the consequences for the theory of income distribution where wages are residual and passive? Secondly: another Keynes-Kaldor teaching is that the velocity of circulation of money is variable in the short period, but stable in the long period because of the endogeneity of the money supply. The optimum Central Bank policy is just to accommodate the supply of money to the exogenous nominal growth of income (growth plus cost inflation), otherwise it would be worse off on the output side and not better off on the inflation side.

On this ground it seems to me that two extreme policies are held: on the one side is the mechanical Friedman rule to prevent inflation rising; on the other side is the adaptive Kaldor rule to prevent output falling. In both cases an active monetary policy is not required. It seems to me that Keynes had a different opinion on the behaviour or role of the central banker. My question is: (a) does Kaldor suggest an adaptive monetary policy also in an open economy, and in an economy with a growing Public Sector deficit? (b) was Keynes wrong in his activism, or have some major changes occurred in the last decades?

(5) My final question is on Kaldor's thesis of the terms of trade. The classics (Smith and Ricardo, but also Marshall) held

that in the long run the relative price of agricultural goods tends to rise. After World War II, Singer and Prebisch held the opposite. Both classics and those modern economists had a *theory of long term trends* of the terms of trade. I would add also Professor Sylos Labini who has held that the first theory is suitable for the 19th century and the second theory for the 20th century. I wonder if I am correct in thinking that Kaldor's theory (based on the two-sector growth model dealt with here in Lecture 3) does not share this view and rather explains an *oscillatory* behaviour of the terms of trade which is more in accordance with some recent empirical investigations (J. Spraos, *Economic Journal* 1980; P. Ercolani, *Moneta e Credito*, 1983).[1]

1. There was no reply to Professor Targetti.

NICHOLAS KALDOR, A BIOGRAPHY
by A. P. Thirlwall

NICHOLAS KALDOR
1908-1986
by A. P. Thirlwall

1. *Introduction*

PROFESSOR LORD KALDOR[1] was one of the most distinguished economists of the twentieth century, who will be recorded in the history of economic thought as a brilliant theoretician and applied economist, surpassed in originality only by Keynes and Harrod among British economists this century. He was a dominant influence in economic debates on the world stage for over fifty years, and hardly a branch of economics escaped his pen. At the London School of Economics (LSE) in the 1930s, while still in his twenties, he emerged as one of the country's leading economic theoreticians making fundamental contributions to controversies in the theory of the firm and in capital theory; to trade cycle theory and welfare economics, and to Keynesian economics by 'generalizing' Keynes's *General Theory,* which nearly fifty years later led Sir John Hicks to remark: 'I think that your (1939) paper was the culmination of the Keynesian revolution in *theory.* You ought to have had more honour for it.'[2] His reputation was such that in 1938, and still only thirty, he was offered a Chair by the prestigious University of Laussane – the home of Walras and Pareto – which he reluctantly declined. Keynes thought extremely highly of him. In a letter to Jesus College, Cambridge in 1943 suggesting Kaldor as an Economics Fellow, Keynes wrote: 'I put him very high among the younger economists in the country.... He is of the calibre which would justify the immediate election to a Readership.... He is a brilliant talker and one of the most attractive people about the place.'[3] The influence of Keynes, and the exigencies of the Second World War, turned

---

1. This memoir draws heavily on my book, *Nicholas Kaldor,* Brighton: Wheatsheaf Books Ltd., 1987.

2. Letter dated 20 May 1936. He was referring to 'Speculation and Economic Stability', *Review of Economic Studies,* October 1939.

3. Letter to Eustace Tillyard, 25 June 1943.

Kaldor into one of the country's leading applied economists, and he continued to mix theoretical and applied analysis thereafter. In the early 1950s as a member of the Royal Commission on the Taxation of Profits and Income, he became one of the world's leading experts on tax theory and policy, writing, amongst other things, a minor classic on the case for an expenditure tax.[1] At the same time, he was the joint architect, with Joan Robinson and Richard Kahn, of the post-Keynesian school of economics which extended Keynesian modes of thought to the analysis of growth and distribution, challenging the prevailing neo-classical orthodoxy of the determinants of long-run steady growth and distributive shares based on factor substitution and marginal productivity pricing. Kaldor's original models of growth and distribution, designed to explain the stylised facts of mature capitalist economies, with their stress on the primacy of the investment decision and embodied technical progress, generated an enormous secondary literature, as did his later thinking on the applied economics of growth, with his stress on the importance of the manufacturing sector as the source of increasing returns. He was highly critical of neo-classical value theory, or what he called equilibrium theory, with its basic assumption of non-increasing returns in all activities. Kaldor did not believe it was possible to understand the growth and development process within countries, or between countries in the world economy, without a two-sector model distinguishing between diminishing returns (primarily land-based) activities on the one hand and increasing returns (primarily industrial) activities on the other. The full implications of his novel thinking in this respect have still to be worked out. Finally, in his last years, he was to lead the intellectual assault on the doctrine of monetarism.

Kaldor lived life to the full both as a professional economist and as a family man. He was passionately interested in the world around him, and in the plight of his fellow men, and how the art and practice of economics could make the world a more agreeable and civilised place in which to live. His belief in a fairer distribution of income and wealth in society, and an intolerance of

1. *An Expenditure Tax*, London: Allen and Unwin, 1955.

injustice, made him a life-long socialist. He indulged no hobbies such as music, gardening, or collecting; he preferred to occupy his time embroiled in economic problems and ideas that intrigued and perplexed him at both the theoretical and policy level. As a devisor of ingenious schemes, he had no equal; the last great innovator as Professor Ken Galbraith once described him. His view of economics as a moral science – as a branch of ethics in the Cambridge tradition – motivated much of his writing, and led him into policy-making at the highest level as a Special Adviser to three British (Labour) Chancellors of the Exchequer, and as an adviser to several developing countries.

He did have financial interests which absorbed a lot of his time. He came from a well-to-do family and he married into wealth. In 1959 he joined with Ralph Vickers of Vickers da Costa in founding an Investment Trust, Investing in Success Equities, which led on to other ventures including the Anglo-Nippon Trust, Acorn Securities, and Investing in Foreign Growth Stocks. In 1964, when he became adviser to the Chancellor of the Exchequer, he had to resign from the boards of all these companies, two of which, ironically, were killed by his own hand with the introduction of capital gains and corporation tax.

It was not only his intellect and passion that made Kaldor dominant and controversial; it was also his style, charm, and sense of fun which made it impossible not to listen to what he had to say. He possessed that rare charisma and magnetic quality which made it difficult not to fall under his spell. When he was an adviser in Ghana in 1961, his hold over the President, Dr. Nkrumah, was likened unto the captivating powers of the ju-ju magicians! He could be rude and offend people, but this only seemed to enhance his fascination. In lectures and seminars, he would endear his audience by the heavily accented flow of English prose, which was so much a feature of his personality. His background was Hungarian, but like so many European émigrés, he became more English than the English and reveled in her institutions. The image of a rotund and jovial medieval monk holding forth in intellectual discourse fits him perfectly. Although he was untidy and forgetful in private life, he had an extraordinarily retentive and well-ordered mind that could recall at an instant the issues and controversies of long ago, and he could pluck statistics from the air like rabbits from a hat in support of his case. This gift could make him devastating in debate. He was always a powerful publicist for his views, and by force of personality and sheer perseverance, he would often wear an opponent down, achieving victory by attrition. He shared with Keynes the urge to protest. He was the most prolific newspaper letter-writing economist of his generation, contributing to debates not just on economic matters, but on social issues and defence as well. Kaldor and Keynes had other intellectual traits in common, and in many ways Kaldor took on, consciously or unconsciously, the mantle shed by Keynes. In particular, both possessed that strong intuition which made them more right in their conclusions and implicit presumptions than in their explanations and explicit statements. Much of Kaldor's work on growth and development falls, I believe, into this category.

Kaldor's love for economics was superseded only by the love for his family from which he derived so much of his inner happiness and self-confidence. In 1934 he married Clarissa Goldschmidt, a history graduate of Somerville College, Oxford, who provided the environment of peace and stability conducive to creativity. The four daughters of the marriage gave him particular pleasure, plus his eleven grandchildren. Kaldor was never happier than when the whole family clan was gathered together for festive or other special occasions in the spacious Edwardian family home at 2 Adams Road, Cambridge, or for holidays at the summer home in Le Garde Freinet, France. He loved to joke and play with young and old. Nothing seemed to trouble him, not even noise. Every day, the ever-open front door of his Cambridge home would invariably see a succession of family and friends toing and froing, while Kaldor worked away unperturbed in his ground-floor study off the entrance hall. He might or might not appear depending on the urgency of the task at hand. He liked to compartmentalise his intellectual effort, working intensely for long periods and then relaxing. This made him appear at times egocentric (and he was), but then he could also be very generous with his time, receiving a succession of invited and uninvited guests who travelled to Cambridge to see the great man as if on a pilgrimage to Buddha. His dearest Cambridge friend was Piero Sraffa, who in his prime would cycle round from Trinity College to Kaldor's house every afternoon to discuss economics and topical matters of the day.

During his lifetime, many honours were bestowed on him, in recognition of his contribution to economic science, and he was in constant demand across the world to give public lectures. He received Honorary Doctorates from the University of Dijon (1962) and Frankfurt University (1982). He was elected an Honorary Member of the Royal Economic Society of Belgium (1955); an Honorary Fellow of the LSE (1970); an Honorary Member of the American Economic Association (1975) – a small tribute to your great contribution to economics is how the President, Professor Kenneth Arrow, described it; a Foreign Honorary Member of the American Academy of Arts and Sciences (1977), and an Honorary Member of the Hungarian Academy of Sciences (1979). In 1970 he was President of the Economics Section (Section F) of the British Association for the Advancement of Science, and in 1974 President of the Royal Economic Society, an honour much coveted by the British economics establishment. In 1974 he was made a Life Peer as Baron Kaldor of Newnham in the City of Cambridge. He used his platform in the House of Lords to great effect. Economic historians will find his speeches one of the finest contemporary records of the economic issues of the day, with a pungency on topical matters reminiscent of the polemical style of Keynes.[1] The major honour that eluded him was the Nobel prize. He was, in the words of *The Economist*, the best known economist in the world not to have received the Nobel prize.[2] Why he was overlooked is still something of a mystery. In the first year of the prize, 1969, he was, according to press reports,[3] on a short list of ten names including Friedman, Samuelson, Meade, Perroux, and Kantorovich, but by his challenge to neo-classical orthodoxy he probably upset too many influential people in the economics establishment, including, presumably, the Swedish Nobel Committee. It may be sig-

1. See *The Economic Consequences of Mrs Thatcher*, London: Duckworth, 1983.
2. 20 January 1979.
3. *Financial Times*, 8 August 1969.

nificant (and some consolation) that none of the great British economists working in the Keynesian tradition – including Roy Harrod or Joan Robinson – were honoured.

2. Early Life, 1908-1939

Kaldór Miklós (Miki) was born in Budapest on 12 May 1908 into a comfortable middle-class Jewish family. His father, Gyula, was a successful lawyer, as legal adviser to the German legation in Budapest. His mother, Jamba, was a well-educated, cultured woman, particularly versatile at languages, including English. There was a daughter of the marriage and two earlier sons, both of whom died in childhood. The young Kaldor, as the only surviving son, was undoubtedly spoilt. He first started school at the age of six, and then at ten transferred to Budapest's famous Minta (or Model) Gymnasium, which in those early years of the 20th century produced a galaxy of distinguished academics including Michael Polanyi, Edward Teller, Leo Szillard, Theo von Karman, Nicholas Kurti and Thomas Balogh. The young Kaldor's education was squarely in the classical tradition, and throughout his life he retained a deep knowledge and interest in European culture and institutions. Politics and freelance journalism became his hobbies, and he continued to practise the latter during his student days in Berlin and London. His interest in economics was partly the natural outcome of his fascination with politics and partly inspired by wanting to understand better the German hyper inflation of 1923. His father had also kindled an interest with the purchase of a copy of Keynes' *The Economic Consequences of the Peace*. He enrolled in the University of Berlin in 1925, committed to the study of economics, but stayed only eighteen months. England, he soon learned, occupied the centre of the economic stage, and he arrived in London in April 1927 to register as a General Student at the London School of Economics to sample the lectures and to improve his English. The summer term was enough to whet his appetite and he enrolled for the B.Sc. (Econ.) degree from October 1927. An allowance from his father and fees from journalism financed his studies. The Hungarian newspaper, *Magyar Hirlap*, employed him, and he was the London correspondent of *Pester Lloyd* with his own headed notepaper. He also wrote for the *London General Press* which syndicated his articles in several countries. His speciality was conducting interviews with prominent personalities, particularly in literary circles, including such famous characters as Hilaire Belloc, G.K. Chesterton, Arnold Bennett, H.G. Wells, John Galsworthy, Arthur Conan Doyle, and Rebecca West.

In his first year at the School, Kaldor attended lectures by Hugh Dalton and John Hicks, among others, and his supervisor was the economic historian Eileen Power (later Postan), whom he held in high regard. His first-year examination performance was no more than mediocre, and he failed (and had to retake) mathematics. There was, however, a dramatic change in the subsequent two years as his interest in economics deepened. Allyn Young, the newly appointed Professor of Economics from Harvard, was a dominant influence in his second year, while Lionel Robbins and a young lecturer, Maurice Allen, dominated his thinking and learning in the third year. Kaldor graduated in 1930 with first-class honours, and became the favourite pupil of Robbins, who had been appointed to a Chair in 1929 following the untimely death of Young from pneumonia. Robbins secured for him a £200 research studentship at the School and gave him his first teaching, supervising second- and third-year students in economic theory. The research award lasted for two years, one term of which in 1931 he spent at the University of Vienna. His research project was the Problems of the Danubian Succession States, the main fruits of which were four anonymous articles in *The Economist*;[1] an article in the *Harvard Business Review*;[2] and his first published letter in *The Times* on the dominance of farming in the Danubian States.[3] At the same time he was reading widely in economic theory. He took an early interest in Keynes' *A Treatise on Money*, writing to Keynes asking for clarification over

1. 14, 21, 28 May and 4 June 1932.
2. 'The Economic Situation of Austria', October 1932.
3. 31 March 1932.

his exchange with Dennis Robertson in the *Economic Journal* of 1931.[1]

Friedrich von Hayek, who was induced to London by Robbins as a counterweight to the growing intellectual influence of Keynes and Cambridge, was also a dominant influence on Kaldor's early thinking. His first published paper on 'The Economic Situation of Austria' was almost pure Hayek in its cyclical analysis of the slump conditions of Austrian industry. With his undergraduate contemporary, Honor Croome (née Scott), he had already embarked in 1930 on an English translation from the German of Hayek's *Monetary Theory and the Trade Cycle,* and he also translated a paper by Hayek on "The Paradox of Saving" which *Economica* published in 1931. It was in connection with unanswered questions from this paper that Kaldor first started to lose respect for Hayek's work, and this culminated later in devastating critiques of his trade cycle theories and other work. He felt increasingly uneasy with the narrow dogmatism and libertarian philosophy of the Austrian school, which both Robbins and Hayek represented. Kaldor wanted to escape, and he gradually did so, particularly with the help of John Hicks. Kaldor and Hicks occupied adjacent flats in Bloomsbury and were close friends before their respective marriages in 1934 and 1935. Hicks introduced Kaldor to Walras and Pareto, and Kaldor read various drafts of Hicks' *Value and Capital* that were in preparation between 1930 and 1935. Hicks was also instrumental in introducing Kaldor to the Swedes. Both read in the original Myrdal's "Monetary Equilibrium" published in 1933, which partly prepared them for the Keynesian revolution to come.

Kaldor became increasingly torn between Robbins and Keynes as mentors. In 1932 he was appointed by Robbins to the staff of the LSE as an Assistant in Economics (later renamed Assistant Lecturer) and naturally felt some allegiance to him, but at the same time he began to feel more secure and independent. His relationship with Robbins waned gradually at first and then rapidly worsened to such an extent that Robbins later obstruct-

---

1. See D. Moggridge, (ed.), *The Collected Writings of J. M. Keynes,* Vol. XIII, *The General Theory and After,* Part I, *Preparation,* London: Macmillan, 1973, 238.

ed his promotion from Assistant Lecturer to Lecturer. Robbins was thoroughly hostile to the Keynesian revolution, effectively denying that the 1930s depression had anything to do with a lack of effective demand, and denouncing Keynesian remedies of public works. Kaldor was in the United States on a Rockefeller Research Fellowship when Keynes' *General Theory* appeared, and was an immediate convert. He was to play a major proselytising role in spreading Keynesian modes of thinking to young generations of economists, remaining faithful to the Keynesian tradition for the rest of his life.

In those early years at the LSE, Kaldor's major teaching commitment was a course on the Theory of Costs (later called the Theory of Production). He was a superb teacher.[1] He also lectured in various years on International Aspects of the Trade Cycle; The Theory and Practice of Tariff Making; Advanced Problems of International Trade (shared with John Hicks); Economic Dynamics; Capital and Interest; and Public Finance and the Trade Cycle. As early as 1933, he was beginning to make an academic name for himself. Four major theoretical papers were in embryonic form;[2] he helped to launch the *Review of Economic Studies* and played an active role on the editorial board, and he took an active part in the weekly seminar run by Robbins and Hayek, which in the folklore of the LSE has become as legendary as the Political Economy Club run by Keynes in Cambridge. It was in reading his paper to the seminar on 'A Classificatory Note on the Determinateness of Equilibrium' that the novel felicitous description of 'cobweb theorem' occurred to him, to explain the oscillatory movements of price around its equilibrium value.

The academic year 1935-6 was spent in the United States where he travelled extensively, meeting many of the leading American economists including Joseph Schumpeter, Edward Chamberlain, Jacob Viner, Henry Simons, and Irving Fisher. At the Econo-

---

1. See the essay by Aubrey Jones in J. Abse, ed., *My LSE*, London: Robson Books, 1977.

2. They were: "The Equilibrium of the Firm", *Economic Journal*, March 1934; 'Mrs Robinson's "Economics of Imperfect Competition"', *Economica*, August 1934; 'A Classificatory Note on the Determinateness of Equilibrium', *Review of Economic Studies*, February 1934; and 'Market Imperfection and Excess Capacity', *Economica*, February 1935.

metric Society meetings in New York in December 1935 he read a paper on "Wage Subsidies as a Remedy for Unemployment",[1] and listened to a paper by Henry Simons on the measurement of income which also indicated how expenditure could easily be calculated to form the basis of an expenditure tax. Kaldor was to resurrect this idea later when he turned his attention to tax matters in the 1950s. On return from the United States, his research output continued apace. In the next four years, there appeared his major survey of capital theory;[2] his attack on Pigou's theory of how wage cuts affect unemployment;[3] his critique of Chamberlin and the distinction between monopolistic and imperfect competition;[4] his devastating critiques of Hayek;[5] his generalisation of the General Theory;[6] and his seminal papers in welfare economics,[7] and on trade cycle theory.[8] This massive theoretical outpouring over a short space of years was inventive and innovative in four major areas of economics, and has had a lasting impact. In the theory of the firm, he contributed to the debate over the incompatibility of the assumption of long-period static equilibrium and perfect competition, and developed the notion of "excess capacity" under imperfect competition; he produced a novel (nonlinear) theory of the trade cycle; he laid the foundations of the new welfare economics; and in the field of Keynesian economics, he converted Pigou to Keynes and provided the most convincing rationale for Keynes' theory of the multiplier. Some brief words in each field are in order.

In 1933, Joan Robinson and Edward Chamberlin, in independent contributions,[9] released the theory of firm behaviour from

1. *Journal of Political Economy*, December 1936.

2. 'The Controversy on the Theory of Capital', *Econometrica*, July 1937.

3. 'Professor Pigou on Money Wages in Relation to Unemployment', *Economic Journal*, December 1937.

4. 'Professor Chamberlin on Monopolistic and Imperfect Competition', *Quarterly Journal of Economics*, May 1938.

5. 'Capital Intensity and the Trade Cycle', *Economica*, February 1939. See also 'Profesor Hayek and the Concertina Effect', *ibid.*, November 1942.

6. 'Speculation and Economic Stability', *Review of Economic Studies*, October 1939.

7. 'Welfare Propositions in Economics and Interpersonal Comparisons of Utility', *Economic Journal*, September 1939.

8. 'A Model of the Trade Cycle', *ibid.*, March 1940.

9. J. ROBINSON, *The Economics of Imperfect Competition*, London: Macmillan, 1933, and

the straight-jacket of perfect competition. One of Kaldor's important contributions in a seminal paper "Market Imperfection and Excess Capacity"[1] was to demonstrate that free entry into an industry will only lead to perfect competition if there are non-decreasing returns to scale; otherwise free entry will raise unit costs which will ultimately halt the entry of new firms. Each firm will operate near its break-even point, not where costs per unit of output are at a minimum. This is the famous "excess capacity" theorem. He went on to argue that if scale economies exist, free entry will not necessarily lead to tangency of the demand curve and the average cost curve, because the minimum size of new entry may dilute demand so much that the demand curve facing each individual firm lies below the cost curve, involving all firms in losses. Equally, the threat of this happening may prevent profit being eliminated, so that "pure" profit may still exist in a state of equilibrium. Like Marshall and Sraffa before him, and Hicks later, Kaldor recognised that increasing returns has profound implications for neo-classical price, distribution, and employment theory. With constant costs, however, profits will never be eliminated as long as the demand for output is less than infinitely elastic, and this is why constant costs lead to perfect competition: "no degree of product differentiation and no possibility of further and further product variation will be sufficient to prevent this result, so long as all kinds of institutional monopolies and all kinds of indivisibilities are completely absent." Later, however, he retracted his views on free entry. In debate with Chamberlin[2] over the meaning of "monopolistic competition" he conceded that if the distinguishing feature of monopolistic competition is an infinite range of differentiated products, there cannot strictly speaking be "free entry" since no one else can produce an identical product. There can only be freedom of entry to produce substitutes, which leaves the structure of monopolistic competition intact. In another important contribution "The Equilibrium of the Firm",[3]

E. CHAMBERLIN, *The Theory of Monopolistic Competition*, Cambridge, Mass: Harvard University Press, 1933.

  1. *Economica*, February 1935.

  2. 'Professor Chamberlin on Monopolistic and Imperfect Competition', *Quarterly Journal of Economics*, May 1938.

  3. *Economic Journal*, March 1934.

he developed a novel theory of differences in the size of firms based on the coordinating ability of managers as the only true fixed factor of production. It was not a theory to which he later attached much importance. Instead, he followed Kalecki and the principle of increasing risk, based on the gearing ratio of firms. Profits are crucial for expansion, not only in themselves, but by enhancing the ability of firms to borrow in the market.

During this fertile theoretical period of the 1930s, Kaldor also became heavily involved in debates on the trade cycle, taking up cudgels against Hayek and the Austrians. Their theory was monetary in essence, not dissimilar to Wicksell's, relating to divergences between the money rate of interest and the natural rate of interest. Kaldor was to absorb this theory and eventually to demolish it in a powerful paper "Capital Intensity and the Trade Cycle".[1] Hayek himself changed his mind over movements in capital intensity and the origins of cyclical crisis during the upswing. In *Monetary Theory and the Trade Cycle*[2] he argued that capital intensity increased during the upswing which then caused adjustment problems as credit expansion was curtailed. Later, in *Profits, Interest and Investment* (1939), he argued the exact opposite, that employers would seek more labour intensive methods of production as real wages fell (the Ricardo effect). Kaldor also launched into this *volte face*, for which he was partly responsible in the first place, in another powerful paper "Professor Hayek and the Concertina Effect".[3] Firstly, he objected to Hayek's use of the term "Ricardo effect", since Ricardo's argument concerning factor proportions referred to the relative price of labour and machinery, not to the price of consumption goods affecting real wages. Secondly, he went on to show the special conditions necessary for the Ricardo effect to work, and to argue that if it does work, its quantitative effect would be small. But whatever happens, it can never lead to *less* investment because a rise in the rate of interest, which is a necessary condition for the Ricardo effect to work, will only occur if investment increases. At the empirical level, Kaldor could find no clear cyclical pattern of capital in-

1. *Economica*, February 1939.
2. Translation by Kaldor and H. Croome, London: Jonathan Cape, 1933.
3. *Economica*, November 1942.

tensity (or concertina effect). He joked: "I think the evidence rather suggests that the concertina, whichever way it goes, makes a relatively small noise – it is drowned by the cymbals of technical progress". Kaldor sent Keynes a copy of his 1942 paper to which Keynes replied: "Your attack on poor Hayek is not merely using a sledge hammer to crack a nut, but on a nut which is already decorticated". Kaldor reminded Keynes that Hayek had spent the whole of the summer term in Cambridge discussing with students his paper on the Ricardo effect "creating an unwholesome muddle in the minds of the young".

Kaldor's brush, and ultimate break, with the Austrians led him to examine the meaning and determination of the concept of the "investment period" in a major survey of capital theory published in *Econometrica* in 1937.[1] Kaldor concluded that the investment period concept is really nothing more than one way of measuring the ratio of capital to labour, but since there is no unique measure of capital, there is no unique measure of the capital to labour ratio. It is possible, however, to construct *ordinal* measures. He criticised conventional measures which were sensitive to changes in the relative price of inputs and outputs without any change in the real structure of production having taken place, and proposed himself an index of the ratio of "initial cost" to "annual cost" in the production of output. In this major contribution to the capital theory debate, Kaldor also anticipated von Neumann's famous result that the rate of interest represents the highest potential rate of growth of an economy which would obtain if nothing were withdrawn from the economic system for unproductive consumption.[2]

Kaldor's own original contributions to trade cycle theory came in two papers "Stability and Full Employment,[3] and 'A Model of the Trade Cycle",[4] in which he argued that instability is inherent in the economic system itself because there is no rea-

---

1. 'The Controversy on the Theory of Capital', *Econometrica*, July 1937. Also 'On the Theory of Capital: A Rejoinder to Professor Knight', *ibid.*, April 1938.

2. See J. von Neumann, 'A Model of General Economic Equilibrium', *Review of Economic Studies*, no. 1, 1945.

3. *Economic Journal*, December 1938.

4. *Ibid.*, March 1940.

son why the division of income for consumption and saving should be in the same proportion as the division of output. All booms must come to an end, either through credit restrictions, rising interest rates, excess saving, or, in the final analysis, through a shortage of labour. The trade cycle is the price to be paid for a high rate of economic progress, which was also the view of Dennis Robertson. Mechanisms do exist, however, that may bring about a stable equilibrium, and in 'Stability and Full Employment', there are to be found the early seeds of Kaldor's macro-theory of distribution which did not fully germinate until 1956. Kaldor first started thinking about trade cycle theory when he gave four lectures on the international trade cycle at the LSE in 1933-4. He realised that the task was to explain oscillations between a low and a high level equilibrium and that this could not be done using a linear accelerator. An S-shaped investment (and savings) curve would be a plausible hypothesis, however. At low levels of output, increased output will not induce more investment because there is excess capacity, and at high levels of output there will be no inducement to invest if increases in output are impossible. Saving is also likely to be a non-linear function of output, but probably more sensitive than investment at both high and a low levels of output.[1] With these two functions, Kaldor showed that the economic system can reach stability at either a high or low level of economic activity.[2] Shifts in the curves then produce limit cycles: at high levels of output, the investment curve shifting down and the savings curve up, and *vice versa* at low levels of output.

Another of Kaldor's original insights at this time was in the field of welfare economics. With Hicks, although with prior claim, he was the founder of what came to be called "the new welfare economics". Kaldor's short seminal paper "Welfare Propositions in Economics and Interpersonal Comparisons of Utility"[3] was a reaction against the nihilism of Robbins and the

1. Kaldor effectively anticipated Duesenberry's relative income hypothesis of a 'customary' standard of living below which people dissave drastically and above which they save a lot.
2. 'A Model of the Trade Cycle', *Economic Journal*, March 1940.
3. *Ibid.*, September 1939.

Paretian school that, if an economic change makes some people better off, but others worse off, it is impossible to make a judgement about whether the change is desirable (in the sense of increasing welfare) because individual utilities cannot be compared. Kaldor interpreted Robbins' stance as support for the *laissez-faire* approach to economic affairs, and as a recipe for economic paralysis. Kaldor's innovation was to introduce the idea of compensation tests: that if the gainers from a policy change could *potentially* compensate the losers and still be better off, the economist should be able to endorse the policy change since output must have increased. The compensation test would allow the economist to say something positive about output, although not about its distribution. A similar distinction between efficiency and distribution had been made by Pigou in his writings on welfare economics, and Hicks endorsed the Kaldor test.[1] The Kaldor-Hicks criterion gave rise to a vast literature, but with no resolution, not least because interpersonal comparisons of utility are still needed if welfare judgements are to be made. There could be changes which satisfy the Kaldor compensation test but which leave the community worse off than before because the income distribution is more "undesirable", in some sense. This later formed the basis of the attack on the new welfare economics led by Ian Little.[2] There is no solution to the problem of deciding whether one distribution of income is worse or better than another unless a social welfare function is specified which makes explicit value judgements about the income distribution. This was Kaldor's original intuition, which he confirmed in a paper in 1946,[3] and which partly explains why he never participated in the subsequent debates.

In the field of macro-economics, concerned with employment and the Keynesian revolution, Kaldor's first paper was on wage subsidies and employment.[4] It reflected his neo-classical back-

1. J. HICKS, 'The Foundations of Welfare Economics', *Economic Journal*, December 1939.

2. *A Critique of Welfare Economics* (Oxford: Clarendon Press, 1950).

3. 'A Comment on W. J. Baumol's Community Indifference', *Review of Economic Studies*, XIV, no. 1.

4. 'Wage Subsidies as a Remedy for Unemployment', *Journal of Political Economy*, December 1936.

ground and training – although he tried, at the same time, to forge a bridge between Keynes and the classics. Well before Keynes' *General Theory* was published in 1936, the emerging "Keynesian" consensus was against money wage cuts because this would simply reduce prices leaving real wages and employment unchanged. Kaldor believed wage subsidies to be a (compromise) alternative, since subsidies do not reduce money demand and therefore should not affect prices. When Kaldor wrote to Joan Robinson about his scheme, she claimed not to understand the argument unless subsidies raised the propensity to consume through a redistribution of income to labour. They would, but that was not Kaldor's point. Kaldor replied in exasperation: "I fear that Cambridge economics is beyond me!"[1] Kaldor was later to join the Cambridge fold, but not before two major contributions which helped to seal the Keynesian revolution. The first was his attack on Pigou, which converted Pigou to Keynesian ways of thinking. This was a notable victory. The second was the generalisation of the *General Theory* explaining why it is output and not prices (the rate of interest) that adjusts savings to investment. Pigou was the defender of the classical faith in Cambridge and was quick into print following Keynes' demolition of classical full employment theory. Pigou continued to maintain that a cut in money wages could increase employment in the aggregate independently of a fall in the rate of interest, and published a paper to this effect in the *Economic Journal*.[2] The paper had been accepted by Dennis Robertson, standing in for Keynes as editor, who was ill. On reading the paper, Keynes described it as "outrageous rubbish beyond all possibility of redemption", and castigated Robertson for publishing it.[3] The sentiments were shared by Kahn, Shove, and Sraffa. It was Kaldor, however, who persuaded Pigou of the error of his ways, as Pigou later conceded. Kaldor showed in his response to

1. Unpublished letter to Joan Robinson, 3 June 1935, King's College Library, Cambridge.

2. A. C. Pigou, 'Real and Money Wage Rates in Relation to Unemployment', *Economic Journal*, September 1937.

3. For all the correspondence see D. Moggridge, ed., *The Collected Writings of John Maynard Keynes*, Vol. xiv, *The General Theory and After*, Part ii, *Defence and Development*, London: Macmillan 1973.

Pigou[1] that the new equilibrium after a wage cut *must* imply a lower rate of interest. Kaldor modified Pigou's model to make saving a function of income in addition to the rate of interest, and showed that there is no way in which a change in money wages by itself could so alter savings and investment to ensure equality of the two at a *given* rate of interest. Kaldor was the first economist (after Keynes) to use rigorously what later came to be called "the Keynes effect". He recognised explicitly that a fall in money wages is exactly analogous to an increase in the nominal quantity of money or a reduction in liquidity preference. Keynes also replied to Pigou, but when Pigou responded to his critics and conceded the argument, it was Kaldor he addressed. He paid him the compliment of saying that "the theory of the relation between money wages and employment, via the rate of interest, was invented by Kaldor". Keynes was naturally annoyed by this, having devoted Chapter 19 of the *General Theory* to this very topic. It needs to be stressed, however, that Pigou conceded to Kaldor not on grounds of liquidity preference but on the assumption that an increase in output must reduce time preference and hence the equilibrium rate of interest. This led to the contention by some that a Keynesian conclusion had been accepted, in effect, by a non-Keynesian route. This was an understandable reaction, but Kaldor cleared up the confusion pointing out that liquidity preference considerations need only be invoked to explain why a reduction in time preference (which must occur) *fails* to produce a fall in the rate of interest.[2] Otherwise, with a normal classical savings function the interest rate is bound to fall.

The paper that gave Kaldor most intellectual satisfaction, however, and his most notable, but neglected, contribution to the immediate Keynesian revolution, was "Speculation and Economic Stability"[3] (including 'Keynes's Theory of the Own-Rates of Interest', originally written as an appendix, but pub-

1. 'Professor Pigou on Money Wages in Relation to Unemployment', *Economic Journal*, December 1937.

2. 'Money Wage Cuts in Relation to Unemployment: A Reply to Mr. Somers', *Review of Economic Studies*, June 1939.

3. *Review of Economic Studies*, October 1939.

lished much later).[1] It addressed three important questions.
First, why does an increase in saving not necessarily lead to an increase in investment; in other words, what are the necessary, if
not sufficient, conditions for the workings of the income multiplier? Secondly, what determines the structure of interest rates?
Thirdly, what asset sets the ultimate limit on employment by limiting the willingness to invest, and why? Kaldor's answer to the
first question was the stabilising influence of speculators. The
greater the stability of price, the greater the instability of income.
Kaldor believed that in the real world, the most important type
of asset whose price is stabilised through speculation is long-term
bonds bought with savings. The less price fluctuates, the stronger
Keynes' theoretical conclusion that savings and investment will
be equated by a change in the level of income rather than by the
rate of interest. The question then is what determines the "normal" price of bonds, i.e. what anchors the long-term rate of interest? Dennis Robertson, it will be remembered, accused
Keynes of leaving the long-term rate of interest "hanging by its
own bootstraps". Kaldor addressed this question providing a
'bottom up' theory of the rate of interest in which the term structure of interest rates is determined by the convenience yield on
money plus a risk premium on assets of different maturities. He
repeated and defended this view many years later in his evidence
to the Radcliffe Committee on the Working of the Monetary
System (1959). Finally, it must be the asset, money, which sets
the ultimate limit to employment because only the money rate of
interest cannot be negative whereas the own-rates of interest on
other assets can be negative, and therefore cannot set the limit on
investment. Kaldor was reacting against Keynes' suggestion in
the *General Theory* that the desire in the past to hold land might
have kept the interest rate too high, and that the desire to hold
gold might do so in the future.

1. *Collected Economic Essays*, II, London: Duckworth, 1960.

3. *The War and Immediate Post-war Years*

The theoretical outpouring at the LSE before the war established Kaldor as one of the world's leading young economic theoreticians. At the outbreak of war he was still only thirty-one years old. The war had two major impacts on his future career. First, the evacuation of the LSE to Peterhouse, Cambridge, brought him into direct contact with the Cambridge Keynesians. Joan Robinson, Richard Kahn, and Piero Sraffa became close academic friends, and together they formed the "war circus", which later became the "secret seminar" (although everybody knew of its existence!). Cambridge became his natural spiritual home, to which he was later invited to return, and he did so permanently in 1949. Secondly, the imperatives of war, and the necessity to plan for peace, switched his mind from pure theory to applied economics, and he rapidly became one of the leading applied economists of his generation. Apart from pure academic research, including new projects on the economics of taxation and of advertising under the auspices of the National Institute of Economic and Social Research, he became actively involved in the economic aspects of the war in three important fields: the finance of the war effort; national income accounting; and the problems of post-war reconstruction particularly in relation to Beveridge's proposals on Social Insurance and on Full Employment. He became friendly with Keynes and they communicated on a regular basis over a variety of matters connected with war finance and national income accounting. In particular, Kaldor made a number of practical suggestions on how Keynes' compulsory savings scheme might be made operational, and offered many constructive suggestions on the papers Keynes was writing on the estimation of national income. After the first White Paper on National Income appeared,[1] Kaldor's annual reviews of them in the *Economic Journal*[2] became a much-awaited event in the economics cal-

---

1. The first was *Analysis of the Sources of War Finance and Estimates of the National Income and Expenditure in 1938 and 1940*, Cmnd. 6261, London: HMSO, 1941.

2. See *Economic Journal*, June-September 1941, June-September 1942, and June-September 1943.

endar in Britain and abroad. His detailed grasp of national income accounting, and his attempts at forecasting, proved invaluable when it came to the assessment of the financial burden of the *Beveridge Report on Social Insurance and Allied Services* published in December 1942;[1] a plan which aroused great controversy. Opponents of extended State insurance claimed that it would be necessary to raise employer' contributions and the standard rate of income tax to over 50 per cent, with devastating effects on export performance and work effort. Kaldor showed convincingly that the price to be paid for comprehensive insurance against old age, sickness, and unemployment – what Beveridge labelled 'Freedom from Want' – would not be more than "ten [old] pence on income tax or six pence on income tax and a penny on a pint of beer".[2] Kaldor was the most influential economist to pave the way for the political acceptance of one of the great social advances of the modern age. The theme of the second Beveridge Report on full employment[3] was "Freedom from Idleness'. Kaldor's contribution to the Report, contained in the now-famous Appendix C, was to calculate (with Tibor Barna) the revenue and expenditure implications of the Government pursuing a fiscal policy to maintain full employment, and in doing so he developed what was virtually the first mini-econometric model of the economy. The meticulous analysis received high praise from all quarters in Britain and abroad, although there was some questioning of the arithmetic and the optimism over the required levels of taxation for post-war reconstruction.[4] As it turned out, he was too optimistic about the assumed increase in real national income after the war, and underestimated the expansion of public spending on non-social and non-military items.

Kaldor did not confine himself solely to domestic issues. He took a keen interest in the war effort of Germany, and followed closely the economies of the allied countries. He also played a

1. Cmnd. 6404, London: HMSO, 1942.

2. 'The Beveridge Report II: The Financial Burden', *Economic Journal*, April 1943.

3. W. BEVERIDGE, *Full Employment in a Free Society*, London: George, Allen and Unwin, 1944.

4. It was calculated that only a 6 per cent rise in tax rates would be required to 'finance' full employment. For a critique of the arithmetic see *The Economist*, 24 February 1945.

prominent role in public discussion of the international economic issues confronting the world economy at the time, including the Bretton Woods plan for a new international monetary system, and the American loan to Britain.

When the war ended, Kaldor wanted some of the war-time controls retained, to ease the transition to peace and to prevent the prospect of a short-lived boom followed by slump, which characterised the aftermath of World War I. He identified three major objectives of economic reconstruction: full employment; the elimination of poverty; and improved efficiency. The Beveridge proposals, which he campaigned for, were designed to secure the first two objectives. In pursuit of the third, he favoured the retention of building and import controls, and advocated the continuation and extension of utility production to reap economies of scale.

The reputation that Kaldor built up during the war as an incisive applied economist led to numerous offers of jobs and advisory posts after the war, when the LSE had returned to London. He was made a Reader in Economics at the LSE in 1945, but was more than receptive to outside work, having become increasingly disenchanted with what he perceived to be the right-wing atmosphere of the School. At home, he was employed for a short time in 1946 as an economic adviser by the Air Ministry and Ministry of Supply to assist the British Bombing Survey Unit. He also became a regular contributor to *The Manchester Guardian* writing articles on aspects of post-war recovery. Abroad, he undertook three important missions. The first in 1945 was to act as Chief of the Planning Staff of the U.S. Strategic Bombing Survey of Germany under the overall direction of Kenneth Galbraith. In that capacity, he interviewed many of the German generals, including Halder, and helped to show that it was not the U.S. Air Force that won the war, but rather the ground troops which proved decisive.[1] In 1946 he served as an adviser to the Hungarian government on its new Three Year Plan, and in 1947 he was invited to assist Jean Monnet at the French Commissari-

---

1. See *The Effects of Strategic Bombing on the German War Economy*, US Strategic Bombing Survey, Washington, 1945.

at Général du Plan in preparing a plan for the financial stabilisation of France. A whole new series of tax measures was
proposed,[1] very similar to the reforms he later advocated in the
context of developing countries.

Then came the invitation from Gunnar Myrdal to become the
first Director of the Research and Planning Division of the newly created Economic Commission for Europe (ECE) in Geneva.
There were difficulties in him taking leave from the LSE, and he
consequently resigned his teaching post at the School after twenty years as student and don. The two years he spent in Geneva
were among the happiest and most stimulating of his professional career, living in elegance on the shores of Lake Geneva with a
young family, and in charge of a talented handpicked staff – including Hal Lary, Robert Neild, Esther Boserup, Helen Makower, and P.J. Verdoorn. Kaldor worked like a Trojan, with the
specific task of preparing an annual *Economic Survey of Europe*.
When the first (and subsequent) *Surveys* appeared they attracted
widespread international interest and were treated as the au-
thoritative account of the economic conditions and trends in
both Eastern and Western Europe.

While in Geneva, Kaldor also became involved in several special assignments including acting as adviser to the U.N. Technical Committee on Berlin Currency and Trade established in the
winter of 1948-9 in an attempt to end the Soviet blockade of
Berlin, and serving on a U.N. Expert Committee in 1949 to prepare a Report on National and International Measures for Full
Employment. In the former capacity, he cross-examined repre-
sentatives of the big-four powers in the light of the evidence of
each, and then drafted the Report recommending the Soviet
mark as the sole currency for Berlin. In the event, the stance of
the western powers hardened as the blockade began to be
breached, and the blockade was eventually lifted unconditional-
ly. The widely acclaimed *Report on National and International Measures for Full Employment*[2] was largely drafted by Kaldor, and its
adoption by such a wide diversity of interests represented at the

1. "A Plan for the Financial Stabilisation of France" in *Collected Economic Essays*, VIII,
London: Duckworth, 1980.
2. United Nations, Geneva, 1949.

United Nations owed much to his verbal dexterity. Much of the Report was devoted to a discussion of the international propagation of cyclical disturbances, and the necessity for countries to strive for balance of payments equilibrium to avoid trade restrictions and deflationary bias in the world economy. *Plus ça change, plus c'est la même chose!* Such was the impact of the Report that Kaldor was asked by the Council of Europe to chair a Working Party on how the recommendations of the Report might apply to Europe. The outcome was a further influential document, *Full Employment Objectives in Relation to the Problem of European Co-Operation,*[1] which recommended, amongst other things, a European Investment Bank and import controls, if necessary, to secure simultaneous internal and external balance. Kaldor's contribution to the international campaign in pursuit of full employment impressed Hugh Gaitskell, the Labour Chancellor of the Exchequer (1950-1), and led in 1951 to his appointment to the Royal Commission on the Taxation of Profits and Income. This was Kaldor's entrée to the role of adviser at the highest level in the United Kingdom and abroad.

Kaldor had not been long in Geneva when he was approached by King's College, Cambridge, to accept a Fellowship there. King's was short of economists, as Keynes and Gerald Shove had recently died, and Kahn was busy administering Keynes's estate. The *New York Times Magazine* described such an appointment as "being one of such honor and prestige for an economist that there are not five posts in the world more coveted by a man of that profession".[2] Cambridge was his natural intellectual home, and he accepted the offer provided he could postpone his arrival in order to complete his work for the ECE. He finally started teaching in Cambridge in January 1950, with a University Lectureship also conferred on him. King's, and the Cambridge Economics Faculty, remained his academic base for the rest of his life. He was made a Reader in Economics in 1952 and elevated to a Chair (with Joan Robinson) in 1966. Unlike Keynes, he chose not to play an active role in College life; nor did he assume any major

1. Council of Europe, Strasbourg, 1951.
2. 12 September 1948.

administrative role in the Economics Faculty. He preferred to devote his time exclusively to research and writing, and later to politics and the role of adviser in several capacities.

4. *Tax Matters*

Kaldor and John Hicks were the only two academic economists appointed to the Royal Commission on the Taxation of Profits and Income in 1951, with Kaldor much more radical in his approach to tax matters. His immersion in issues of taxation for the next four years turned him into one of the world's leading tax experts. The Memorandum of Dissent to the Commission's Report,[1] which he drafted, and his book *An Expenditure Tax* (1955), became minor classics in the literature on taxation. The American public finance expert, Arnold Harberger, described the latter as "one of the best books of the decade in public finance, ranking with the classic works of Edgeworth, Pigou, Simons and Vickrey".[2] Kaldor's campaign for a comprehensive definition of income, as the basis for a more equitable tax system, made him more and more influential in Labour Party circles, which culminated in his appointment in 1964 as Special Adviser on tax matters to the Chancellor of the Exchequer and led to a flood of invitations from developing countries to advise on tax matters, starting with India in 1956. Perhaps more than any other economist of his generation, Kaldor had an abiding faith in the power of taxation to alter significantly the performance of an economy. The desire to see social justice was also a strong motivating factor behind all his advice. In the 1960s and 1970s in the United Kingdom, he was the proposer and inventor of a variety of ingenious new tax schemes to enhance equity and to improve the performance of the British economy.

The equity of a tax system is to be judged by whether people with the same taxable capacity, or ability to pay, pay the same amount of tax. By this criterion, Kaldor viewed the U.K. tax sys-

1. Cmnd. 9474, London: HMSO, June 1955, also signed by George Woodcock and Mr H. L. Bullock.

2. *Journal of Political Economy*, February 1958.

tem as "absurdly inequitable" in the sense that the tax burden on some people was very heavy while on others it was very light according to how income was earned; whether or not they were property owners, and so on. Income by itself, however, is not an adequate measure of ability to pay because however comprehensively income is defined, it ignores taxable capacity that resides in property as such. This constituted for Kaldor an argument for measuring ability to pay by spending power rather than by income, but consideration of an expenditure tax was outside the Royal Commission's terms of reference. Kaldor's Memorandum of Dissent confined itself, therefore, mainly to existing inequities in the tax system relating to the exemption from tax of capital gains and to the differential treatment of the self-employed and others. A flat rate capital gains tax was recommended and this later became official Labour Party policy. Company taxation also came in for criticism. Kaldor wanted a single corporation tax but not an end to tax discrimination against distributed profits until a capital gains tax was introduced. Kaldor's name is identified most closely, however, with the advocacy of an expenditure tax. The idea of an expenditure tax was not new – it had been discussed in the past by Hobbes, J.S. Mill, Marshall, Pigou, and Keynes – but no one before Kaldor had exposed so comprehensively the weaknesses of income as a measure of taxable capacity. Moreover, if wealth is not taxed, inequity is even more acute, and Kaldor wanted to see the taxation of wealth too. A wealth tax became Labour Party policy, but was never implemented. An expenditure tax has never found favour with any political party in the United Kingdom. India and Sri Lanka (on Kaldor's advice) have been the only two field experiments, and in both countries the tax was withdrawn within a few years of implementation.

After finishing his work with the Royal Commission, Kaldor took a sabbatical year from Cambridge in 1956 and embarked on a world tour with his family, giving lectures wherever he went. He spent half the year in India and the Far East and then went to Latin America as consultant to the Economic Commission for Latin America (ECLA) in Santiago at the invitation of Raul Prebisch, visiting Mexico and Brazil on the same trip. He delivered thirteen lectures in Chile on "The Theory of Economic De-

velopment and Its Implications for Economic and Fiscal Policy"
and five lectures at the University of Rio de Janeiro on the
"Characteristics of Economic Development" at the invitation of
Roberto Campos. He returned to England via the United States
where for a short time he was Seager Visiting Lecturer at Co-
lumbia University.

His journeys round the world as a tax adviser started in India
in 1956, and his classic report on Indian tax reform is by far the
most comprehensive.[1] It contains one of the clearest statements
ever made of the case for wealth taxation. Many of the recommendations made for India to tighten up the tax system to provide a basis for social justice, efficiency, and growth, are found in
his later proposals for other countries with suitable modification
for individual country circumstances. He gave tax and budgetary advice to Ceylon (1958), Mexico (1960), Ghana (1961),
British Guiana (now Guyana) (1961), Turkey (1962), Iran
(1966), and Venezuela (1976). The proposed reforms and advice
invariably received a hostile reception from vested interests, but
he never wavered from the conviction that "progressive taxation
is the only alternative to complete expropriation through violent
revolution". The proposals for India, some of which were repeated for other countries, were: a) that all income (including
capital gains) should be aggregated and taxed progressively with
a maximum marginal rate of 50 per cent (Kaldor did not believe
in "confiscatory" taxation for social justice); b) a progressive
personal expenditure tax imposed on rich individuals where
income tax leaves off; c) a wealth tax; d) a gifts tax; e) a corporation tax imposed at a single rate; and f) a comprehensive and
self-enforcing reporting system, and a more professional tax administration with highly paid officials immune from the temptation of bribes. The Indian Report received a generally hostile reception in the country itself, but was highly praised by tax
experts. Ursula Hicks described it as "an outstanding and remarkable achievement".[2] Kaldor became embroiled in political

1. *Report of a Survey on Indian Tax Reform*, Ministry of Finance, Government of India,
Delhi, 1956.
2. U. Hicks, 'Mr Kaldor's Plan for the Reform of Indian Taxes', *Economic Journal*,
March 1958.

controversy almost everywhere he went. In 1958 he was called to advise the Prime Minister of Ceylon, Mr Bandaranaike. A Report was prepared and accepted, but, owing to racial and other disturbances at the time, it was not published until 1960 – ironically by the newly elected right-wing United National Party who attempted to show that Bandaranaike (and his successor) had failed to implement fully the desirable recommendations relating to the extension of the tax base and the reduction of tax rates. His mission to Mexico in 1960 to make a study of the 'Possibilities and Conveniences of Modifying the Structure and Organisation of the Mexican Tax System' was so sensitive that to write the Report he remained *incognito* for a month locked away in the hills outside Mexico City. The Report was never published,[1] the government fearing opposition and trouble from vested interests. A year later he went to Ghana to advise President Nkrumah. The country was in financial crisis, arising largely from the extravagance and corruption of its Government. There was an urgent need for tax reform and to increase savings. Kaldor's proposed compulsory savings scheme, and the taxation of multinational companies, caused a wave of political protest and strikes. Later in the same year he was requested by Dr. Cheddi Jagan, the Prime Minister of British Guiana, to undertake a comprehensive review of the tax system there with a view to increasing revenue and distributing the burden more equitably. British Guiana was also in a financial crisis with a lack of confidence both at home and abroad, manifesting itself in heavy capital outflows. The budget proposals designed by Kaldor, again including compulsory saving and anti-tax avoidance measures, provoked a general strike and serious anti-Government riots which had to be quelled by British troops. Sixty thousand demonstrators stormed the Parliament building and there were five deaths. A Commonwealth Commission appointed to inquire into the origins of the disturbances, however, exempted Kaldor's budgetary proposals from *direct* blame; it was, the Commission concluded, a case of spontaneous combustion fermented by a number of forces, in-

1. At least not in Mexico. It was published much later in Kaldor's *Collected Economic Essays*, VIII.

cluding an opportunity to protest against Dr. Jagan and his Government.[1] His mission to Turkey in 1962 at the request of the State Planning Organization was to prepare a memorandum on the problems of fiscal reform for use by the Prime Minister, Mr. Ismet Inonu. Most of the proposals, including a novel land tax on the productive *potential* of land, were opposed by the Cabinet representing the landed interest and nothing was done, which led four top officials of the State Planning Organization to resign in protest. Despite these setbacks, Kaldor firmly believed that the job of an adviser is to advise to the best of his professional ability leaving the politicans to decide whether to implement the recommendations or not.

5. Growth and Development

The 1950s in Cambridge was perhaps the most fruitful period in Kaldor's academic life. While still immersed in tax matters, he began the daunting task, aided by Joan Robinson, Richard Kahn, and (later) Luigi Pasinetti, of rethinking the whole of growth and distribution theory on non-neoclassical, Keynesian lines. He was profoundly dissatisfied with both the neoclassical theory of distributive shares, based on the perfectly competitive assumptions of constant returns to scale and marginal productivity factor pricing, and (later) with the neo-classical theory of long-run equilibrium growth based on an exogenously given rate of growth of the labour force and technical progress, with adjustment to equilibrium growth brought about by a smooth change in factor proportions. He was also unhappy with the generally pessimistic nature of the "classical" growth models of Ricardo, Mill, and Marx, which appeared to be at variance with the facts of historical experience. In a remarkable series of papers between 1956 and 1966[2] Kaldor helped to lay the founda-

1. *Report of the Commission of Inquiry into Disturbances in British Guiana in February 1962*, Colonial White Paper No. 354, London: HMSO, 1962.

2. E.g. 'Alternative Theories of Distribution', *Review of Economic Studies*, XXIII, no. 2 (1956); 'A Model of Economic Growth', *Economic Journal*, December 1957; 'Capital Accumulation and Economic Growth' in F. Lutz ed., *The Theory of Capital* London:

tions of the neo- or post-Keynesian school of economics, with adherents and disciples throughout the world. This was the start[1] of the famous neo-Keynesian – neo-classical controversies between Cambridge, England, and Cambridge, Massachusetts, USA, which captivated and preoccupied large sections of the economics profession throughout the 1960s. Kaldor and Joan Robinson became the *bêtes noires* of the American economics establishment. As Ford Visiting Professor at the University of California in 1959, Kaldor acquired the affectionate nickname of "enfant terrible of the Bay Area"!

One of Kaldor's earliest attacks on classical pessimism was a bold lecture on Marx that he delivered in Peking in 1956 (which he visited from India), in which he rejected the view that unemployment, cyclical fluctuations, and growing concentrations of economic power are the inevitable features of capitalist evolution. The fact that money wages may rise as the reserve army of unemployed disappears does not imply a fall in profits because *real* wages may fall (or not rise as fast as productivity in a growing economy). Money wages and real wages are determined by different forces, and there can be no presumption of crisis based on a falling rate of profit. He went on to expound his own unique macro-theory of distribution (published a few months before in the *Review of Economic Studies*), which originated from a meeting of the 'secret seminar' at the end of 1955, and which derived its inspiration from the insight in Keynes's *Treatise on Money*, vol. I, (1930) that profits are the result of the expenditure decisions of entrepreneurs, not the cause: the so-called "widow's curse". Kalecki had the same insight but used it to show why the level and fluctuations of output are particularly dependent on entrepreneurial behaviour, not specifically as a theory of the share of profits in output.[2] He relied instead on the concept of the "degree of monopoly". Kaldor's model is beautiful in its simplicity, and

Macmillan, 1961; 'A New Model of Economic Growth', *Review of Economic Studies*, June 1962, with J. Mirrlees; and 'Marginal Productivity and the Macro-economic Theories of Distribution: Comment on Samuelson and Modigliani, *ibid.*, October 1966.

1. See also J. ROBINSON, 'The Production Function and the Theory of Capital', *ibid.*, XXI, no. 2, 1954.

2. M. KALECKI, 'A Theory of Profits', *Economic Journal*, June-September 1942.

it will surely rank in the history of economic thought as one of the fundamental new theoretical breakthroughs of the twentieth century. In words, the model states that, given that investment is autonomous and determines saving and given that the propensity to save out of profits is greater than out of wages, there will be a unique equilibrium distribution of income between wages and profits associated with that level of investment. Full employment is assumed, and this was regarded by some as a weakness, but as Sen,[1] Harcourt[2] and Wood[3] have shown, the model can be generalised to non-full employment situations. Kaldor's theory of distribution spawned an enormous literature, including the famous Pasinetti Paradox, which showed that even if workers save and receive profits, the theory remains intact with only the distribution of income between workers and capitalists affected, not the equilibrium share of profits in income.[4] Samuelson and Modigliani challenged Pasinetti's elegant generalisation of Kaldor's model, and argued that if realistic parameter values are assumed for the model, the workers' saving propensity will exceed the investment ratio, and capitalists would disappear entirely.[5] In this case, the steady state conditions *would* be determined by the workers' propensity to save out of profits. Kaldor replied with his famous neo-Pasinetti theorem,[6] which was never challenged by the Cambridge, Massachusetts, school. The new model of distribution also provided within limits an alternative mechanism to that of neo-classical theory for equilibrating the warranted and natural growth rates. If the warranted rate lay above the natural rate, with planned saving in excess of planned investment, the share of profits would fall reducing the savings ratio, and *vice versa*. This seemed infinitely more plausible

1. A. SEN, 'Neoclassical and Neo-Keynesian Theories of Distribution', *Economic Record*, March 1963.

2. G. Harcourt, 'A Critique of Mr Kaldor's Model of Income Distribution and Economic Growth', *Australian Economic Papers*, June 1963.

3. A. WOOD, *A Theory of Profits*, Cambridge: Cambridge University Press, 1975.

4. L. PASINETTI, 'Rate of Profit and Income Distribution in Relation to the Rate of Economic Growth', *Review of Economic Studies*, October 1962.

5. P. SAMUELSON and F. MODIGLIANI, 'The Pasinetti Paradox in Neoclassical and More General Models', *Review of Economic Studies*, October 1962.

6. "Marginal Productivity and the Macro-Economic Theories of Distribution: Comment on Samuelson and Modigliani", *ibid*.

to the Cambridge, England, school than the idea (as Joan Robinson once graphically put it) of the existing stock of "jelly" [capital] being spread out or squeezed up to employ all available labour.

In 1957 and 1958, armed with his distribution theory, Kaldor set out to build a growth model to explain what he regarded to be the "stylised facts" of capitalist economic history: a steady trend rate of growth of labour productivity; a steady increase in the capital-labour ratio; a steady rate of profit on capital; the relative constancy of the capital-output ratio; a roughly constant share of wages and profits in national income; and wide differences in the rate of growth of output and productivity between countries with similar capital-output ratios and distributive shares. Kaldor wanted to show how these various tendencies and "constancies" are the consequence of endogenous forces operating in capitalist economies, and that it is not satisfactory to explain them on the basis of chance coincidence and unsupported assumptions such as neutral disembodied technical progress; constant returns to scale; and a unitary elasticity of substitution between capital and labour. Apart from his distribution theory, the other main novel feature of Kaldor's growth models was the idea of a technical progress function to overcome the artificial distinction implicit in the production function between movements along a function (due to relative price changes) and shifts in the whole function (due to technical progress). Technical progress, for the most part, requires investment, and investment normally embodies new ways of doing things. The technical progress function thus relates the rate of growth of output per worker to the rate of growth of capital per worker, with the shape of the function dependent on the degree to which capital accumulation embodies new techniques which improve labour productivity. Shifts in the function will change the relation between capital and output, but at the same time will set up forces, through a change in investment, which restore the capital-output ratio to its equilibrium level. Steady long-run growth is determined by the parameters of the technical progress function incorporating both exogenous and endogenous forces. With the long-run equilibrium growth rate determined, the equilibrium investment ratio, the profits share and the profit rate can all be derived, providing an explanation of the "stylized" facts of capitalist development.

As Kaldor grew older (and perhaps wiser?), he lost interest in theoretical growth models and turned his attention instead to the applied economics of growth. Two things particularly interested him: first, the search for empirical regularities associated with "interregional" (country) growth rate differences, and secondly, the limits to growth in a closed economy (including the world economy). The distinctive feature of all his writing in this field was his insistence on the importance of taking a sectoral approach, distinguishing particularly between increasing returns activities on the one hand, largely a characteristic of manufacturing, and diminishing returns activities on the other (namely agriculture and many service activities). Kaldor's name is associated with three growth "laws" which have become the subject of extensive debate.[1] The first "law" is that manufacturing industry is the engine of growth. The second "law" is that manufacturing growth induces productivity growth in manufacturing through static and dynamic returns to scale (also known as Verdoorn's Law). The third "law" sates that manufacturing growth induces productivity growth outside manufacturing, by absorbing idle or low productivity resources in other sectors. The growth of manufacturing itself is determined by the growth of demand, which must come from agriculture in the early stages of development, and from exports in the later stages. Kaldor's original view[2] was that Britain's growth rate was constrained by a shortage of labour, but he soon changed his mind in favour of the dynamic Harrod trade multiplier hypothesis of a slow rate of growth of exports in relation to the income elasticity of demand for imports, the ratio of which determines a country's balance of payments constrained growth rate. Because fast growing "regions" automatically become more competitive vis-à-vis slow growing regions, through the operation of the second "law", Kaldor believed that growth would tend to be a cumulative disequilibrium

1. See A. P. Thirlwall, ed., 'Symposium on Kaldor's Growth Laws', *Journal of Post-Keynesian Economics*, Spring 1983.

2. See *Causes of the Slow Rate of Economic Growth of the United Kingdom*, Cambridge: Cambridge University Press, 1966.

process – or what Myrdal once called a "process of circular and cumulative causation", – in which success breeds success and failure breeds failure. He articulated these ideas in several places, most notably in two lectures: his Inaugural Lecture at Cambridge in 1966,[1] and in the Frank Pierce Memorial Lectures at Cornell University in the same year.[2] Most of the debate concerning Kaldor's growth laws has centred on Verdoorn's Law and the existence of increasing returns. Kaldor drew inspiration for the theory from his early teacher, Allyn Young, and his neglected paper "Increasing Returns and Economic Progress".[3] Young, in turn, derived his inspiration from Adam Smith's famous dictum that productivity depends on the division of labour, and the division of labour depends on the size of the market. As the market expands, productivity increases, which in turn enlarges the size of the market. As Young wrote "change becomes progressive and propagates itself in a cumulative way", provided demand and supply are elastic. Hence increasing returns is as much a macro-economic phenomenon as a micro-phenomenon, which is related to the interaction between activities, and cannot be adequately discerned or measured by the observation of individual industries or plants. Kaldor was convinced by theoretical considerations and by his own research, and that of others, that manufacturing is different from agriculture and most service activities in its ability to generate increasing return in the Young sense.

The difference in the laws of production governing the output of manufactured goods and primary products, and the different conditions under which manufactured goods and primary products are priced and marketed, also lay at the heart of his two-sector model of economic development, in which the ultimate constraint on the growth of a closed economic system is the rate of land-saving innovations in agriculture (or more generally land-based activities) as an offset to diminishing returns.[4] Within a

1. *Id.*

2. *Strategic Factors in Economic Development*, New York: Cornell University, Ithaca, 1967.

3. *Economic Journal*, December 1928.

4. E.g. see his paper 'Equilibrium Theory and Growth Theory' in M. BOSKIN, ed., *Economics and Human Welfare: Essays in Honour of Tibor Scitovsky*, New York: Academic Press, 1979. For a formalization of the model see A.P. THIRLWALL, 'A General Model of Growth and Development on Kaldorian Lines', *Oxford Economic Papers*, July 1986.

framework of reciprocal demand, the growth of industry and agriculture must be in a particular relationship to each other, and it is the function of the terms of trade to equilibrate supply and demand in both markets for growth to be maximised. In practice, the industrial terms of trade may be "too high" or "too low", in which case industrial growth becomes either demand-constrained or supply-constrained. Kaldor was highly critical of neo-classical development theory with its emphasis on allocation and substitution to the neglect of the complementarity between activities, with its prediction that long-run growth is determined by an exogenously given rate of growth of the labour force in efficiency units. He was equally critical of classical development theory with its focus on the supply side of the economy to the neglect of demand. Keynes undermined Say's Law at the aggregate level. Kaldor showed that Say's Law is equally invalid at the sectoral level because there is a minimum below which the industrial terms of trade cannot fall, set by the minimum subsistence wage in industry.

Like Keynes, Kaldor believed that the uncontrolled movement of primary product prices was a major source of instability in the world economy, and that some intervention was desirable. This was the theme of his Presidential Address to the Royal Economic Society in 1976,[1] but he had addressed the issue before. He foresaw the collapse of the Bretton Woods system based on the U.S. dollar as the key currency, and in 1964 he had prepared a Report for UNCTAD,[2] proposing an international commodity reserve currency, backed by thirty commodities, which would replace the dollar and anchor the price level at the same time. The Report received short shrift, but he never altered his view that such a scheme was desirable. After the introduction of Special Drawing Rights (SDRs) in 1970, he recommended the use of SDRs to finance buffer stocks of key commodities on lines similar to Keynes' Commod Control[3] scheme proposed at the time of Bretton Woods, but never adopted.

1. 'Inflation and Recession in the World Economy', *Economic Journal*, December 1976.
2. *The Case for an International Commodity Reserve Currency*, with A. HART and J. TINBERGEN: UNCTAD, Geneva, 1964.
3. See D. MOGGRIDGE, ed., *The Collected Writings of John Maynard Keynes*, Vol. XXVII,

6. *Adviser to Labour Governments 1964-70 and 1974-6*

When the Labour Party assumed office in 1964, Kaldor was the natural choice of adviser to the Chancellor of the Exchequer. Hugh Gaitskell, who died in 1963, had promised him such a position if and when Labour was returned to power, and James Callaghan kept the pledge, appointing him as Special Adviser on the Social and Economic Aspects of Taxation Policy. His friend Robert Neild, replaced Alec Cairncross as Chief Economic Adviser to the Treasury, and his Hungarian compatriot, Thomas Balogh, was appointed as adviser to the Prime Minister, Harold Wilson. The appointment of two Hungarians to influential positions in the machinery of government provoked a hostile reaction in the press, as if a sinister Eastern European plot was about to be launched on the British people. Kaldor was portrayed as a tax ogre intent on squeezing the rich. The Labour Government inherited a serious balance of payments deficit, and the immediate question was whether sterling should be devalued. Kaldor favoured some form of flexible exchange rate, but Wilson and other influential members of the Cabinet were against any form of exchange depreciation, hoping that a combination of controls and improved industrial efficiency would bring the balance of payments back into the black. As so many times in the past, deflation was eventually resorted to as a substitute for devaluation. Robert Neild was disillusioned and resigned his post. Callaghan approached Kaldor to take the job as Chief Economic Adviser to the Treasury, but he, too, was out of sympathy with the emphasis on deflation. When the Government had no option but to devalue in November 1967, Callaghan resigned, and Roy Jenkins became Chancellor. Kaldor stayed on as Special Adviser, but Jenkins distanced himself from him, and in September 1968 Kaldor decided to return to Cambridge full time, staying on in the Treasury as an unpaid consultant and working with research assistants on several research projects including the relationship between budget

Activities 1940-1946, Shaping the Post-War World: Employment and Commodities, London: Macmillan, 1980.

deficits and the balance of payments (the 'New Cambridge' theory), and the relationship between employment, output, and productivity growth, pursuing the ideas put forward in his Inaugural Lecture. In November 1969 he returned to office as Special Adviser to Richard Crossman at the Department of Health and Social Security, where he was responsible, amongst other things, for persuading the government to increase family allowances substantially but at the same time to "claw back" some of the increase through the tax system – benefiting the poor at the expense of the rich.

As Special Adviser to the Chancellor, Kaldor exerted a considerable influence on tax policy. In the Inland Revenue, where he was first based, he enjoyed a good working relationship with the Head, Alexander Johnston, and with most of the civil servants. Sir Douglas Wass, later Permanent Secretary to the Treasury, has described him as "the only economic adviser to Government that I have worked with who studied the administrative system and sought to fashion his ideas to what the system could bear".[1] Understanding the art of the possible, he never pressed hard for a wealth tax, and never mentioned the introduction of an expenditure tax. He was heavily involved, however, with the introduction and implementation in 1965 of the new capital gains and corporation tax, and with several other new tax initiatives. To encourage investment, particularly in depressed regions, he was instrumental in the replacement of investment allowances by investment grants differentiated regionally, and he played a major part in plugging various tax loopholes to reduce avoidance and evasion. He will be best remembered, however, as the inventor of the Selective Employment Tax, to encourage the diversion of resources from services to manufacturing activity, coupled with the Regional Employment Premium to give an extra boost to manufacturing employment growth in depressed regions. The inspiration for the Selective Employment Tax was based on the theory that manufacturing output growth was constrained by a shortage of labour, and that a tax on labour in ser-

1. See the Foreword to my book, *Nicholas Kaldor*, Brighton: Wheatsheaf Books Ltd., 1987.

vices would not be passed on to the consumer in the form of higher prices but be paid for either out of profits or by increased productivity. It turned out to be an ideal tax: it raised substantial revenue for the Exchequer, at no "cost" to the consumer as predicted. It is hard to show that manufacturing output at the time was constrained by a shortage of labour, but productivity in services improved substantially.

Even as a Special Adviser to the Chancellor, he continued to travel widely giving lectures and seminars, and advising foreign Governments in an unofficial capacity. In the summer of 1967 he toured four countries, giving his first lecture in Russia; delivering several lectures in Japan; advising the Indian Planning Commission on the budgetary implications of the Fourth Five Year Plan; and holding talks with officials of the Central Bank of Israel.

While in office, Kaldor was prevented from pronouncing publicly on topical matters of the day. Out of office in 1970 he took full advantage of his freedom with a flood of newspaper letters and articles on a whole variety of subjects. He was highly critical of Conservative economic policy between 1970 and 1974 – its monetary profligacy, and its encouragement of consumption to the neglect of the foreign trade sector. He also became heavily embroiled in the Common Market debate, and became the foremost academic critic of Britain's entry on the proposed terms. Armed with statistical ammunition on the "true" costs of entry, and with his theory of circular and cumulative causation, he warned that Britain could become "the Northern Ireland of Europe". The Common Agricultural Policy (CAP) came in for particular attack, but his most devastating critique was contained in a *New Statesman* article 'The Truth about the "Dynamic Effects"',[1] in which he showed the balance of payments costs of entry to be close to one billion pounds, and argued that if deflation were necessary to pay for these costs, the assumed dynamic effects of entry would be negative. Many of Kaldor's prognostications on the costs and consequences of EEC entry have materialised. CAP has absorbed more and more of the

1. 12 March 1971.

Community's resources; Britain's budgetary contribution has been massive, and the balance of payments costs have contributed to the destruction of large sections of manufacturing industry. The dynamic benefits of entry promised by the 1970 White Paper have proved to be illusory.[1]

When the Labour Government was returned to power in 1974, Kaldor resumed the role of Special Adviser to the Chancellor, this time to Denis Healey. Once again, the Conservative legacy was a severe balance of payments crisis. Since the floating of the pound in 1972, Kaldor had become sceptical of the efficacy of exchange rate changes as a means of reconciling internal and external balance (one of the few major issues on which he changed his mind), and he campaigned instead for various forms of import controls. Without some form of action, other than exchange rate depreciation, he forecast an 'IMf budget', and this is exactly what transpired in 1976. As far as the broad thrust of economic policy is concerned, Kaldor's influence on Healey was minimal. Disillusioned, he resigned his post in the summer of 1976, and took his seat in the House of Lords. He was, however, responsible for two major tax initiatives: firstly, stock appreciation tax relief which saved several companies from bankruptcy, and secondly capital transfer tax to replace death duties (including unrealised capital gains on death).

7. Monetarism

The 1960s witnessed the recrudescence of interest in the doctrine of the quantity theory of money which lay at the heart of what came to be called "monetarism" and which spread like a plague from the United States to infect susceptible academic communities and eventually the conduct of economic policy in several countries. Its appeal was deceptively attractive. Through control of the money supply it promised a reduction in inflation with hardly any loss of output or employment and without having to

---

1. *Britain and the European Communities: An Economic Assessment,* Cmnd. 4289, London: HMSO.

talk to the trade unions. Kaldor led the intellectual assault against monetarism, in both the U.K. and abroad, describing the doctrine as "a terrible curse"... "a visitation of evil spirits"... "a euphemism for deflation". His view of monetarism was reminiscent of what Keynes felt about economic policy in the 1920s when in attacking the return to the gold standard in 1925 at the pre-war parity, he described monetary policy as "simply a campaign against the standard of life of the working classes", operating through the "deliberate intensification of unemployment – by using the weapon of economic necessity against individuals and against particular industries – a policy which the country would never permit if it knew what was being done".[1]

Kaldor was not a monetary economist in the sense of Keynes or Robertson. Monetary analysis did not infuse the major part of his work. He was, however, a powerful witness before the Radcliffe Committee on the Working of the Monetary System which reported in 1959; and, as Harrod noted in a review of Kaldor's *Collected Essays*,[2] the Committee's conclusions seemed to reflect Kaldor's evidence, namely that monetary policy is an uncertain instrument of economic policy on account of changes in the velocity of circulation of money and the insensitivity of expenditure to changes in the rate of interest. Kaldor fully concurred with the Committee's attack on the mechanistic quantity theory of money, although, in his own review of the Report, he regretted that it failed to probe more fully into the reasons for the behaviour of monetary velocity.[3] Like Keynes, he believed that prices could rise quite independently of prior increases in the money supply, resulting from wage (and other cost) increases. His explanation of the Phillips curve, however, was a profits-based theory of wage increases,[4] which he later turned into a productivity-based theory of wage determination arising from leading sectors in the economy.

1. JOHN MAYNARD KEYNES, *The Economic Consequences of Mr Churchill*, Hogarth Press, 1925.
2. *Economic Journal*, December 1965.
3. 'The Radcliffe Report', *Review of Economics and Statistics*, February 1960.
4. 'Economic Growth and the Problems of Inflation' Parts I and II, *Economica*, August and November 1959.

Kaldor's first major attack on the doctrine of monetarism was in a lecture at University College London, in 1970, directed at Milton Friedman, the undisputed father of modern monetarism.[1] During the 1970s and 1980s, during which his intellectual assault became a crusade, there followed a series of other lectures, including the Page Lecture at Cardiff University, 1980;[2] the Radcliffe Lectures at Warwick University, 1981; The Chintaman Deshmukh Memorial Lecture at the Reserve Bank of India, 1984,[3] and culminating in his magnificent polemic *The Scourge of Monetarism*,[4] reminiscent in style, topicality and pungency of Keynes' *Economic Consequences of the Peace*. This volume contains his masterly Memorandum of Evidence on Monetary Policy to the Select Committee on the Treasury and Civil Service, 1980, brilliant for its marshalling of the theory and facts relating to the core propositions of monetarism.

The key propositions of monetarism which formed the basis of the application of monetarism in the U.K., and which Kaldor attacked, were as follows. First that the stock of money determines money income. This has at least two important corollaries: that the money supply is exogenously determined, and that the demand for money is a stable function of money income. Secondly, that government borrowing is a major source of increases in the money supply. Thirdly, that government spending crowds out private spending, making government stabilisation policy redundant, and fourthly there is, in any case, a natural rate of unemployment, and if governments try to reduce unemployment below the natural rate, there will be ever-accelerating inflation. Kaldor found all three propositions wanting, either theoretically or empirically. He was adamant that there is a fundamental difference between commodity-backed money and credit money, and that in a credit economy, such as advanced capitalist economies, it can never be true to say that expenditure rises *because* of an increase in bank money held by the public since credit money only comes into existence because it is demanded. Money is en-

1. 'The New Monetarism', *Lloyds Bank Review*, July 1970.
2. *Origins of the New Monetarism*, Cardiff: University College Cardiff Press, 1981.
3. *The Failures of Monetarism*.
4. Oxford: Oxford University Press, 1st edn., 2nd edn., 1986.

dogenous, not exogenous. Thus changes in the supply of money must be regarded as the *consequence* of changes in money income not the cause. The endogenous nature of money also accounts for studies that find the demand for money to be a stable function of money income. Indeed, contrary to the monetarist proposition that stability is evidence of the potency of monetary policy, for Kaldor it was precisely the opposite, i.e. that supply responds to demand and proves the impotence of monetary policy. Friedman's initial retort to Kaldor was: "if the relation between money and income is a supply response . . . how is it that major differences among countries and periods in monetary institutions and other factors affecting the supply of money do not produce widely different relations between money and income?"[1] The short answer is that they do, which Kaldor amply demonstrated in his evidence to the Treasury Select Committee of 1980.

Whether government borrowing is a major source of monetary expansion is essentially an empirical question. Kaldor showed for the U.K. that between 1968 and 1979 there was no relation between the size of the Public Sector Borrowing Requirement (PSBR) and the growth of broad money (M_3). Changes in the money supply were dominated by bank lending to the private sector which is demand-determined.

Whether government spending crowds out private spending is also an empirical matter. If there exist unemployed resources, there cannot be resource crowding out. Indeed there should be crowding in through the Keynes multiplier. Financial crowding out owing to higher interest rates to finance government deficits is a possibility, but not inevitable. Higher interest rates may not be necessary and, even if they are, private expenditure may be relatively insensitive. Kaldor found no evidence for the U.K. that a higher PSBR required ever-rising interest rates.

Kaldor dismissed the concept of the natural rate of unemployment, based as it is on the classical labour market assumptions of diminishing returns to labour and that workers are always on their supply curve, ruling out the possibility of involuntary unemployment, and was contemptuous of the doctrine of

1. MILTON FRIEDMAN, 'The New Monetarism: Comment', *Lloyds Bank Review*, October 1970.

"rational" expectations: "the rational expectations theory goes beyond the untestable basic axioms of the theory of value, such as the utility-maximising rational man whose existence can be confirmed only by individual introspection. The assumption of rational expectations which presupposes the correct understanding of the workings of the economy by all economic agents – the trade unionists, the ordinary employer, or even the ordinary housewife – to a degree which is beyond the grasp of professional economists is not science, nor even moral philosophy, but at best a branch of metaphysics."[1]

8. *The Challenge to Equilibrium Theory*

No account of Kaldor's life and work would be complete without more detailed reference to his challenge to neo-classical value theory (or what he called equilibrium theory), which preoccupied him in later life and which will remain one of his lasting memorials. Few economists are willing or able to attack orthodoxy from within, but Kaldor had the courage and tenacity to do so in a remarkable series of lectures and papers. It was not the concept of equilibrium that he objected to, but the formulation of economic theory within an equilibrium framework and neoclassical modes of thinking with their static emphasis on the allocation and substitution role of the price system to the neglect of the dynamic process of growth and change based on increasing returns. His complaint, also shared by Kornai,[2] was quite simply that the framework of competitive equilibrium, within which so much contemporary economic theory is cast, is barren and irrelevant as an apparatus of thought for an understanding of how capitalist industrial economies function in practice. His war of words with the neo-classical school started in 1966 with his response to Samuelson and Modigliani in which he declared: "it is high time that the brilliant minds of

---

1. 'A Keynesian Perspective on Money', with J. Trevithick, *Lloyds Bank Review*, January 1981.

2. J. KORNAI, *Anti-Equilibrium: On Economic Systems Theory and the Tasks of Research*, Amsterdam: North Holland, 1971.

MIT were set to evolve a system of non-Euclidean economics which starts from a non perfect, non-profit maximising economy where ... [neoclassical, general equilibrium] abstractions are initially unnecessary". His assault gathered momentum in the 1970s with provocative essays on "The Irrelevance of Equilibrium Economics"[1] and "What is Wrong with Economic Theory",[2] and culminated in his 1983 Okun Memorial Lectures on *Economics Without Equilibrium*,[3] and his 1984 Mattioli Lectures on *Causes of Growth and Stagnation in the World Economy*. There were three major strands to his critique of equilibrium theory. The first was methodological; the second concerned the lack of realism about the way markets function in practice; and the third related to the implications of the neglect of increasing returns.

At the methodological level, Kaldor was strongly against the deductive method of building models on *a priori* assumptions without any firm empirical basis. For models to be useful, the assumptions must be verifiable, not axiomatic – which makes theories tautological. Many of the assumptions of equilibrium theory, e.g. non-increasing returns, optimising behaviour, perfect competition, etc., are either empirically false or unverifiable. The methodological critique paralleled the disquiet that many economists had been expressing for a long time concerning the use of mathematics in economics, which, for the sake of scientific precision, invariably substitutes elegance for relevance.

Kaldor's second major objection to neo-classical equilibrium theory was its emphasis on the principle of substitution and on the allocative function of markets to the neglect of the creative function of markets and the complementarity between activities. Complementarity, rather than substitution, is much more important in the real world – between factors of production, such as capital and labour, and between activities such as agriculture and industry or industry and services. Static neo-classical analysis is dominated by the idea that one thing must always be at the expense of something else – a "tangential" economics as Allyn

1. *Economic Journal*, December 1972.
2. *Quarterly Journal of Economics*, August 1975.
3. Cardiff: University College Cardiff Press, 1985.

Young once described it; yet there are a variety of mechanisms whereby the expansion of activities can take place simultaneously. It is equally misleading to think of the market as simply a mechanism for the allocation of resources. Much more important is the role of markets in transmitting the impulses for change when tastes, technology, and factor endowments are constantly changing. Nor are market prices the *deus ex machina* by which decentralised market economies function in the real world. Equally important are quantity signals. Loyalty, custom, goodwill, and other intangible relations play an important part in market transactions, the more so where the product is not homogeneous and producers are price makers. In these markets prices are also relatively sticky, determined by costs plus a markup, and notions of fairness and goodwill stop prices from being adjusted to take advantage of (temporary) conditions of excess demand.

Finally there is the problem for equilibrium theory of increasing returns. Marshall, Sraffa, Hicks, among the great economists, all recognized the difficulty. Competitive equilibrium requires perfect competition which is impossible if long-run marginal cost is below price. Hicks admitted in *Value and Capital* (1939): "unless we can suppose that marginal costs generally increase with output at the point of equilibrium . . . the basis on which economic laws can be constructed is shorn away". The evidence for increasing returns in manufacturing industry is overwhelming from empirically estimated production functions; from Verdoorn's Law; from the very existence of oligopolies and monopolies; and from the fact that although the capital-labour ratio differs between countries, the capital-output ratios of countries are very similar. Increasing returns, based on the division of labour, lay at the heart of Adam Smith's vision of economic progress as a self-generating process, and Kaldor used to joke that economics went wrong from Chapter 4, Book I, of the *Wealth of Nations*, when Smith dropped the assumption of increasing returns. The concept lay dormant until Allyn Young revived it in 1928.[1] In the meantime, however, the damage was done; the foundations of neo-classical value theory were laid. Kaldor kept

1. 'Increasing Returns and Economic Progress', *Economic Journal*, December 1928.

harping back to Young's paper. The implications and consequences of increasing returns for how economic processes are viewed are indeed profound and far-reaching. First, what is the meaning of "general equilibrium", if increasing returns cause everything in the equilibrium system to change – resource availabilities, technology, tastes, prices, and so on? Secondly, once increasing returns are admitted, the concept of an optimum allocation of resources loses its meaning since the position of the production possibility curve itself depends on how resources are allocated. Thirdly, increasing returns undermine the notion that at any moment of time, output must be resource constrained. Finally, if supply and demand interact in the presence of increasing returns, in the manner described by Young, many of the treasured theorems of equilibrium economics become untenable. There is no reason why free trade should equalise factor prices; there is no reason why factor migration should equalise unemployment between regions; and there is no reason why growth rates between countries and between regions should converge.

Kaldor admitted that as a young man he was caught in the equilibrium trap, but he did eventually escape. In his own recollections as an economist[1] he confesses: "most of my early papers were based on the deductive *a priori* method and concentrated on unresolved inconsistencies of general equilibrium theory but without questioning the fundamentals . . . Such was the hypnotic power of Walras' system of equations that it took me a long time to grasp that this method of making an abstract model still more abstract by discovering unsuspected assumptions implied by the results is an unscientific procedure that leads nowhere . . . It was a long journey".

9. *Conclusion*

Kaldor was one of the most original, inspiring and controversial economists of his day; a unique figure in twentieth-century eco-

---

1. 'Recollections of an Economist', *Banca Nazionale del Lavoro Quarterly Review*, March 1986.

nomics. His many contributions to economic theory and applied analysis will ensure his place in the history of economic thought. It is perhaps a matter for regret that he never wrote a grand Treatise in the tradition of Smith, Mill, Ricardo, Marx, or Marshall. The reason he did not do so was not because he lacked the vision, intellect, or ability to write, but because he succumbed to the temptation to become involved in too many projects at the same time, and never found the time to sit down for long concentrated periods which such a *magnum opus* requires. His nine volumes of *Collected Essays* are some substitute, however; they give a coherence to his work, and provide a lasting monument to his energy, creativity, and endeavour. Kaldor died at Papworth Hospital near Cambridge on 30th September, 1986, aged 78. At his Memorial Service in King's College Chapel on 17 January 1987, there were over 400 people in attendance from all walks of life including one Prime Minister, ambassadors, civil servants, politicians, and economists from all over the world. This is some measure of the affection and esteem in which he was held.

A. P. THIRLWALL

BIBLIOGRAPHY
of the Works of Nicholas Kaldor
compiled by Ferdinando Targetti

Not included in this bibliography are Kaldor's numerous letters to *The Times* (which over the thirty years between 1932 and 1986 numbered around 260), his articles for *The Economist*, the *Financial Times*, the *Guardian*, the *Manchester Guardian*, and many other newspapers. The exceptions are those written for *The Times* and republished in his Collected Papers or in special booklets. Translations of Kaldor's books and articles into Italian, French, Spanish, and German are included, but not translations into other languages.

Works published over several years are listed under the first date of publication; published speeches and reports are listed according to the date when the speech or report was delivered.

Books and articles

Collected Editions

Collected Papers (London, Duckworth, 1960-89), vols., I-IX:
  I. *Essays on Value and Distribution* (1960; 2nd edn., 1980);
  II. *Essays on Economic Stability and Growth* (1960; 2nd edn., 1980);
  III. *Essays on Economic Policy* (vol. I) (1964; 2nd edn., 1980);
  IV. *Essays on Economic Policy* (vol. II) (1964; 2nd edn., 1980);
  V. *Further Essays on Economic Theory* (1978);
  VI. *Further Essays on Applied Economics* (1978);
  VII. *Reports on Taxation* (vol. I) (1980);
  VIII. *Reports on Taxation* (vol. II) (1980);
  IX. *Further Essays on Economic Policy and Theory* (1989).
An Italian edition of collected works has been edited by F. Targetti in two volumes:
  I. *Equilibrio, distribuzione e crescita* (Turin, Einaudi, 1984);
  II. *Inflazione, moneta e tassazione* (Turin, Einaudi, 1986).
Cap. II was translated into Italian as *Saggi sulla stabilità economica e lo sviluppo*, ed. A. Chiancone (Turin, Einaudi, 1965).

1931

'The Paradox of Saving', trans. of F. von Hayek, *Gibt es einen Widersinn des Sparens, EC* (May).

1932

'A Case against Technical Progress', *EC* (May).
Review of C. Landauer, *Planwirtschaft und Verkehrswirtschaft, EJ* (June).
'The Economic Situation of Austria', *HBR* (Oct.).
Review of E. Lederer *Aufris de ökonomischen Theorie, EC* 12.

1933

Two letters to *NeN* (22 July and 5 Aug.) on Keynes' article 'National Self-Sufficiency', *NeN* (8 and 15 July 1933).
Monetary Theory and the Trade Cycle (London, Johathan Cape, and New York, Kelley, 1966), trans. (with H. Croome) of F. Hayek, *Geldtheorie und Konjunktur-theorie* (Vienna, 1929)

1934

'A Classificatory Note on the Determinateness of Static Equilibrium', *RES* (Feb.); cap. 1; It. edn. 1.
'The Equilibrium of the Firm', *EJ* (Mar.); cap. 1; It. Trans., 'L'equilibrio dell'impresa', in G. Zanetti (ed.), *Contributi per un'analisi economica dell'impresa* (Naples, Liguori, 1980); It. edn. 1.
'Mrs Robinson's Economics of Imperfect Competition', *EC* (Aug.); cap. 1.

1935

'Market Imperfection and Excess Capacity', *EC* (Feb.); repr. in *Readings in Price Theory: Selected by a Committee of American Economic Association* (Chicago, R. D. Irwin, 1952); cap. 1; Ger. trans. in *Wettbewerbtheorie* (Neue Wissenschaftliche Bibliothek, Wirtschafts-Wissenschaften, 77; Cologne, 1975); It. edn. 1.
'Wages Subsidies as a Remedy for Unemployment', lecture to the Conference of the Econometric Society, New York, Dec.; pub. in *JPE* (Dec. 1936); cap. III.

1936

Review of E. Schneider, *Theorie der Produktion, EC* (Feb.).

Review of H. Stackelberg, *Marktform und Gleichgewicht, EC* (May).

Review of O. Morgenstern, *Die Grenzen der Wirtschaftpolitik, EJ* (Dec.).

1937

'Limitational Factors and the Elasticity of Subsitution', *RES* (Feb.).

'The Recent Controversy on the Theory of Capital', *ECTR* (July); cap. I.

Exchange of letters between Keynes and Kaldor, 27 Sept.-1 Nov. (in preparation for the article cited immediately below), in *Collected Writings of John Maynard Keynes* (London, Macmillan for Royal Economic Society, 1973), XIV. 215-23, 240-50.

'Professor Pigou on Money Wages in Relation to Unemployment', *EJ* (Dec.); cap. II; It edn. II.

1938

'Addendum: A Rejoinder to Professor Knight', *ECTR* (Apr.); cap. I.

'Professor Chamberlin on Monopolistic and Imperfect Competition', *QJE* (May); cap. I.

'Mr Hawtrey on Short- and Long-Term Investment', *EC* (Nov.); cap. II.

'Stability and Full Employment', *EJ* (Dec.); cap. II; Ger. trans. in *Koniunktur und Beschäftigungstheorie* (New Wissenschaftliche Bibliotek, Wirtschafts-Wissenschaften, 14; Cologne, 1967).

1939

'Capital Intensity and the Trade Cycle', *EC* (Feb.); cap. II.

Review of A. H. Hansen, *Full Recovery or Stagnation, EJ* (Mar.).

'Money Wage Cuts in Relation to Unemployment: A Reply to Mr Somers', *RES* (June).

'Principles of Emergency Finance', *BK* (Aug.)

'Welfare Propositions in Economics and Interpersonal Comparison of Utility', *EJ* (Sept.); repr. in K. J. Arrow and T. Scitovsky (eds.), *Readings in Welfare Economics* (London, Allen & Unwin, 1969); cap. I; It. edn. II.

Review of W. Marget, *The Theory of Prices: An Examination of the Central Problem of Monetary Theory*, I, *EJ* (Sept.).

'Speculation and Economic Stability', *RES* (Oct.); cap. II; It. edn. II.

'Keynes' Theory of the Own-Rates of Interest'; cap. II; It. edn. II.

1940

'The Trade Cycle and Capital Intensity: A Reply', *EC* (Feb.).

'A Comment on a Rejoinder of H. M. Somers (on Kaldor's Money Wage Cuts in Relation to Unemployment)', *RES* (Feb.).

'A Model of the Trade Cycle', *EJ* (Mar.); cap. II; It. edn. I.

Review of M. Abramowitz, *An Approach to a Price Theory in a Changing Economy*, *EJ* (July-Sept.).

'A Note on the Theory of the Forward Market', *RES* (June).

'A Note on Tariffs and the Terms of Trade', *EC* (Nov.); repr. in A. M. Page (ed.), *Utility Theory: A Book of Reading* (New York, Wiley, 1968); cap. I; It. edn. II.

1941

'Rationing and the Cost of Living Index', *RES* (June).

'The White Paper on National Income and Expenditure', *EJ* (June-Sept.)

'Employment and Equilibrium – A Theoretical Discussion', *EJ* (Dec.); repr. in cap. II as 'Pigou on Employment and Equilibrium'.

1942

'The Income Burden of Capital Taxes', *RES* 9; 2 (June); pub. in part as 'The Estimation of the Burden of Death Duties' in G. F. Shirras and L. Rostas (eds.), *The Burden of British Taxation* (Cambridge, Cambridge University Press, 1943), cap. VII; It. edn. II.

'The 1941 White Paper on National Income and Expenditure', *EJ* (June-Sept.).

'Models of Short Period Equilibrium', *EJ* (June-Sept.).

'Professor Hayek and the Concertina Effect', *EC* (Nov.); cap. II.

Economic Reconstruction after the War (with M. Joseph) (London, Association for Education in Citizenship).

1943

'Budgeting for Employment, National Income and State Finance, Closing the Deflationary Gap', in *Full Employment* (10 articles from TT '1942-3'); (London, The Times Publishing Company).

'The Beveridge Report II. The Financial Burden', *EJ* (Apr.).

Review of A. H. Hansen, *Fiscal Policy and Business Cycles*, *EJ* (Apr.).

'Export Costs and Export Price Policy', *BK* (June).

1944

The 1943 White Paper on National Income and Expenditure (with T. Barna), *EJ* (June-Sept.); Fr. trans. (Paris, Imprimerie de l'Agence France Press, 1946).

Planning for Abundance (with J. Robinson, A. A. Evans, E. F. Schumacher and P. Lamartine Yatts), papers by the economists present at the meeting organised by the National Peace Council on 'Interrelation of National and International Reconstruction' held in Oxford; (London, Peace Aims Pamphlet, 21, National Peace Council).

'The Quantitative Aspects of the Full Employment Problem in Britain', memorandum submitted to Sir William Beveridge's Committee on Full Employment, pub. as appendix C to Sir W. Beveridge, *Full Employment in a Free Society* (London, Allen & Unwin); cap. III.

1945

The Effects of Strategic Bombing on the German War Economy, prepared by US Strategic Bombing Survey (Washington, DC).

'Obituary of Erwin Rothbarth' (with D. G. Champernowne), *EJ* (Apr.).

1946

'The German War Economy', speech to the Manchester Statistical Society, 22 May; pub. in *MS* (Sept.) and *RES* 13:1 (1945-6); cap. IV.

1947

'A Note on W. J. Baumol's Community Indifference', *RES* 14:1 (1946-7).
'A Plan for the Financial Stabilization of France', report prepared for the Commissariat Général du Plan (Paris, Mar.-May); cap. VIII.

1948

'The Theory of Distribution', in *Chambers Encyclopedia*; It. trans. 'La teoria della distribuzione', in I. Musu (ed.), *I neokeynesiani* (Bologna, Il Mulino, 1980).
'A Statistical Analysis of Advertising Expenditure and of the Revenue of the Press' (with R. Silverman) (NIESR Studies, 8; Cambridge, Cambridge University Press).
'A Survey of the Economic Situation and Prospects of Europe: 1947', prepared by the Economic Committee for Europe, Research and Planning Division, under the direction of Kaldor (Geneva, U.N.).

1949

'A Survey of the Economic Situation and Prospects of Europe, 1948', prepared by the Economic Commitee for Europe, Research and Planning Division, under the direction of Kaldor (Geneva, UN).
National and International Measures for Full Employment (with J. M. Clark, A. Smithies, P. Uri and R. Walker) (New York, U.N.); It. trans., *Politiche della piena occupazione*, introd. by Tremelloni (Milan, Istituto per gli studi economici, 1950).

1950

'The Economic Aspects of Advertising', *RES* 18:4 (1949-50).
'A Positive Policy for Wages and Dividends', memorandum sub-

mitted to the Chancellor of the Exchequer, 21 June; cap. III;
It. trans., 'Per un'efficace politica dei salari e dei dividendi'
(introd. added in 1964), in D. Cavalieri (ed.), *La politica dei red-
diti* (Milan, Franco Angeli, 1973); It edn. II.

'Employment Policies and the Problem of International Balance', paper given to the Conference of the International Economic Association, Monte Carlo, Sept.: pub. in *RES* 19: 1
(1950-1); cap. III.

Report on National and International Measures for Full Employment
(with J. M. Clark, A. Smithies, P. Uri and E. R. Walker)
(Geneva, U.N.).

'A Survey of the Economic Situation and Prospects of Europe:
1950', prepared by the Economic Committee for Europe, Research and Planning Division, under the direction of Kaldor
(Geneva, U.N.).

1951

'Mr Hicks on the Trade Cycle', *EJ* (Dec.); cap. II. *Report on Full
Employment Objectives in Relation to the Problem of European Cooperation* (co-author) (Strasburg, European Council).

1952

'Beschäftigungspolitik und das Problem des Internationalen
Gleichgewichtes', *ZN* (15 Jan.).

'The International Impact of Cyclical Movements', paper given
to the Conference of the International Economic Association,
Oxford, Sept.; pub. in E. Lundberg (ed.), *The Business Cycle in
the Post War World* (London, Macmillan, 1955); cap. IV.

'Foreign Trade and the Balance of Payments', written for the
Fabian Society; pub. in cap. IV.

A Reconsideration of the Economics of the International Wheat Agreement,
report prepared for the UN FAO (Commodity Policy Studies,
1; Rome, F.A.O., Sept.); cap. IV.

1953

'Relations entre la croissance économique et les fluctuations cy-
cliques', lecture at the Institut de Sciences Économiques Ap-

pliquées, Paris 23 May; pub. in *EA* (Jan.-June 1954); repr. as 'The Relation of Economic Growth and Cyclical Fluctuations', *EJ* (Mar. 1954); Ger. trans. in *Konjunktur und Beschäftigungstheorie* (Neue Wissenschaftliche Bibliotek, Wirtschafts-Wissenschaften, 14; Cologne, 1967); cap. II.

'Caratteristiche dello sviluppo economico', paper given to the International Conference on Underdeveloped Areas, Milan, 10-15 Oct.; Engl. trans., 'Characteristics of Economic Development', in cap. II.

1955

'The Lessons of the British Experiment since the War: Full Employment and the Welfare State', paper given to the centennial meeting of the Société Royal d'Économie du Belgique, Brussels; cap. III.

'Professor Wright on Methodology: A Rejoinder', *EJ* (Mar.).

'The Economic Effects of Company Taxation', *Transactions of the Manchester Statistical Society*, 1954-5 (23 Mar.).

'Memorandum of Dissent to the Final Report of the Royal Commission on the Taxation of Profits and Income' (with G. Woodcock and H. L. Bullock), pub. with *Final Report of the Royal Commission on the Taxation of Profit and Income* Cmd 9474 (London, HMSO, June); repr. as. *Reforming the Tax System* (Fabian Research Series, 190; London, 1957); cap. VII; partial trans. in It. edn. II.

An Expenditure Tax (London, Unwin University Books, and New York, Macmillan, 1956); pub. in part as 'Taxation and Economic Progress' and 'Income Expenditure and Taxable Capacity' in H. Miffly (ed.) *Public Finance and Fiscal Policy Selected Readings* (Boston, 1966); Ger. trans., *Begründung einer Ausgabesteuer* (Cologne, 1969); It. trans., *Per un'imposta sulla spesa* (Turin, Boringhieri, 1962).

'Alternative Theories of Distribution', *RES* 23: 2 (1955-6); repr. in D. R. Kamerscher (ed.), *Readings in Microeconomics* (Cleveland, World Pub. Co., 1967); repr. in J. E. Stiglitz and H. Uzawa (eds.), *Readings in the Modern Theory of Economic Growth*, (Cambridge, Mass., MIT Press, 1969); repr. in I. Rima (ed.), *Readings in the History of Economic Theory* (New York, H. R. and

W. Dryden, 1970); cap. I; Span. edn. *RCE* 76 (1956-7); repr. in O. Braun (ed.), *Teoria del capital y la distribución* (Buenos Aires, Editorial Tiempo Contemporaneo, 1973); It. trans., 'Teorie alternative della distribuzione', in G. Lunghini (ed.), *Valore, prezzi ed equilibrio generale* (Bologna, Il Mulino, 1971); It. edn. I.

1956

'Capitalism Evolution in the Light of Keynesian Economics', lecture at the University of Peking, 11 May; pub in *SAN* (May 1957) and *JES* (1957); cap. II; Fr. trans., *EA* (Apr.-Sept. 1957); Port. trans., *EB* 2 (1956) and *TE* (July-Sept. 1956); It. trans., *RPE* (Feb. 1958).

Indian Tax Reform: Report of a Survey, Dept. of Economic Affairs, Ministry of Finance (New Delhi, June); repr. in R. Bird and O. Oldman (eds.), *Readings on Taxation in Developing Countries* (Baltimore, Johns Hopkins Press, 1964); cap. VIII.

'Problems Económicos del Chile', essay written for the UN ECLA, Santiago del Chile, July-Sept.; pub. in *TE* (Mexico, Apr.-June, 1959); Engl. trans., cap. IV.

'Characteristics of Economic Development', *AS* (Nov.); It. trans. *IS* (May 1958).

1957

Four essays in *RBE* (Mar.): 'Caracteristicas do desenvolvimento económico: Crescimento equilibrado e disequilibrado'; 'O problema do crescimento acelerado'; 'Inflação e desenvolvimento económico'; 'Tributacão e desenvolvimento economico'; It. trans. of 1st, 3rd, and 4th essays, *IS* (June, July, Aug. 1958).

'The Reform of Personal Taxation', paper given to the Conference of the Society of Chartered Accountants, London, 29 Oct., pub. in *ACC* (12 Apr.); cap. III.

'La inflación chilena y la estructura de la producción' *PaE* (Nov.).

'A Model of Economic Growth', *EJ* (Dec.); Sp. trans., *TE* (Apr.-June 1958); Fr. trans., *EA* (Aug.-Sept.), cap. II; It. trans., 'Un modello dello sviluppo economico', in G. Nardozzi and V. Valli (eds.), *Teoria dello sviluppo economico* (Milan, Etas Kompass, 1971).

'Community Indifference, A Comment', *RES*, 14: 1.

1958

Review of P. Baran, *The Political of Growth*, *AER* (Mar.).

Suggestions for a Comprehensive Reform of Direct Taxation in Ceylon (Colombo, Ceylon Government Publications, Bureau, 1960); cap. VIII.

'The Reform of Personal Taxation', *ACC* (12 Apr.).

'Observations on the Problem of Economic Development in Ceylon', essay written at the request of Prime Minister Mr S. R. W. Bandaranaike, 18 Apr.; pub. in *Papers by Visiting Economists* (Colombo, National Planning Council, Government Press, 1959); cap. IV.

'Monetary Policy, Economic Stability and Growth', memorandum submitted to the Committee on the Working of the Monetary System, 23 June *Memoranda of Evidence*, pp. 146-53, and *Minutes of Evidence*, pp. 712-18, Cmnd 827 (London, HMSO); cap. III; It. edn. II.

'Risk Bearing and Income Taxation', *RES* (June).

'Capital Accumulation and Economic Growth', paper given at the Conference of the International Economic Association, Corfu, Aug.; pub. in F. A. Lutz and P. C. Hague (eds.), *The Theory of Capital* (London, Macmillan, 1961); repr. in *AER* (June 1962); cap. V; It. edn. I.

'Problems of the Indian Third Five Year Plan', memorandum written for the Secretariat of the Plan Bureau, New Delhi, Sept.; cap. IV.

'Comment on a Note on Kaldor's Speculation and Economic Stability', *RES* (Oct.).

'Tax Reform in India', essay submitted to the Indian Parliamentary Committee, 16 Dec.; pub. in *EWA* (Jan. 1959); repr. in Bird and Oldman (eds.), *Readings on Taxation in Developing Countries*; cap. III.

'The Growing Disparity between Rich and Poor Countries', in *Problems of United States Economic Development* (New York, Committee for Economic Development).

1959

'Economic Growth and the Problem of Inflation', lectures given at the LSE, 3 and 13 Feb.; pub. in *EC* (Aug. and Nov.); cap. III; Sp. trans., *TE* 28 (1961); Fr. trans. ed. Institut pour le développement économique de la Banque Internationale pour la Reconstruction et le Développement (Paris, 1963); It. edn. II.

'The Radcliffe Report'; pub. in *REST* (Feb. 1960); cap. III; It. edn. II.

'El concepto de ingreso en la teoria económica', *TE* (July-Sept.).

1960

'A Rejoinder to Mr Atsumi and Professor Tobin', *RES* (Feb.).

'Economic Growth and Distributive Shares: A Rejoinder to Mr Findlay', *RES* (June).

'La Rôle de l'instrument monétaire en matière de croissance et de stabilité économique', *BID* (Aug.).

'Report on Mexican Tax Reform', essay written for the Finance Ministry of Mexico, Sept.; cap. VIII.

Introduction to cap. I.

Introduction to cap. II.

1961

'Increasing Returns and Technical Progress: A Comment on Professor Hicks's Article, *OEP* (Feb.).

Ensayos sobre el desarrollo económico, written for CEMLA (Mexico, July; 2nd edn., Nov. 1964).

'Proposals for a Reform of Taxation in British Guiana', written for the Ministry of Finance of British Guiana, (Georgetown, 30 Dec.); cap. VIII.

1962

'A Proposal for a Levy on the Advertising Revenue of Newspapers', (with R. R. Neild) written for the Royal Commission on the Press, Feb.; cap. VII; It. edn. II.

'A New Model of Economic Growth' (with J. Mirrlees), *RES* (June); cap. V; Ger. trans. in *Sonderdruck aus Heinz Köning*,

Wachstum und Entwicklung der Wirtschaft; It. trans., 'Un nuovo modello di sviluppo economico', in M. G. Mueller (ed.), *Problemi di macroeconomia* (Milan, Etas Kompass, 1966); It. edn. 1.

'Report on the Turkish Tax System', written for the State Planning Organization of the Turkish Government, Ankara, Apr.; cap. VIII.

'Symposium on Production Functions and Economic Growth: Comment', *RES* (June).

The Choice of Taxes in Developing Countries, paper given to the Nyasaland Economic Symposium on 'Economic Development in Africa', Blantyre, 18-28 July (Oxford, Basil Blackwell, 1965).

'Overdeterminateness in Kaldor's Growth Model: A Comment', *EJ* (Sept.).

'The Role of Taxation in Economic Development' paper for the Conference of the International Economic Association on 'Fisical Policy and Organization of American States', (Santiago, Chile, Dec.); cap. III.

'Will Underdeveloped Countries Learn to Tax?'; pub. in *FA* (Council of Foreign Relations) (Jan. 1963); repr. in Bird and Oldman (eds.), *Readings on Taxation in Developing Countries* (3rd edn. 1975); cap. III.

'Stabilizing the Terms of Trade of Underdeveloped Countries', written for the UN ECLA; pub. in Eng. and Sp. in *EBLA* (Mar. 1963); It. trans., *MA* (Apr. 1964) cap. IV.

1963

'Comment on I. Svennilson's Paper on "Economic Growth and Technical Progress", OECD conference on 'Residual Factors and Economic Growth' (Château de la Muette, Paris, 20-22 May).

'A Memorandum on the Value Added Tax', memorandum submitted to the Committee on Turnover Taxation, July; cap. III; It. edn. II.

'Taxation for Economic Development', *JMAS* (Mar.); repr. in H. E. Smith (ed.), *Readings on Economic Development and Administration in Tanzania* (Nairobi; Institute of Public Administration, University College, Dar-es-Salaam, Tanzania, 1966).

'El papel de la imposición e el desarrollo económico', *IE*, 37-96.

'The Case for an International Commodity Reserve Currency' (with A. G. Hart and J. Tinbergen), submitted to the UN Conference on 'Trade and Development', Geneva, Mar.-June 1964; cap. IV.

'Prospects of a Wages Policy for Australia', essay written as Consultant Economist to the Australian Central Bank; pub. in *ER* (June 1964); cap. IV.

1964

'Las reformas del sistema fiscal en México', *CEX* (Apr.).

'The Problem of International Liquidity', *BOIES* (Aug.); cap. VI.

'Dual Exchange Rates and Economic Development', *EBLA* (Sept.), in Eng. and Sp. cap. IV.

'International Trade and Economic Development', in 'Problems of Foreign Aid', papers for the conference on 'Public Policy' held in Dar-es-Salaam, Tanzania, Nov.; pub. in *JMAS* (Dec.).

Kaldor's speech at the conference pub. in W. Baer and I. Kerstenetzky (eds.), *Inflation and Growth in Latin America* (Homewood, Irwin, The Economic Growth Center, Yale University).

Introduction to cap. III.

Introduction to cap. IV.

1965

'The Relative Merits of Fixed and Floating Exchange Rates'; pub. in cap. VI.

'Les Prélèvements fiscaux dans les pays en voie de développement', paper for the Réhovoth Conference, 18 Aug., pub. in *Les Problèmes fiscaux et monétaires dans les pays en voie de développement* (Paris, 1967).

1966

'Marginal Productivity and the Macro-Economic Theories of Distribution: Comment on Samuelson and Modigliani', *RES* (Oct.); cap. V; It. edn. I.

'Economic and Taxation Problems in Iran', written for the Prime Minister of Iran, Tehran, June; cap. VIII.

Causes of the Slow Rate of Economic Growth in the United Kingdom, inaugural lecture at the University of Cambridge (Cambridge, Cambridge University Press); Fr. trans. *EA* (Mar. 1967); Russ. trans., *Mirovaja Ekonomika i Mezdunarodnye Otnösenija* (Moscow, Institut Mirovoj Ekonomiki, 1968); cap. v; It. edn 1.

Strategic Factors in Economic Development, Frank Pierce Memorial Lecture at Cornell University, Oct. (Ithaca, Cornell University Press, 1967); It. partial. trans., 'Problemi di industrializzazione nei paesi in via di sviluppo', in B. Jossa (ed.), *Economia del sottosviluppo* (Bologna, Il Mulino, 1973).

Une politique monétaire pour l'Amérique Latine (with P. Uri, R. Ruggles, and R. Triffin) (Paris, Institut Atlantique); Sp. trans. for CEMLA (1966); Eng. trans., *A Monetary Policy for Latin America* (New York, Praeger, 1968).

1968

'Productivity and Growth in Manufacturing Industry: A Reply', *EC* (Nov.).

1969

'The Role of Modern Technology in Raising the Economic Standards of Less Developed Countries', paper given to the conference held in Jerusalem, 14-18 Apr.; proceedings pub. under conference title: W. L. Hodges and N. A. Kelley (eds.), *Technological Change and Human Development* (Ithaca, New York State School of Industrial and Labour Relations, Cornell University, 1970).

'The Choice of Technology in Less Developed Countries', *MLR* (Aug.).

1970

'Some Fallacies in the Interpretation of Kaldor', *RES* (Jan.).

'Europe's Agricultural Disarray', lecture given to the International Press Institute, Paris, 13 Jan., as pub. 'Europe's Agricultural Disarry – ECC Farm Policy is Fundamentally Misconceived', *NS* (3 Apr.); cap. VI; It. trans., 'La politica agricola della Cee è forse fondamentalmente sbagliata?', in T. Joshing and R. Pasca (eds.), *Analisi economica e politica agraria* (Bologna, Il Mulino, 1981).

'The Case for Regional Policies', lecture given at Aberdeen University as the 5th Annual Scottish Economic Society Lecture (Feb.); pub. in *SJPE* (Nov.); cap. V.

'The New Monetarism', lecture given at University College London, 12 Mar.; pub. in *LLBR* (July 1970); cap. VI; Ger. trans., *IST* 16: 1-2 (1970); It. trans., 'Il nuovo monetarismo', in G. Bellone (ed.), *Il dibattito sulla moneta* (Bologna, Il Mulino, 1972); It. edn. II.

'Conflicts in National Economic Objectives', Presidential Address to Section F of the British Association for the Advancement of Science, Durkheim, Sept.; pub. in *Conflicts in Policy Objectives* (Oxford, Basil Blackwell, 1971); repr. in *EJ* (Mar. 1971); cap. V; It. edn. I.

'A Rejoinder to Professor Friedman', *LLBR* (Oct.).

Un avenir pour l'Europe agricole (co-author), ed. P. Uri (Paris, L'Institut Atlantique); It. trans., *Un futuro per l'agricoltura europea*, intro. by G. La Malfa (Milan, Franco Angeli, 1971).

1971

'The Existence and Persistence of Cycles in A Non-Linear Model: Kaldor's 1940 Model Re-Examined: A Comment', *RES* (Jan.).

'The Role of Industrialization in Latin American Inflations', paper given to the conference on Latin America (Gainesville, Fla., Feb.); pub. in D. T. Geithman (ed.), *Fiscal Policy for Industrialization and Development in Latin America* (Gainseville, Fla., University of Florida Press, 1974; repr. Cambridge, Cambridge University Press, 1976); cap. VI.

'The Truth about the "Dynamic Effects" of the Common Market', *NS* (12 Mar.); repr. in *Destiny or Delusion? Britain and the Common Market* (London, 1971); cap. VI.

'Le Professeur Kaldor relance le débat sur le coût de l'entrée de la Grande Bretagne dans le Marché Commun', *PE* (May).

'The Money Crisis: Britain's Chance', *NS* (14 May).

'The Distortions of the 1971 White Paper', *NS* (16 July); cap. VI.

'The Economic Effects of Alternative Systems of Corporation Tax', memorandum submitted to the Select Committee of the House of Commons of the Corporation Tax; cap. VII; It. edn. II.

'Bretton Woods and After', *TT* (6, 7, 8 Sept.); repr. as 'The Dollar Crisis', in cap. VI.

'The Common Market – A Final Assessment', *NS* (22 Oct.); cap. VI.

'Functioning and Economic Perspectives of the EEC', seminar on 'The Trade Unions and the European Economic Community', Julsminde, Denmark, 31 Oct.-6 Nov.

1972

'Advanced Technology in a Strategy of Development: Some Lessons from Britain's Experience'; Eng. repr. in *Automation and Developing Countries* (Geneva, ILO); Sp. trans. in D. Alejandro (ed.), *Politica económica en centro y periferia (Ensayos en honor a Felipe Pazos)* (Mexico, Jeritel & Tokman, Fondo de Cultura Económica, 1976); repr. as 'Capitalism and Industrial Development: Some Lessons from Britain's Experience', *CJE* 1 (1977); cap. VI.

'Notes on a Talk to VAT Conference', *Financial Times* conference, London, 25 Apr.

'Mr Heath's New Socialism', *ST* (8 Oct.).

'The Irrelevance of Equilibrium Economics', lecture at the University of York as the Goodricke Lecture, 10 May; pub. in *EJ* (Dec.); cap. V; Sp. trans., *ICE* (1975); It. trans., 'L'irrilevanza della teoria dell'equilibrio economico', in M. D'Antonio (ed.), *La crisi post-keynesiana* (Turin, Boringhieri, 1975); It. edn. I.

The Common Market: Its Economics Perspective (Trade Unions against the Common Market and NATSOPA).

'Money and Gold', *Acta Oeconomica*, 9: 2.

1973

'Teoria del equilibrio y teoria del crecimiento', lecutre at the University of Barcelona, Apr.; pub. in *CE* 2 (May-Aug. 1974);

pub. in Eng. as 'Equilibrium Theory and Growth Theory', in M. Baskin (ed.), *Economics and Human Welfare – Essays in Honour of Tibor Scitovski* (New York, Academic Press, 1979); It. trans., in G. Caravale (ed.), *La crisi delle teorie economiche* (Milan, Franco Angeli, 1983); It. edn. 1.

'La estrategia del desarrollo industrial en los países menos avanzados', in 'La financiación del desarrollo en los países en proceso de crecimiento', 3rd Sermana Económica Internacional, organised by Mondo, Documento Económico 7, Barcelona.

'Problems and Prospects of International Monetary Reform, *BK* (Sept.); cap. VI.

'Tax Credits: A Critique of the Green Paper's Proposals', essay submitted to the Select Committee of the House of Commons on Tax Credit; cap. VII.

'Per una riforma monetaria internazionale: necessità di un nuovo indirizzo', lecture held at the Banca d'Italia, 12 Dec.; pub. in *BAN* (Mar. 1974); Eng. trans., cap. VI.

1974

'Mr Health's Road to Ruin', *NS* (22 Feb.); repr. (Cambridge, DAE reprint series no. 396).

'The Road to Recovery', *NS* (Mar.), repr. (Cambridge, DAE reprint series no. 396).

'Managing the Economy: The British Experience', the David Kinley Lecture given at the University of Illinois, 18 Apr.; pub. in *QREB* 3.

'What is Wrong with Economic Theory', a Political Economy Lecture given at Harvard University, 29 Apr.; pub. in *QJE* (Aug. 1975; repr. Cambridge, Cambridge University Press, 1976); cap. V; Sp. trans., *TE* (Apr.-June 1976); It. edn. 1.

'The Case for Nationalizing Land' (with J. Brockebank, J. Maynard, R. Neild and O. Sutchbury) (Campaign for Nationalizing Land, London).

1975

'Economic Growth and the Verdoorn Law: A Comment on Mr Rowthorn's Article', *EJ* (Dec.).

'Why are Regional Policies Necessary?', paper given at the conference organised by the Deutscher Wirtschaftwissenschaftlicher Forschungsinstitut, Bonn, 15-16 May; pub. in *Regionalpolitik und Agrarpolitik in Europa* (Berlin, Dunker & Humboldt).

1976

'Inflation and Recession in the World Economy', Presidential Address to the Royal Economic Society, 22 July; pub. in *EJ* (Dec.); cap. v; Fr. trans., *PE* (1977); It. trans., 'Inflazione e recessione nell'economia mondiale', in *Rassegna sulla letteratura dei cicli economici*, 3 (Istituto per la Congiuntura, 1977) and in *REA* (1977); It. edn. II.

'The Economic Outlook', European Banking Conference, Stockholm, 2-3 Nov.

'Observations on Fiscal Reform in Venezuela', written for the Ministry of Economic and Planning Coordination (Caracas, Dec.); cap. VIII.

1977

'The Nemesis of Free Trade', lecture given at the University of Leeds, 21 Mar.; cap. VI.

'The Effects of Devaluation on Trade in Manufacture', cap. VI.

'Is Capital Shortage a Cause of Mass Unemployment?', paper for the Kiel Symposium; pub. in H. Giersch (ed.), *Capital Shortage and Unemployment in the World Economy* (Institut für Weltwirtschaft an der Universität Kiel, Tübingen, 1978).

Comment on 'Capital Requirements for Full Employment and Economic Growth in Developed Countries', paper given to the Kiel Symposium by K. Wernerschatz; pub. in Giersch (ed.), *Capital Shortage and Unemployment in the World Economy*.

1978

'A New Look at the Expenditure Tax', paper given to the Brooking Institution conference on 'Income versus Expenditure Taxes', Washington, DC, Oct.; cap. VII; It. edn. II.

'Uzroci svetske inflacije i posledice na zemlje u razvoju' (The Effect of International Inflation on the Economies of Developing Countries), paper given to the Conference of the Interna-

tional Organization of Bank Sciences held at Dubrovnik, 31
Oct.-5 Nov.; proceedings pub. under the conference title:
Medunarodno finansiranje ekonomskovo razvoja (International Fi-
nancing to Economic Development) (Belgrade).

'Public or Private Enterprise: The Issue to be Considered', lecture in Mexico City (Jan.); pub. in W. G. Baumol (ed.), *Public and Private Enterprise in a Mixed Economy* (Londo, Macmillan,
1980).

'The Foundations of Free Trade Theory and their Implications
for the Current World Recession', paper given to the Conference of the International Economic Association held Bischen-
berg, France; proceedings pub. under the conference title: E.
Malinvaud and S. P. Fitoussi (eds.), *Unemployment in Western
Countries* (London, Macmillan, 1980); repr. in J. Los *et. al.*,
(eds.), *Studies in Economic Theory and Practice*, essays in honour of
E. Lipinski (Amsterdam, North Holland, 1981); cap. IX.

'Structural Causes of the World Economic Recession', in *Mondes
en développement* (Central Nationale de la Recherche
Scientifique, 22; Paris).

Introduction to cap. V.

Introduction to cap. VI.

1979

'Inflation: an Endemic Problem of Modern Capitalism', mimeo
(Cambridge); repr. in *WG* 8: 2 (1982).

'Economic Policy Dimension for Restructuring Industrial
Economies', paper given to the Varenna conference, Sept.

'An Introduction to "A Note on the General Theory" by J. de
Largentaye', *JPKE* 1.

'The Role of Fiscal and Monetary Policies in Latin American
Inflations', in *Interamerican Institute of Capital Markets* (Caracas).

'What is De-Industrialization?', comment on the article by Sir
Alec Caincross, in F. Blackorby (ed.), *De-Industrialization*
(London, Heinemann).

Collected Economic Essays (New York, Holmes & Mayer).

1980

'The Role of Increasing Returns, Technical Progress and Cumulative Causation in the Theory of International Trade', lecture, Paris, Feb.; pub. in *EA* 34: 4 (1981); cap. IX.

'Le difficili vie dello sviluppo', interview given to F. Targetti, *RI* (6 June).

'Memorandum of Evidence on Monetary Policy' (17 July) (London, HMSO).

'The World Economic Outlook', paper given to the 6th World Congress of the International Economic Association, Mexico City, Aug.; pub. in *Human Resources, Employment and Development* (London, Macmillan, 1983).

'Problems of Energy Self Sufficient Countries', lecture given in Oaxaca, Mexico, Sept.

'Gemeinsamkeiten und Unterschiede in den Theorien von Keynes, Kalecki und Rüstow', lecture given in Starnberg, Bavaria, 16 Oct.; pub. in *IST* 29: 1 (1983).

'Keynes as an Economic Adviser', lecture given at Canterbury, Nov.; pub. in A. P. Thirlwall (ed.), *Keynes as a Policy Adviser* (London, Macmillan, 1982); It. trans., *PEE* 4 (1983).

'Monetarism and United Kingdom Monetary Policy', *CJE* (Dec.).

'Origins of the New Monetarism', Page Fund Lecture, Cardiff, 3 Dec. (Cardiff, University College Cardiff Press, 1981); It. edn. II; cap. IX.

'What are the Threatening Economic Issues?', paper given to the *Financial Times* conference on 'European Banking', Amsterdam, Dec.

General Introduction to cap. I (2nd edn.).

Introduction to cap. VII.

Introduction to cap. VIII.

'I guasti del monetarismo', *MO* 12 (Dec.).

'The Economics of the Selective Employment Tax', memorandum to the NIESR; pub. in F. Shirras and L. Rostas (eds.), *The Burden of Taxation* (London, NIESR); cap. VII; It. edn. II.

1981

'Discussion of "Verdoorn's Law, the Externalities Hypothesis, Kaldor's Proposition and Economic Growth in the U.K." by

M. Chatterji and M. Wickens', in D. Currie *et. al.* (eds.), *Macroeconomic Analysis* (London, Croom Helm).

'A Keynesian Perspective on Money' (with J. Trevithick), *LLBR* 139 (Jan.); It. edn. II; cap. IX.

'Fallacies of Monetarism', lecture given in Basel, 16 Feb.; pub. in W. Ehrlicher and H.-J. Krümmel (eds.), *Kredit und Kapital* (Berlin, Dunker & Humboldt).

'Theoretische Grundlagen der europäischen Wohlfahrstaaten', paper given to the conference on 'Systemkrisen in Ost und West' at the Creditanstalt Bankverein of Vienna, 22-4 Apr.

'The Radcliffe Report in the Light of Subsequent Developments in Monetary Theory', two Radcliffe Lectures given at the University of Warwick, 18-19 May; repr. in *Scourge of Monetarism.* cap. IX.

'Inflation: An Endemic Problem of Modern Capitalism', lecutre at the University of Reykjavik, 8 June; pub. as *Verdbólgan – Prálát vandamál, nútíma efnahagslífs* (Reykjavik, Isafoldar-pentsidja HF, 1982); and in *WG* 2.

'La dama di ferro: una frana – Mitterrand: un modello', *EL* (28 Nov. and 5 Dec.); repr. in *Incontri* (Radiotelevisione della Svizzera italiana, 1982).

1982

The Scourge of Monetarism (Oxford, Oxford University Press); Fr. trans. with introd. (Paris, Economica, 1984); Jap. trans. with introd. (Tokyo) (Nihon Keizai Hyron Sha Ltd., 1984); It. trans. with the same Fr. introd., *Il flagello del monetarismo* (Turin, Loescher, 1984).

'The Role of Devaluation in the Adjustement of Balance of Payment Deficit', UNCTAD (Apr.).

'Limitations of the General Theory', Keynes Lecture in Economics, British Academy, London, 12 May; pub in *British Academy Acta*, 68 (1982).

'Economic Prospects of the '80s', lecture at the European University of Florence, Fresole, 11 Sept.; pub. in *EN* (May).

'La rivoluzione keynesiana e i suoi limiti', *MO* (May).

'Conclusion of Todays Discussion', lecture at the Centre d'Études Perspectives et d'Informations Sociales, Paris, 17 May.

Inflation: An Endemic Problem of the Twentieth Century, lecture at the Johann Wolfgang Goethe University, Frankfurt, 23 June, on the occasion of receiving his honorary degree (Johann Wolfgang Goethe University, Frankfurt-on-Main).

Grenze der 'General Theory', two Merton Lectures given at the Johann Wolfgang Goethe University, Frankfurt, June (Berlin, Springer, 1983).

'A Plan for Securing Equilibrium in the Balance of Payments under a Policy of Economic Expansion', report to the French Budget Ministry (4 Oct.).

'The Role of Commodity Prices in Economic Recovery', lecture in Brussels, Nov.; pub. in *LLBR* (July 1983) and in *World Development* (June-July 1987); cap. IX; It. trans. in *ENR* 3 (1984).

1983

The Economic Consequences of Mrs Thatcher (Fabian Tract, 486; Jan.; repr. London, Duckworth).

Review of *The Collected Writings of John Maynard Keynes*, XXVII. *Activities 1940-1946: Shaping the Post-War World: Employment and Commodities*, *EJ* (Mar.).

'Keynesianism in the '80s', lecture at the Creditanstalt Bankverein, Vienna, Apr.

'Devaluation and Adjustment in Developing Countries', report to the Group of 24, IMF; pub. in *FeD* (June); cap. IX.

'The End of the Keynesian Era', *G* (8 June).

'Keynesian Economics after Fifty Years', lecture at the Keynesian Centennial, Cambridge, July; pub. in D. Worswick and J. Trevithick (eds.), *Keynes and the Modern World* (Cambridge, Cambridge University Press, 1983); cap. IX.

'Le occasioni mancate dell'economia inglese', *MO* (July-Aug.).

'The Role of Effective Demand in the Short Run and in the Long Run', lecture on Keynes, Paris, Sept.; cap. IX.

'The Futility of General Equilibrium Theory', lecture at Harvard University, 28 Oct., mimeo.

Economics without Equilibrium, three Okun Lectures given at Yale University, Nov. (Armonk, New York, M. E. Sharpe Inc., 1985); It. trans., *Economia senza equilibrio* (Bologna, Il Mulino, 1988).

'Obituary of Piero Sraffa', address at Trinity College, Cambridge, 19 Nov.; pub. in *CR* (July 1984).

'The Changing Situation of the World Economy: Possibilities and Limits of Adjustment', lecture, Rome, Nov.

1984

'The Failure of Monetarism', Chintaman Deshmukh Memorial Lecture, Reserve Bank of India, Bombay, 18 Jan.

'Causes of Growth and Stagnation of the World Economy', four Mattioli Lectures at the Università Bocconi of Milan, 21-5 May (forthcoming).

Paper at the conference 'Un intellettuale europeo del XX secolo: Piero Sraffa, 1898-1983', held at Istituto Gramsci, Turin, May; It. trans., 'Sraffa come critico della teoria economica', in R. Bellofiore (ed.), *Tra teoria economica e grande cultura europea: Piero Sraffa* (Milan, Franco Angeli, 1986).

'Joan Robinson Obituary', *KCAR* (July).

'An Exchange Rate Policy for India', *EPW* (14 July).

'Lessons of the Monetarist Experiment', lecture at the conference 'Monetary Eruditions for Economic Recovery', held at University of Amsterdam, 14-16 Nov.; pub. as 'How Monetarism Failed', *CH* (May-June 1985); repr. in C. Van Ewijk and J. J. Klant (eds.), *Monetary Conditions for Economic Recovery* (Dordrecht, Martinus Nijhoff); cap. IX; It. edn II.

'I Tories nell'era Thatcher: da conservatori a reazionari', *PEE* (Dec.).

'Se il dollaro cade: L'economia della instabilità', Kaldor's intervention at a Round Table, pub. in *RI* (22 Dec.).

1985

Review of P. Sylos-Labini, *The Forces of Economic Growth and Decline*, *EJ* (Dec.).

'The Changing Situation of the World Economy: Possibilities and Limits of Adjustment', Cambridge, Mar., mimeo.

Paper given to the Symposium 'In Search of Ways to Eliminate Economic Frictions' for the 50th anniversary of the Asahi Shinbun, Nagoya, Japan, 19 May.

'Viaggio attraverso il mondo: 3. L'economia', interview given to
    F. Targetti for *MO* (Aug.).
'John von Neumann (1903-1957)', (Cambridge, July); pub. in
    cap. IX.
'Piero Sraffa (1898-1983)', *Proceedings of British Academy*, 81
    (1985); It. trans., *BNLMC* (Sept. 1986); cap. IX.
'Advantages of EMS Membership', mimeo (Cambridge).
'Limits on Growth', Hicks Lecture given in Oxford, 28 Nov.;
    pub. in *OEP* 38 (1986); cap. IX.

1986

Ricordi di un economista, ed. M. C. Marcuzzo (Milan, Garzanti).
'Recollections of an Economist', *BNLQR* (Mar.); It. trans.,
    'Reminiscenze di un economista', *BNLMC* (June), repr. in *Il
    mestiere di economista* (Turin, Einaudi, 1988); cap. IX.
'The Impact of Import Restrictions in the Interwar Period',
    (with M. Kitson), mimeo (Cambridge, June).
'The Rise and Decline of Monetarism' (Labour Institute for
    Economic Research, Discussion Paper, 46; Helsinki).

Speeches to the House of Lords

Debate on the Address, 25 Nov. 1976
The Economic Situation, 20 July, 1977.
Debate on North Sea Oil, 22 May 1978.
Debate on the Economic Situation, 2 Nov. 1978.
Industrial Recovery, 17 Jan. 1979.
Economic and Social Policies: Industrial Strategy, 13 June 1979.
Debate on the Budget, 19 June 1979.
Debate on the Oil Crisis, 4 July 1979.
Economic Policy, 11 July 1979.
Debate on the Government's Policies, 7 Nov. 1979.
Inflation and Employment: Policies, 4 Dec. 1979.
Gas and Electricity Price Increase, 30 Jan. 1980.
Economic Policy, 13 Feb. 1980.
Domestic Economic Strategy, 16 Apr. 1980.
BSC: Appointment of Chairman, 14 May 1980.
Employment Bill: Second Reading Debate, 20 May 1980.

Monetary Policy, 11 June 1980.
Employment Bill: Third Reading Debate, 14 July 1980.
Debate on the Address: Economic Affairs, 27 Nov. 1980.
Industry: The Public Sector, 4 Feb. 1981.
Motion: Unemployment, 4 Mar. 1981.
Debate on Cuts in Education, 18 Mar. 1981.
Debate on Defence, 21 July 1981.
Debate on Address, 12 Nov. 1981.
The Arms Race and the Economy, 16 Dec. 1981.
European Monetary System, 27 Jan. 1982.
The Economic Situation and National Recovery, 3 Feb. 1982.
Unemployment and Industrial Recovery, 17 Mar. 1982.
Debate on the Address, 10 Nov. 1982.
Causes of Unemployment, 16 Nov. 1982.
The ECC Internal Market, 13 Dec. 1982.
The Policy on Deterrence, 16 Feb. 1983.
World Economy and Currency Stability, 23 Mar. 1983.
Oil and the Decline of Manufacturing, 29 June 1983.
Comment on ACARD/ABRC Report (decline of industry), 10
    Feb. 1984.
Debate on Redeployment of Resources, 22 Feb. 1984.
Future Financing of the Community, 15 Mar. 1984.
Unemployment, 9 May 1984.
Policies for Employment, 13 Nov. 1984.
Causes of Unemployment, 12 Dec. 1984.
Social and Economic Policies, 23 Jan. 1985.
Government Policy and New Technology, 14 Nov. 1985.
Overseas Trade: Select Committee Report, 3 Dec. 1985.
Economic Situation, 19 Feb. 1986.

APPENDIX

BIBLIOGRAPHY OF WORKS CITED

Allen, G.C., *The Industrial Development of Birmingham 1816–1927* [no publisher *or date* given: see p. 56]

Beveridge, W., *Full Employment in a Free Society*, London: George Allen & Unwin, 1944

Chamberlin, E., *The Theory of Monopolistic Competition*, Cambridge, Mass: Harvard University Press, 1933

Denison, E., *Accounting for Slower Growth*, Washington DC: Brookings Institution, 1979

Friedman, M., 'The New Monetarism: Comment', *Lloyds Bank Review*, October 1970

Harcourt, G., 'A Critique of Mr Kaldor's Model of Income Distribution and Economic Growth', *Australian Economic Papers*, June 1963

Harrod, R., *International Economics*, London: Macmillan, 1933

Hicks, J., 'The Foundations of Welfare Economics', *Economic Journal*, December 1936

Hicks, U., 'Mr Kaldor's Plan for the Reform of Indian Taxes', *Economic Journal*, March 1958

Hufbauer, G.C., *Synthetic Materials and the Theory of International Trade*, London: Duckworth, 1966

Jones, Aubrey, in J. Abse (ed.), *My LSE*, London: Robson Books, 1977

Kalecki, M., 'A Theory of Profits', *Economic Journal*, June–September 1942

Kendrick, J.W. (ed.), '*International Comparisons of Productivity and Causes of the Slowdow*', Cambridge, Mass: Ballinger, 1986

Keynes, J.M., *The Economic Consequences of Mr Churchill*, London: Hogarth Press, 1925

General Theory, ed. 1936

'The Policy of Government Storage of Foodstuffs and Raw Materials', *Economic Journal*, September 1938, pp. 440–460

Kornai, J., *Anti-Equilibrium: On Economic Systems Theory and the Tasks of Research*, Amsterdam: North Holland, 1971

Lewis, W.A., 'World Production, Prices and Trade, 1870–1960', *Manchester School*, May 1952

Malthus, T., *An Essay on the Principle of Population*, 2nd edition, London: J. Johnson, 1803

Matthews, R.C.O. (ed.), *Slower Growth in the Western World*, London: Heinemann, 1982

McCombie, J.S.L. and A.P. Thirlwall, *Economic Growth and the Balance of Payments Constraint*, London: Macmillan, 1994

Moggridge, D. (ed.), *The Collected Writings of J.M. Keynes*, Vol. XIII, *The General Theory and After, Part I, Preparation*, London: Macmillan, 1973
The Collected Writings of J.M. Keynes, Vol. XIV, *The General Theory and After, Part II, Defence and Development*, London: Macmillan, 1973
The Collected Writings of J.M. Keynes, Vol. XXVII, *Activities 1940–1946 Shaping the Post-War World: Employment and Commodities*, London: Macmillan, 1980

Neumann, J. von, 'A Model of General Economic Equilibrium', *Review of Economic Studies*, no. 1, 1945

Pasinetti, L., 'Rate of Profit and Income Distribution in Relation to the Rate of Economic Growth', *Review of Economic Studies*, October 1962

Pigou, A.C. (ed.), *Memorials of Alfred Marshall*, London: Macmillan, 1925
'Real and Money Wage Rates in Relation to Unemployment', *Economic Journal*, September 1937

Prebisch, R., *The Economic Development of Latin America and itd Principal Problems*, New York: ECLA, U.N. Department of Economic Affairs, 1950

Robinson, J., *The Economics of Imperfect Competition*, London: Macmillan, 1933

Samuelson, P. and F. Modigliani, 'The Pasinetti Paradox in Neoclassical and More General Models', *Review of Economic Studies*, October 1962

Sen, A., 'Neoclassical and Neo-Keynesian Theories of Distribution', *Economic Record*, March 1963

St Clair Grondona, L., *Economic Stability is Attainable*, London: Hutchison Benham, 1975

Sylos Labini, P., 'On the Instability of Commodity Prices and the Problem of Gold', in A. Quadrio-Curzio (ed.), *The Gold Problem: Economic Perspectives*, Oxford: Oxford University Press, 1982

Thirlwall, A.P., 'The Balance of Payments Constraint as an Explanation of International Growth Rate Differences', *Banca Nazionale del Lavoro Quarterly Review*, March 1979

'Symposium on Kaldor's Growth Laws', *Journal of Post-Keynesian Economics*, Spring 1983

'A General Model of Growth and Development on Kaldorian Lines', *Oxford Economic Papers*, July 1986

Nicholas Kaldor, Brighton: Harvester Wheatsheaf Press, 1987

Weintraub, Roy, 'On the Existence of a Competitive Equilibrium, 1930–1957', *Journal of Economic Literature*, March 1983

Wood, A., *A Theory of Profits*, Cambridge: Cambridge University Press, 1975

Young, Allyn, 'Increasing Returns and Economic Progress', *Economic Journal*, December 1928

List of Abbreviations

ACC	*Accountant*
AER	*American Economic Review*
AS	*Asian Studies*
BAN	*Bancaria*
BID	*Bulletin d'Information et de Documentation National* (Bank of Belgium)
BK	The *Banker*
BNLMC	*Banca Nazionale del Lavoro, Moneta e Credito*
BNLQR	*Banca Nazionale del Lavoro, Quarterly Review*
BOIES	*Bulletin of Oxford Institute of Economics and Statistics*
CBI	Confederation of British Industry
CE	*Caudernos de Economia*
CEMLA	Centro de Estudios Monetarios Latinoamericanos
CEX	*Comercio Exterior*
CH	*Challenge*
CJE	*Cambridge Journal of Economics*
CP	Kaldor, Collected Papers (London, Duckworth, 1960-89), 9 vols.
CR	*Cambridge Review*
DAE	Department of Applied Economics
EA	*Économie Appliquée*
EB	*Econômica Brasileira, Clube de Economistas*
EBLA	*Economic Bulletin for Latin America, Exclusive Secretariat of the Economic Commission for Latin America, United Nations*
EC	*Economica*
ECLA	Economic Commission for Latin America
ECTR	*Econometrica*
EJ	*Economic Journal*
EL	*Eco di Locarno*
EN	*Economic Notes*
ENR	*Energia*
EPW	*Economic and Political Weekly*
ER	*Economic Record*
EWA	*Economic Weekly Annual*
FA	*Foreign Affairs*
FAO	Food and Agricultural Organization
FeD	*Finance and Development*
G	*Guardian*
HBR	*Harvard Business Review*
HMSO	Her Majesty's Stationery Office
ICE	*Información Comercial Española, Revista de Economia, Ministerio de Comercio*
IE	*Investigación Económica*
IEAB	*International Economic Association Bulletin*
ILO	International Labour Office
IMF	International Monetary Fund
IS	*Informazione Svimez*
ISAB	*International Scienze Association Bulletin*
IST	*Ifo-Studien, Zeitschrift des Ifo Institus für Wirtschaftsforschung* (Berlin)
It. edn. i	Kaldor, *Equilibrio, distribuzione e crescita*, ed. F. Targetti (Twin, Einaudi, 1984)

LIST OF ABBREVIATIONS

It. edn. ii	Kaldor, *Inflazione, moneta e tassazione*, ed. F. Targetti (Twin, Einaudi, 1986)
ITO	International Trade Organization
JES	*Journal of the Economic Society, Hong Kong University*
JMAS	*Journal of Modern African Studies*
JPE	*Journal of Political Economics*
JPKE	*Journal of Post Keynesian Economics*
KCAR	*King's College Annual Report*
LLBR	*Lloyds Bank Review*
LSE	London School of Economics
MA	*Mondo Aperto*
MLR	*Monthly Labor Review, US Dept. of Labor, Bureau of Labor Statistics*
MO	*Mondoperaio*
MS	*Manchester school*
NeN	*New Statesman and Nation*
NIESER	National Institute for Economic and Social Research
NS	*New Statesman*
OEP	*Oxford Economic Papers*
PaE	*Parorama Económico*
PE	*Problèmes Économiques*
PEE	*Politica ed Economia*
QJE	*Quarterly Journal of Economics*
QREB	*Quarterly Review of Economics and Business*
RBE	*Revista Brasileira de Econômia*
RCE	*Revista de Ciencias Económicas*
REA	*Rivista di Economia Agraria*
RES	*Review of Economic Studies*
REST	*Review of Economics and Statistics*
RI	*Rinascita*
RPE	*Rivista di Politica Economica*
SAN	*Sankhya* (The Indian Journal of Statistics)
SJPE	*Scottish Journal of Politcal Economy*
ST	*The Sunday Times*
TE	*Trimestre Económico* (Fondo de Cultura Económica)
TT	*The Times*
UNCTAD	United Nations Committee on Trade and Development
WG	*Wirtschaft und Gesellschaft, Kammer für Arbeiter und Angestellte für Wien*
ZN	*Zeitschrift für National ökonomie*

INDEX

INDEX

Advertising 163
agriculture
  competitive market 50-1
  price determination 51-2
  price support programmes 75
  production 25-6
  surplus 28, 40
  terms of trade with industry 45-6,
    49-50, 105, 135, 140-1, 177
  see also buffer stocks; economic models;
    primary sector
Allen, M. 151
Amato, A. 95-6
An Expenditure Tax 168
asymmetries 125
auctioneer 10, 124
Austria 90

Balance of payments 68, 87
  UK 83-4
  US 78-9
Balogh, T. 179
'bancor' 111
Bandaranaike, Mr. 171
banking 129-30
Barna, T. 164
Becattini, G. 97-101
Bellone, G. 129
Beveridge Report 163-5
Biasco, S. 120-23
bond issue 95-7
Boserup, E. 166
Bowley, A. L. 100
Bretton Woods system 77, 79, 178
Budapest 150
budget deficit 95-7, 139-40
buffer stocks 52-4, 88, 107-8, 111, 122,
    136-7, 178

Cairncross, A. 179
Callaghan, J. 179
Cambridge 172
  Jesus College 145
  King's College 167
  Peterhouse 163
  'secret seminar' 163
Cambridge Controversies 172

capital accumulation 28-9
  and culture 99
  determined by production 31
  and technological progress 116
  in two-sector model 43-4
capital/labour ratio 28
capital/output ratio 35
Cardani, A. M. 132-4
Cassel, G. 113
centralization 127-8
Chamberlain, E. 153-4
China 27
classical economics 21-30, 31, 62
comparative cost theory 60
compensation test 159
competition
  in agriculture 50-1
  and growth 15
  imperfect 41
  in industry 50-1
  monopolistic 154
  and technical change 18-9
Conservative Party 181
consumerism 117-18
Cozzi, T. 123-6
crisis of 1929 52-4, 117, 119-20
Croome, H. 152
Crossman, R. 180
crowding out and crowding in 96-7,
    185-6
culture 98-9

Dalton, H. 151
dealers expectations 11-2
'dealers' turn' 10-11
decision makers 129
  demand
  effective 31-33
  growth 118
  international 120-21
  for manufactured goods 76
  and output 33
  outside 57
  in two-sector model 44-6
demand management 77
development theory 172-8
disequilibrium 9, 13, 115

distribution theory 173-4
'division of labour' 40, 98, 131
dollar 78-9
Domar, E. 39, 103

Economic agents 6, 9
Economic Commission for Europe
    (ECE) 166
economic growth
  and competition 15
  conditions for 34
  decline after 1973 72
  determinants 3-5
  exogenous assumptions 36-7
  export led 121
  and manufacturing growth 67
  and population growth 27, 113
  sectoral variations 46-7, 106
  and technical progress 15, 116-17, 139
  and trade cycles 134-5, 158-9
economic growth models 41-52
  assumptions 41-44
economic growth rates
  variations in 175-6
  warranted and natural 35-6, 174
economic growth theory 5, 172-8
  classical 21-30
  Keynesian 30, 34-7
Economic Journal 161
economic laws 4
economic models
  general equilibrium 113-14
  two-sector 41-52, 104-6, 112, 146
economic policy, international co-ordi-
    nation 86-91, 127-8
Economic Survey of Europe 166
economic theory
  dynamic and static 4, 9, 22
  multidisciplinary approach 101
  scarcity 21-22
  two objectives 3
  versus empirical research 97-8
economies
  internal and external 130
  of large-scale production 59-60
Edgeworth, F. Y. 9
empirical research, versus theory 97-8
employment
  full 87
  limit on 162-3

energy 82-3
Engel's law 74, 101
equilibria
  continuum 124
  intertemporal 7
equilibrium theory 4-15, 186-89
  cul-de-sac 8
  main purpose of 5
  prices in 5-6, 8-9
  restrictive axioms 6-7, 123, 146
European Community 108, 72-3, 181
  CAP 88, 107, 109
exchange rates 79-80, 121
expectations 11-2, 114-15
exports
  and economic growth 121
  post WWII prices 75
  productivity 106-7
  rate of growth of 67-9

Fallacies in composition 121-22
fertility 23-4
  see also population growth
Filippini, C. 134-6
firm behaviour theory 154-5
France 77, 79, 81, 84
free entry 155
free trade 60-1, 62
  polarisation process 64-6
French Physiocrats 22
Friedman, M. 85, 95, 140, 184-5

Gaitskell, H. 167, 179
Galbraith, K. 147, 165
GDP deflator 16
Germany 77-8, 79, 84, 90
'guest workers' 78

Halder 165
Harberger, A. 168
Harcourt, G. 174
Harrod, R. 34-6, 39, 67-8, 103, 125,
    183
Hayek, F. von 102, 152-3, 154, 155, 156
Healey, D. 182
Hecksher, E. 60, 62
Hicks, Sir J. 145, 151, 152, 155, 158, 168,
    188
Hicks, U. 170
history 4

Hufbauer, G. C. 69

Imports
   controls 183
   income elasticity 67-9
income
   distribution 17, 63
   measurement 16-18
India 27, 168-9
industrial revolution 18-9, 64-5
industrialization
   spread of 65-6
   urban concentration 55, 58
   and wealth generation 56-7
industry 39
   competitive market 41, 51-2
   and economic growth 40, 67, 132, 177
   price determination 51-2
   terms of trade with agriculture 45-6,
      49-51, 105, 135, 140, 178
   see also economic models
inflation 81-2, 88-90
Inonu, I. 172
institutional arrangements 76-7
interest rates
   and growth rates 155
   policy 87
   structure 96-7, 159-60
   volatile 137
international co-ordination 86-91, 127-8
investment
   S-shaped 158
   and savings 43-4
   and share of profits 30
investment period 157
Italy 26, 65-6, 77-8, 84
Iwai, K. 115

Jagan, C. 171
Japan 72
Jenkins, R. 179
Jevons, S. 21
Johnston, A. 180

Kahn, R. 146, 160, 167, 172
Kaldor, C. (née Goldschmidt) 148
Kaldor, N. 145-90
   1908-1939 150-161
   adviser to Labour politicians 147,
      167-8, 179-82

   at the LSE 145, 150-2, 153, 163-4
   in British Guiana 170
   in Cambridge 160, 166-7, 172
   in Ceylon 168-9
   in the Common Market debate 181-2
   on equilibrium theory 186-89
   financial interests 147
   in Ghana 170
   growth and development theories
      172-8
   honours 149
   in India 168-9
   interest in politics 149
   intuition 148
   journalism 151-2
   marriage 148
   in Mexico 170
   on monetarism 182-6
   on taxation 180
   in Turkey 170
   in the USA 153
   war and immediate aftermath 162-7
Kalecki, M. 30, 138, 173
Kennedy, J. F. 77
Keynes, J. M. 5, 11, 31-34, 39, 53, 77, 85,
      88, 97, 99, 102, 107, 111, 140, 145, 148,
      152-5, 157, 160-63, 165, 173, 178
Keynes effect 160
Keynesians versus monetarists 95-6
Knight, F. H. 114
Korean War 75
Kornai 186

Labour
   and capital 28
   constraint 106-8
   cost of reproduction 24
   division of 40, 98, 131
   mobility 26
   natural price 24
   surplus 42-3, 47
Labour Party 147, 166, 168-9, 179-82
land constraint 61
Lary, H. 166
Law of Diminishing Returns 24
Leontief, W. 104
Lewis, W. A. 71, 106
liquidity 96-7
liquidity preference 161
Little, I. 159

LLoyd George, D. 97
locomotive country 122
Lombardini, S. 112-19
London School of Economics 102, 145,
    152-53, 154-5, 164-5
long run 95

Makower, H. 165
Malthus, T. 22, 23, 27
markets
    adjustment 13-4
    functions of 189-90
    imperfect 64
    oligopolistic 14-5
    primary and secondary sectors 41, 50-
        1, 178
Marshall, A. 21, 64, 99, 100, 130, 190
Marx, K. 4, 22-3, 24, 29-31, 110, 134
mathematics 21, 99-100, 190
Meade, J. 113
Menger, K. 21
methodology 189
Mexico 108, 171
Mill, J. S. 22, 31, 60
Modigliani, F. 174, 186
Moggridge, D. 111
monetarism 84-5, 95-6, 184-7
monetary reform 111, 122
money 140
    commodity-backed and credit 186
    endogenous 186
    importance of 32
Monnet, J. 165
monopoly 64
Monti, M. 127-8
multiplier 57
    income 160-1
    international 79
    trade 67-8, 177
Myrdal, G. 64, 152, 166, 177

National income accounting 162-3
Neild, R. 166, 179
neo-classical economics 5, 22, 62
    see also equilibrium theory
neo-Pasinetti theory 174
newly industrialized countries 70
Nixon, President 80
Nkrumah 147, 171
Nobel Prize 149-50

Ohlin, B. 60, 62
oil
    North Sea 83-4, 108
    price hike 82-3
Onida, F. 130-1
OPEC 82-3, 86
organizational innovation 126
output
    determination 33-4
    and productivity 132-5
    real 16-18

Pareto, V. 116, 152
Pareto-optimality 6
Pasinetti, L. 101-107, 172
Pasinetti Paradox 174-5
Pasinetti-Kaldor inequality 38
Pigou, A. C. 154, 158, 159, 160
plans, five-year 77
'polarisation process' 64-6
population growth 25, 27, 113
    see also fertility
population law 23-4
Portugal 60-62
post-WWII
    boom 71-2, 74, 117-18
    reconstruction 162, 164
Power, E. 151
Prebisch, R. 169
Prebisch Effect 74
preferences 56
price determination 41
    agriculture 51-54
    auction 9-10
    industry 51-2
    mark-up 139
    in oligopolistic markets 14-15
    primary sector 74
    professional intermediaries role 10-2
price variation, and stocks 11-2
price-leadership 14
prices
    equalization 62
    in equilibrium theory 5-6, 8-9
    and market adjustment 13-4
    normal 11-2
    oil 82-3
    post-WWII exports 75
    primary products 52-4, 80-1, 88,
        119-20, 136-8, 181

role of 113-15
short run fluctuations 136-8, 177-8
signals 189-90
in two-sector model 45-6
primary commodities
price fluctuations 81, 88, 136-8, 181
speculation in 80
see also buffer stocks
primary sector 39, 110
effect of productivity increase 74
market form 125
production growth 73-4
see also agriculture
principle of circular and cumulative causation 64, 179
product development 69
production
agricultural 25-6
and capital 31
constant costs of 60
potential 26
surplus 29-30, 32
productivity
declining growth 72-3
export sector 106-7
and market size 40
and output 132-5
and wages 49
profits
acceleration factor 99
importance of 32-3
as income 36-7
and investment 30
rate 29
retained 37
source of savings 37-8
programme of recovery 86-9, 127-9
Public Sector deficit 139-40

Quantity signals 14, 188

Radcliffe Committee 184
rational expectations theory 186
Reagan, R. 129
recession 52-4, 82-3, 120
Report on National and International Measures for Full Employment 164-5
reserve currency 78-9
residual country 121-22
resource endowment 56

restructuring 104, 118-19
returns
constant 62
diminishing 61, 110, 112
increasing 19, 59-60, 63-4, 100, 112, 125-6, 146, 154, 177, 190-1
Ricardo, D. 4, 22, 24, 25, 26, 30, 31, 60, 108, 110, 112
Ricardo effect 155-6, 190
Robbins, L. 102, 150, 151, 152, 157
Robertson, D. 109, 156, 159, 161
Robinson, J. 104, 146, 153, 159, 162, 173
Rostow, W. W. 135
Royal Commission on the Taxation of Profits and Income 146, 166, 168

St Clair Grondona, L. 12
Salant, S. 137
Samuelson, P. A. 60, 108, 174, 186
savings
and investment 43-4
profits as 37-8
S-shaped 157
Say's law 31-32, 178
scale economies 130-32
see also returns
Schumpeter, J. A. 109, 117, 119, 134
secondary sector see industry
Sen, A. 174
services 40, 31
short run 95
Shove, G. 166
Simons, H. 152
slump 52-4, 82-3, 120
Smith, A. 4, 22, 24, 28, 40, 98, 99, 110, 112-13, 129-31, 188, 190
social class 128
Solow, R. 102
specialisation 131, 135-6
speculation 137-8
Sraffa, P. 104, 147, 162, 188
stability analyses 123-5
stagflation 82
stocks
buffer 52-4, 88, 107-8, 111, 122, 136-7, 179
food 75-6
and price variation 11-12
structural change 104, 118-19
'stylized facts' 146, 175-6
supply 31-32, 120

supply policy 119
Sylos-Labini, P. 13, 80, 109-11, 141

Tabellini, G. 136-8
Targetti, F. 138-41
tastes 7-8, 116-17
  see also wants
'tatonnement' 10
tax 162, 168-72
  capital gains 181
  capital transfer 183
  corporation 169, 181
  expenditure 128, 169
  interest equalization 87-8
  Selective Employment 180-1
  stock appreciation relief 183
  wealth 169-70
technical progress 7-8
  and accumulation 116
  and competition 18-19
  and culture 99
  and economic growth 15, 116-17, 139
  embodied 28
  exogenous 29
  labour-saving 19, 47-8
  land-saving 24-5, 27, 47, 110, 129, 139,
    178
  and population growth 25
  product development 69
  role of 132-5
technical progress function 125, 176
terms of trade 45-6, 49-51, 74-5, 105, 135,
    140-41, 178
Thatcher, M. H. 83-4, 85, 95, 108
The Manchester Guardian 165
The Scourge of Monetarism 184
Thirlwall, A. P. 67
trade 106, 108
  effect on income distribution 63
  free 60-62, 64-6
  low wage/technological lead split
    69-70
  protection 66, 122-3, 126, 183
  regulation 87
trade cycles 73, 155

and economic progress 134-5, 156-7
  Kondratief long wave 117, 135
trade unions 88-90
transport revolution 64-5

Un Technical Committee on Berlin
    Currency and Trade 165-6
unemployment 26, 73, 187
United Kingdom 77, 85-6
United States 72-3, 75-9, 85-7, 121, 129,
    152
urban concentration 55, 58

Verdoorn, P. J. 166
Verdoorn's Law 48, 177, 188
Vickers, R. 147
Vietnam War 79
Volcker 85
von Neumann 104, 106, 113, 156

Wages 30
  determination 174
  differentials 110-11
  money 81-82
  and productivity 49
  settlement systems 88-90
  subsidies 158-9
Walras, L. 5-6, 8-10, 12, 21, 113, 115, 152,
    191
wants
  specification 98-9
  see also tastes
war finance 162
Wass, Sir D. 181
wealth
  distribution 55-6, 106-8
  generation 56-7
welfare economics 157-8
White Paper on National Income 162
widow's cruse 174
Wilson, H. 180
Wood, A. 174

Young, A. 18-19, 58-9, 98-9, 101-102,
    130-31, 150, 177, 188-9

RAFFAELE MATTIOLI LECTURES

SCIENTIFIC COMMITTEE (*to be renewed*): Sergio Steve, Chairman; Carlo Filippini, Mario Monti, Adalberto Predetti, Sergio Siglienti, Franco Venturi; Enrico Resti, Secretary.

ORGANIZATION: Banca Commerciale Italiana-Università Commerciale Luigi Bocconi · Milano.

ADMINISTRATION: Banca Commerciale Italiana · Milano.

PUBLISHER: Cambridge University Press · Cambridge.

RAFFAELE MATTIOLI FOUNDATION
Fondazione Raffaele Mattioli
per la Storia del Pensiero Economico

Published

RICHARD F. KAHN, *The Making of Keynes' General Theory* (First edition: May 1984; Japanese edition, Tokyo: Iwanami Shoten, Publishers, April 1987).

FRANCO MODIGLIANI, *The Debate over Stabilization Policy* (First edition: July 1986).

CHARLES P. KINDLEBERGER, *Economic Laws and Economic History* (First edition: December 1989; Italian edition, Bari: Laterza, 1990; Spanish edition, Barcelona: Editorial Crítica, December 1990).

ALAN PEACOCK, *Public Choice Analysis in Historical Perspective* (First edition: March 1992).

SHIGETO TSURU, *Institutional Economics Revisited* (First edition: January 1993).

KARL BRUNNER - ALLAN H. MELTZER, *Money and the Economy. Issues in Monetary Analysis* (First edition: June 1993).

PAUL P. STREETEN, *Thinking About Development* (First edition: May 1995).

NICHOLAS KALDOR, *Causes of Growth and Stagnation in the World Economy.* (First edition: January 1996).

To be published

ERIK F. LUNDBERG, *The Development of Swedish and Keynesian Macroeconomic Theory and its Impact on Economic Policy.*

HERBERT A. SIMON, *An Empirically Based Microeconomics.*

RICHARD STONE, *Some British Empiricists in the Social Sciences.*

Lightning Source UK Ltd.
Milton Keynes UK
UKOW021046140413

209105UK00005B/109/A